Michel de Certeau

Key Contemporary Thinkers

Michel de Certeau

Interpretation and its Other

JEREMY AHEARNE

Stanford University Press
Stanford, California
1995

Stanford University Press
Stanford, California
© 1995 Jeremy Ahearne
Originating publisher: Polity Press,
    Cambridge, in association with
    Blackwell Publishers
First published in the U.S.A. by
    Stanford University Press, 1995
Printed in Great Britain
Cloth ISBN 0-8047-2670-1
Paper ISBN 0-8047-2672-8
LC 95-70478
This book is printed on acid-free paper.

Contents

Acknowledgements

I would like to thank especially Ian Maclean and Luce Giard for their discerning and generous guidance over the course of this project. I would also like to thank Malcolm Bowie, Maddi Dobie, Alex Dracobly, Pierre-Antoine Fabre, Mike Holland, Ann Jefferson, Jacques Le Brun, Jacques Revel and Wes Williams for reading and commenting on earlier drafts from this work, and Christina and Bernard Howells for directing me towards Michel de Certeau's work in the first place. I am grateful to John Thompson for asking me to write this book and to Ann Bone for her deft and expert copy-editing.

This book is dedicated to my parents, with particular thanks also to Katy and Molly for new perspectives.

The author and publishers gratefully acknowledge permission to quote from the following: Michel de Certeau, *The Writing of History*, tr. Tom Conley, copyright © 1988 by Columbia University Press; Michel de Certeau, *The Mystic Fable*, tr. Michael B. Smith, copyright © 1992 by The University of Chicago; Michel de Certeau, *The Practice of Everyday Life*, tr. Steven Rendall, copyright © 1984 by The Regents of the University of California. They are also grateful for permission to use a number of translated quotations from Michel de Certeau, Dominique Julia and Jacques Revel, *Une politique de la langue. La Révolution française et les patois*, copyright © Éditions Gallimard 1975.

Abbreviations

I shall refer to Certeau's major texts using the following abbreviations.

AH	*L'Absent de l'histoire*
CP	*La culture au pluriel*
E	*L'Étranger ou l'union dans la différence*
FC	*La faiblesse de croire*
H	*Heterologies: Discourse on the Other*
HP	*Histoire et psychanalyse entre science et fiction*
MF	*The Mystic Fable*, vol. 1 (French: *La fable mystique*, vol. 1)
PE	*The Practice of Everyday Life* (French: *L'Invention du quotidien*, vol. 1: *Arts de faire*)
PL	*La possession de Loudun*
PP	*La prise de parole et autres écrits politiques*
UPdL	*Une politique de la langue. La Révolution française et les patois*
WH	*The Writing of History* (French: *L'Écriture de l'histoire*)

Publication details for these editions are given in the bibliography. Wherever possible, I have given references to English translations. In abbreviated references I cite first the abbreviated title, then a page reference to the English translation, then a page reference to the French edition. Thus (*MF* 295/407) refers to a passage which can be found on page 295 of *The Mystic Fable*, and on page 407 of *La fable mystique*. Where a passage or article can be found in translation in the collection *Heterologies* (which does not correspond directly to a French volume), then the reference takes the form (*H* 119/*CP* 45). Where only one page reference is given (i.e. *UPdL* 15), this means unless otherwise indicated that no translation is yet available.

I have used the excellent published translations where they exist, though I occasionally modify them in order to emphasize particular nuances or connotations contained in the French. Otherwise I have produced my own translations.

Introduction

To each their strangers
Julia Kristeva

Michel de Certeau died on the 9 January 1986, leaving behind him the memory of an 'intelligence without bounds' (Roger Chartier), but also 'without fear, without fatigue and without arrogance' (Marc Augé), of 'one of the boldest, the most secret and the most sensitive minds of our time' (Julia Kristeva), and of a 'spoken word bathed today in shadow and light' whose writings 'continue to call to us in our most intimate recesses' (Edmond Jabès).[1] Since 1984, with the translation of *The Practice of Everyday Life*, his writings have begun to circulate increasingly across a plurality of disciplines throughout the English-speaking world.[2] The present book represents the first full-length study of Certeau's thought, and is designed as a guide to draw out the exceptional range but also the overall coherence of a challenging and incisive body of work. My book presupposes no prior knowledge of Certeau's thought, but should also be of particular interest for those readers who are already acquainted with at least one facet of his prismatic work and who wish to explore how their understanding of this may be reconfigured by a reading of the oeuvre as a whole.

Certeau was born in Chambéry in 1925. He obtained degrees in classics and philosophy at the universities of Grenoble, Lyon and Paris and, rather later, a doctorate in religious science at the Sorbonne in 1960. He joined the Jesuits in 1950 (with the hope of working in China), and was ordained in 1956. Asked to undertake research into the origins of the Jesuit order, he had become by the mid-1960s a leading specialist in early modern religious history (working notably on Pierre Favre, a companion of Ignatius, and then on Jean-Joseph Surin, a strange seventeenth-century mystic). At this time he was editing and contributing regularly to a number of broadly Catholic reviews (in particular *Christus* and *Études*, Jesuit journals devoted respectively to spirituality and to culture). In 1968, he published a seminal analysis of the symbolic 'revolution' of that year, entitled *La prise de parole. Pour une nouvelle culture* [Starting to speak: Towards a new culture]. In retrospect, this can be seen to have heralded a watershed in his intellectual itinerary, confirmed by the publication in 1970 of the historical study *La possession de Loudun* [The possession of Loudun]. While many of the fundamental questions informing his thought would remain, their expression no longer bore the marks of an orthodox religious affiliation. Likewise his writings henceforth became disseminated across heterogeneous social, political and intellectual sites (*Annales ESC*, *Politique Aujourd'hui*, *Recherches de Science Religieuse*, *Esprit*, *Traverses*, *Le Débat*, *Le Bloc-Notes de la Psychanalyse*, to list only some of the journals in which his later work appeared). His writings were now clearly situated in relation to a range of contemporary problematics, and cut across issues in psychoanalysis (Certeau was a member of Jacques Lacan's École Freudienne from its inception in 1964), historiography, epistemology, semiotics and the social sciences. At the same time, in the wake of *La prise de parole*, Certeau had been drawn into a number of official and unofficial interlocutory networks addressing questions relating to contemporary cultural practices and policies.[3] Some of these investigations emerged in book form as *La culture au pluriel* [Culture in the plural] (1974) and *The Practice of Everyday Life* (1980). The course of his work also took him across Europe, the United States and South America (he occupied a full-time post in California from 1978 to 1984). The extraordinary intelligence at work in his thought from the late 1960s onwards is the product of this untiring textual, cultural and interlocutory 'travel', coupled with a form of interior distancing or 'quiet' born of a life-long immersion in the demanding texts of the Christian mystics. This singular combination of engagement and detachment reverberates through his more properly erudite and historiographical production of the period: *L'Absent de l'histoire* [The absent of history] (1973), *The Writing of History* (1975), *Une politique de la langue. La Révolution française et les patois* [A politics of language: The French Revolution and patois] (1975), and the first volume of *The Mystic Fable* (1982).

Certeau has left us, in the words of Jean Louis Schefer, with 'the image of an open work'.[4] He was not interested in producing a systematic doctrinal edifice, nor did he set himself up as the guardian of an erudite preserve. Indeed, I shall argue that his intellectual strategy consisted precisely in an endeavour to discern and to make ethical and aesthetic space for particular forms of interruption. His work was conceived as an ongoing response to a series of appeals and solicitations addressed to him directly or indirectly by others. In the light of this, I shall not myself extract an interpretative system from Certeau's work. In the mode perhaps of a 'travelogue', I have sought rather to map out and to correlate a set of intellectual itineraries which took Certeau through an intriguing combination of intellectual fields. I show how these itineraries are organized by a recurrent set of questions, and I explore how the different treatments which these questions receive can be used to shed unexpected light on each other.

The reading contained in this study is by no means the only way of moving across and analysing Certeau's work. It could have taken a very different form. It could, for example, have followed the route mapped out by Wlad Godzich in his introduction to *Heterologies*, a collection of Certeau's articles translated into English and published in 1986. Godzich inscribes Certeau's work in a philosophical 'countertradition' which 'in shorthand, could be described as being deeply suspicious of the Parmenidean principle of the identity of thought and being' (*H* vii). He invokes the writings of Friedrich Nietzsche, Martin Heidegger, Georges Bataille, Maurice Blanchot and Jacques Derrida, as well as Emmanuel Lévinas, Michel Foucault, Clifford Geertz and Edward Said, and uses them as a framework through which to articulate the nature of Certeau's work on alterity. This is a legitimate and helpful exercise. It corresponds to the way in which Certeau has often been received by anglophone readers, and even constitutes a viable research project. The danger which it runs, however, is that of flattening or erasing the specificity of Certeau's oeuvre. As Godzich himself observes, few of the authors cited above (with the notable exception of Foucault) are explicitly at issue in Certeau's thought. I have therefore opted for a different approach. If nothing else, this should provide an interesting detour to be undertaken before reinscribing Certeau into a comprehensive heterological 'countertradition'.

I have concentrated in this study on those intertexts which work most powerfully in Certeau's major writings. These comprise, broadly speaking, contemporary French historiographical production; the writings of early modern mystics and travellers; Michel Foucault and Pierre Bourdieu; Freud read in a somewhat oblique manner (itself marked by Certeau's critical participation in Lacan's École Freudienne); the linguistics of 'utterance' and a range of work on contemporary cultural practices. The principal objective of my work has not, however, been to produce a general comparative study based on a flow-chart of influence and critique. I have sought rather to draw out a set of problematics which are distinctive either in their form or their treatment to Certeau: the history of early modern and modern 'economies' of writing, reading and speech; the gap between representations and practices; the relation between 'strategic' social and intellectual programmes and 'tactical' political or poetic activity; the question of religious belief and desire; the operations of thought in their bodily complication (psycho-analysis and socio-analysis); the development of what might be called an ethics/ aesthetics. I have organized my study around one central problematic – 'interpretation and its other' – which cuts a transversal line across the multiplicity of Certeau's intellectual engagements. The interpretation in question is generally a 'certified' form of interpretation (the homophony may possess more than a passing significance), institutionally based and founded on a set of written authorities. I examine Certeau's reflection on the relations between such practices of interpretation and that which lies 'outside' them, either historically or culturally, and which they aspire in various ways to control.

In the course of my analyses, I will endeavour to gloss a variety of terms which are peculiar in their usage or connotations to Certeau's writing, and which are liable to unsettle a first-time reader ('scriptural economies', 'fables', 're-employments', 'formalities', 'operations', 'insinuations', *'poeisis'*, 'strategies', 'tactics', etc.). I will also introduce for the purposes of demonstration a number of my own categories. These are designed to help clarify my reading of Certeau's work on alterity, and to prevent the term from becoming an undifferentiated catch-all or rhetorical device. They enable me to elucidate more effectively just what Certeau is doing at different points when he refers or appeals to otherness. I will talk therefore of 'implicit' forms of social or historical alterity, of a transcendent Other, a projected 'other', a fantasmatic *other*, a 'virtual' or 'secreted' other, etc. It will be most helpful to unpack these terms as and when they are needed. I would like here simply to emphasize their limits. They are themselves conceived not as a fantasmatic or technical nomenclature for alterity. I use them rather to distinguish particular forms of 'alteration' as they are analysed by Certeau. As concepts, they cannot themselves remain immune from the complex and ubiquitous effects of alteration for which they provide a necessary schematization. Indeed, I should also alert the reader to the organizing presence in my own writing of the lexis of 'complication' (implication, explication, complex, complicity, multiplicity, duplicity, etc.). The etymological force of these terms (from the Latin, *plicare*) provides a means of approach to the vertiginous and properly mani-fold interweaving of alterity and identity which emerges from Certeau's work.

I have focused on the work which Certeau published from 1970 onwards. This date marks what Certeau himself might have called a 'founding rupture' (*rupture instauratrice*).[5] His work broke away from the restricted networks in which it had circulated throughout the previous decade, and entered into a more 'common life'. This is by no means to say that one should disregard the work which led up to this turning point. In many ways it prefigures the 'shattering' (*éclatement*) which was to follow, and I will frequently use it as a means of illuminating his later work.[6] Neither should one overlook the haunting presence in his writing of Surin, whom Certeau was later to call 'the ghost who has haunted my life'.[7] Nevertheless, the body of his writings after 1970 constitutes the principal object of this book. Given the nature of Certeau's intellectual activities, it is hardly possible to treat these writings in a strictly chronological manner. At any one time, Certeau would be working in a heterogeneous set of intellectual spaces. He would produce texts (or 'communications') for different publications and addressees, and would intermittently combine ('re-employ') these texts with other writings in order to form coherent books. I have based my study for the most part on these books, supplemented by the posthumous collections of Certeau's essays edited by Luce Giard, *La faiblesse de croire* [The weakness of believing] and *Histoire et psychanalyse entre science et fiction* [History and psychoanalysis between science and fiction]. I have produced a thematic analysis, treating my corpus as though it were a synchronic collection, while also introducing diachronic nuances. This seems the most helpful way of introducing the reader in a limited space to both the breadth and rewarding complexity of Certeau's thought.

Part I
Implications

1

The Historiographical Operation

Michel de Certeau's analysis of contemporary historiographical production provides a useful starting point for an introduction to his work. Notoriously difficult to categorize as a thinker, Certeau tended when pressed by institutional necessity to define himself primarily as a 'historian'.[1] I will show in this chapter how there emerges from his encounter as a practising historian with the alterity of the past a combination of questions concerning interpretation and otherness which will help us to elucidate the broader range of his writings.

Figuring Interpretation

Certeau conceives his historiography as a treatment for absence. He analyses it as an activity which is irredeemably separated from the presence of its object. This thwarted relation to its object constitutes for Certeau both the starting point and the vanishing point of historical interpretation. I shall begin by examining how such an existential situation is figured in his writing in a particular series of tropes. These tropes convey important information about Certeau's understanding of the interpretative act, at a level prior to subsequent formal analysis.

The first set of figures I want to consider concerns the 'sea' and its uncertain and moving borders with the 'land'. These figures

present in a quasi-mythical form the interpreter's initial encounter
with the historical inscription which he or she must endeavour to
render intelligible. They also place the interpreter's relation to this
'other' in the shadow of a transcendent Other:

> Like Robinson Crusoe on the shore of his island, before 'the vestige
> of a naked foot imprinted upon the sand', the historian travels along
> the borders of his present; he visits those beaches where the other
> appears only as a *trace* of what has *passed*. Here he sets up his industry.
> On the basis of imprints which are now definitively mute (that which
> has passed will return no more, and its voice is lost forever), a litera-
> ture is fabricated. (*AH* 8–9)

The 'literature' of the historian, a 'fabrication' (whose metaphors I
will go on to examine), brings us only a trace of a trace (here that
of the footprint, which so obsesses Crusoe). Certeau returns repeatedly to such figures of the 'trace'.[2] Yet it is equally characteristic
that he should place the apprehension of this trace at the borders
of that which has withdrawn its presence, which will return – in
another of its protean guises – to erase the trace, and which finally
exceeds and dissolves, in its vast and fluctuating indeterminacy,
the determined limits of both trace and interpretation. The place of
the interpreter emerges in Certeau's writing as precarious, fleeting and finite. His apprehension of the other which he aspires to
understand is both given to him and taken away by a larger Other
which, precisely, can never be apprehended as such:

> The violence of the body reaches the written page only across absence,
> through the intermediary of documents that the historian has been
> able to see on the shore from which the presence that left them behind
> has been washed away, and through a murmur that lets us hear – but
> from afar – the unknown immensity which seduces and menaces our
> knowledge. (*WH* 3/9)

The cumulative effect of such figures, or what one might call
their performative force, is considerable. Certeau's writing continually wears away at deep-rooted visually based models of interpretation, according to which the past might through the workings
of exegesis reveal itself to the naked eye.[3] In the quotation above,
what the historian can see is destabilized by what he or she can
at best indistinctly hear (it is a 'murmur'). The visible 'proofs' of
the historian's trade (indispensable as they are) seem to assume

an uncertain, flickering status against the encroaching background of what is invisible. Certeau challenges myths of interpretative transparency and mastery. He sets against these, in the very texture of much of his writing, the resistance of an opaque corporeal struggle, the confusion of distant voices and the mute unintelligibility of 'hieroglyphs' (*MF* 17/29). In the first instance, such figures disarm interpretation. They overturn the figure of the European conqueror which stands as a frontispiece to *The Writing of History*.[4] At the same time, however, in the relationship full of menace and seduction which they establish between the interpreter and his object, they introduce into Certeau's writing a diffuse 'erotics' of interpretation.

Such figures represent myths of historical interpretation in so far as they stage its activity in a 'place' which has no effective existence other than that of its poetic figuration. In more concrete terms, the flotsam and jetsam evoked above are the documents and archival traces which constitute the standard material basis for the work of the historian or literary critic. Certeau seeks elsewhere actively to reduce the relationship between the interpreter and this documentation to a peculiar kind of material banality. He adopts, so to speak, a cultivated naivety which paradoxically demands from us a certain intellectual effort if we are to break with habitual conceptions about our relation to 'historical' material.[5] Certeau subjects this relation to a form of estrangement.

Generally, we think of these relics and inscriptions which come down to us as 'belonging' to the past. Given this a priori categorization (which one could hardly say is simply wrong), it would be the historian's task to refine the 'arrangement' of these traces according to their originary provenance or respective position in time – time here being intuitively understood as an ordered geometrical space which one could lay out before oneself. Certeau problematizes this conception of time. He underlines that it represents not an adequate grasping of historical temporality, but rather a construction in and of the present. All those residual items which we come across – in museums, in archives, in books – do not really belong to the past. Whenever we apprehend them, they have always already been preselected and configured according to the structures of perception which govern our present. The vestigial organizations thereby produced are not history itself. We are given not the past in its immediacy, but rather a series of objects laid out and dispersed in the flatness of a present. Before such objects can in Certeau's terms be called properly 'historical', they must become the object of a particular kind of treatment. They must be turned around, reordered:

> No doubt it is an overstatement to say that 'time' constitutes the 'raw material of historical analysis' or its 'specific object'. Historians treat according to their methods the physical objects (papers, stones, images, sounds, etc.) that are set apart within the continuum of perception through the organization of a society and through the systems of relevance which characterize a 'science'. They work on materials in order to transform them into history. (*WH* 71/82)

Certeau defamiliarizes the historical artefacts which we perceive, foregrounding their status as artifices of contemporary systems of meaning. Furthermore, by bracketing, as it were, our common figuration of time as an organizing (and simultaneously reassuring, identificatory, consolidatory) principle, he emphasizes the degree to which the conditions of our temporal existence isolate us in the present, with no certain guidelines as to what to do with the debris we are given as 'history'.

Nevertheless, the principal thrust of Certeau's writings on historiography is precisely that the historian should indeed do something with these traces. Hence the importance of figures of 'fabrication': 'what do historians really fabricate when they "make history"?' (*WH* 56/63).[6] It would be reductive to see such figures, or ways of presenting interpretative activity, merely as figures. Nevertheless, it is useful to begin by juxtaposing them as such to the figures evoked above based on the 'sea' and its borders. If the first set of metaphors, heavy with ontological and even cosmic resonances, serves to disarm interpretation, the second set, in a vigorously down-to-earth and 'debasing' movement (in Mikhail Bakhtin's sense), serves to return interpretative practice to its concrete tasks and conditions of possibility.[7] It is the very movement between such contrasting figures, rather than a harmonious coexistence, which characterizes Certeau's own interpretative practice. Their alternation and combination is itself significant. We distort Certeau's thought if we privilege one of these metaphorical complexes over the other.

Historians, then, 'fabricate' the history which they produce. A disciplinary combination of rules, techniques and conventions defines for Certeau historiographical practice. These determine the treatment to which archival material will be subjected. They also work against the claims of any exclusively personal and intuitive response to the past. Certeau's dissatisfaction with Raymond Aron's classic critique of historical objectivity is revealing here.[8] While Aron argues that all historiography is indeed a function of the specific intellectual 'choices' of the historian, Certeau questions the priority which he sees Aron as giving to the sphere of the conscious ideas which prevail in an intellectual milieu. This approach protects these ideas from – or blinds them to – what are for Certeau key determining instances of historiographical production:

> The plurality of these philosophical subjectivities had . . . the discreet effect of preserving a singular position for intellectuals. As questions of meaning were treated *amongst themselves*, the explication of their differences of thought came to bestow upon the entire group a privileged relation to ideas. None of the noises of production, of social constraints, of professional or political positioning could interfere with the tranquillity of this relation: a silence was the postulate of this epistemology. (WH 59/66–7)

Again, in Certeau's language, the silent assurance of visual contemplation or panoramic control is troubled and set off balance (literally 'disquieted') by 'sounds' – here those of the interpreter's own techniques, and the localized affiliations which these suppose. Certeau stages these putative distractions as what in theatrical terms one might call 'noises off': they figure at first as interruptions to the smooth workings of the interpretative process, while actually pointing to more fundamental aspects of the productions in question. I propose to read such 'noises off' as a first form of 'implicit' alterity which Certeau discerns at work in historical interpretation. I will place under this rubric Certeau's attempts to elucidate the unconscious or tacit effects on historiographical production of contemporary socioeconomic and technical configurations (or 'complexes').

Certeau argues that historical interpretation has often tended to erase its relation to the techniques on which it is founded, whether these comprise its 'auxiliary' sciences (from computer studies to folklore) or its own formal procedures:

> It is as though history began only with the 'noble speech' of interpretation. As though finally it was an art of discourse delicately erasing all traces of labour. In fact, there is a decisive option here: the importance that is accorded to matters of technique turns history

either in the direction of literature or in the direction of science. (*WH* 69/80)

Certainly, much of Certeau's thought, contrary perhaps to the suggestion immediately above, will show that historiography cannot be defined once and for all either as a 'science' or as 'literature' – it is inevitably caught between the two.[9] Equally, we will see in subsequent chapters how Certeau's work questions the 'noble' or 'full' speech of learned interpretation by appealing to an unsettling series of 'voices off'. What needs to be underlined here, however, is Certeau's insistence that historiography is a concrete and limited form of production.[10] Historiography cannot for him be a mirror which would simply reflect the past, and the historian cannot set up his or her discourse in a sphere uncontaminated, so to speak, by the practices which have rendered it possible.

Hence Certeau's somewhat provocative figuration of the historiographical institution: 'like the car turned out by a factory, the historical study is bound to the complex of a specific form of collective fabrication far more than it is the effect of any personal philosophy or the resurgence of some past "reality". It is the *product* of a *place*' (*WH* 64/73). Certeau emphasizes that the historian's 'production' can be separated neither from the techniques and criteria which he or she shares with a larger workforce, nor from the demands addressed to the historiographical 'factory' as a result of its place in a larger whole. This larger whole may be represented in Certeau's thought either by general epistemic configurations, or by larger social structures. Certainly, we should not lean too heavily on the figure of the factory. Certeau is drawn in his work above all to the limits of such social and intellectual 'systems'. He seeks, precisely by delimiting these systems as such, to uncover the often surprising forms of inventiveness and ethical activity which orchestrate or elude in particular ways the objective constraints of a social order.[11] Likewise, Certeau focuses on how the 'I' of the historian may be inscribed in a more conflictual or intimate manner in his or her work.[12] Finally, as we shall see, he considers historical interpretation itself to be engaged in a rather paradoxical relation with regard to systems of productivity. Nevertheless, the lexis of 'fabrication' and 'factories' plays an important role in Certeau's theoretical writing. It returns the practice of interpretation, which often seems to speak as if from an autonomous intellectual sphere, to the social and historical institutions which both limit it and make it possible.

The two sets of figures discussed above – both that referring to finitude and transcendence, and that referring interpretative activity to what it 'fabricates' – will recur in my analyses of Certeau's work. They constitute an immediately striking aspect of his writing,[13] and they betray much about his fundamental conception of what he is doing in this writing. They repeatedly re-present in it both the myth of an Other which 'gives' (and takes) all others, and the localized forms of 'implicit' alterity at work in interpretative practice. In so far as I will be dealing in what follows with historiography conceived as a contemporary 'operation', it will initially be the second set of figures which predominates.

Interpretation as Operation

I shall show over the course of this study how the apparently neutral or disconcertingly technical term 'operation' performs an organizing function in Certeau's thought. He proposes for example in *La culture au pluriel* that 'in cultural matters, we need to direct our research towards the question of operations' (*CP* 221). Certeau's analyses of historical interpretation are formulated in similar terms. He argues that

> in history, everything begins with the move which *sets apart*, which groups together and which transforms into 'documents' certain objects which had been classified in another way. ... The material is created through the concerted actions which cut it out from its place in the world of contemporary usage, which seek it also beyond the frontiers of this usage, and which subject it to a coherent form of re-employment. ... Establishing signs offered up for specific kinds of treatment, this rupture is therefore neither solely nor first of all the effect of a 'gaze'. It requires a technical operation. (*WH* 73/84)

Certeau emphasizes that the interpreter does not passively absorb the traces of the other, but 'operates' on them in such a way as to redistribute them. The material constituted by these founding operations of selection and ordering forms itself moreover the basis for a further series of operations, or 'treatments'. Finally, the results of this treatment must be 'written up' – itself an operation of a particular kind. Certeau takes up all these facets of interpretative practice to present, as it were, a complex and 'layered' account of the 'historiographical operation'. In my analysis of this account, I will examine firstly Certeau's treatment of interpretative operations in so far as they can be 'delimited' by formal analysis, and secondly the forms of social practice implied by these operations. In both cases, I will indicate the modifications which Certeau's employment of the lexis of 'operations' was designed to effect upon prevailing conceptions of historical interpretation.

Delimiting operations

If interpretative acts are to be conceived as operations, the suggestion is that they can, like other operations designed to fabricate other objects, be delimited and broken down into their constituent parts. That is, they can be shown to consist of specific formal rules, procedures and skills. Of course, there are important differences between interpretative practice and other more obviously 'practical' practices. Interpreters are seldom aware of the extent to which, or indeed of exactly how, they are following (or are led by) diverse rules and procedures. Moreover, there is likely to be a resistance on the part of interpreters to having all their mental acts reduced to formal ('abstract') operations.[14] Yet it is precisely as a response to such innate resistance that Certeau sets out to place all interpretative activity under the rubric of 'operations'.[15] He seeks to prise apart any supposed intuitive bond linking the interpreter to his or her object, in order to foreground rather the 'artificiality' and projections (in the psychoanalytic sense) inherent in this relation, and the inevitable misprisions and forceful appropriations which constitute the interpretative act. As Terence Hawkes writes of Roland Barthes's project in *Mythologies*, Certeau aims 'to take us "behind the scenes" as it were of our own construction of the world'.[16] This does not mean, however, that we are given access to a single full and deeper reality beneath the manifest play of interpretation. Certeau's task is more circumscribed:

> By envisaging history as an operation, we may attempt, in a necessarily limited manner, to understand it as the relation between a *place* (a type of recruitment, a milieu, a profession, etc.), analytic *procedures* (a discipline), and the construction of a *text* (a literature). . . . This analysis of the preconditions which its discourse does not take up will allow us to specify the silent laws which organize the space produced as text. (*WH* 57/64)

Certeau is not simply stating as a matter of truistic principle that we approach the documents of the past in terms which are not those of the past. He seeks rather to bring into relief the concrete historiographical processes of dissection and configuration which reorder the traces of the past. By scrutinizing these processes of dissection (or what Foucault calls 'découpes'), Certeau hopes to uncover some of the largely unconscious or unspoken laws which govern contemporary interpretative activity. I want to suggest that these laws constitute for Certeau a first form of 'implicit' alterity at work in learned interpretation. They complicate and overdetermine the relation of the interpreter to the historical 'other' which he or she aspires to comprehend. I shall take up in a summary manner Certeau's tripartite division of the historiographical operation (place, procedures, text), organizing my exposition around examples which are of strategic importance in Certeau's thought. These concern the relations between historiography and the practice and products of writing as such.

(1) The allotted place of historians has for Certeau traditionally been that of 'clerks', dealers of the written word. This has meant that they have privileged written documents – and consequently certain segments of society – in the representations they propose of what is significant in society as a whole. Certeau argues that their disproportionate concern with authoritative writings has led historians to reproduce deep-rooted forms of social hegemony:

> Despite attempts to break down such barriers, the intellectual labour of historians is established within the circle of *writing*: in this written history, it places first and foremost the very people who have themselves written, in such a way that historiographical works reinforce a sociocultural tautology between their authors (a learned group), their objects (books, manuscripts, etc.), and their (cultivated) public. (*WH* 65/74)

We have seen how Raymond Aron does not in Certeau's view take the institutional setting of historiography properly into account, locating the writing of history in an intellectual sphere isolated from the 'noises' of its own and others' production. Certeau maintains in addition that historians have long paid insufficient attention to the far-reaching implications for their interpretative practice of their position precisely among the 'writers' of society.[17]

I will examine critically in chapter 2 Certeau's historical analyses of successive 'circles of writing'. It is worth indicating here, however, an initial complication. Certeau traces how such 'circles' work at one level as a form of implicit alterity in learned interpretation. They seem for him to structure the historian's enterprise like a social unconscious, confronting the historian 'with a praxis which is inextricably both his own and that of the other' (*WH* 45/58). At another level, however, the effect of their operation is precisely to reproduce the 'Same', and to exclude other forms of alterity. This two-way slippage underlines the impossibility of analysing Certeau's work in terms of a single category of alterity. It shows how the 'same' and the 'other' are themselves not stable entities in Certeau's thought, but must always be differentially and positionally defined. The ongoing work of alterity upon identity serves also in Certeau's writing to direct narrowly circumscribed discourses beyond themselves. By delimiting the sociocultural 'tautology' (a repetition of the same) implied by the operations outlined above, he sets up a space – and a desire – for a set of 'heterologies' (discourses 'on' the other). Certeau's own heterological operations address notably questions of orality and of reading. I will explore in subsequent chapters how the supplementary questions which these heterologies provoke are designed to shake the assurances of fellow writers. They reveal what for Certeau constitute unavowed forms of enclosure. He seeks to introduce fragments of alterity into the established edifices of written knowledge, and thereby to alter our conceptions of this knowledge. This is not to say, of course, that Certeau can himself claim to proceed from an abstract sphere removed from the sites of written production.

(2) The procedures deployed by historians to interpret historical material are evidently related, though not reducible, to the places where they work. Certeau isolates notably two modes of interpretation used to analyse the transition from a religiously organized society to a secular society.[18] He calls the first 'literary' or 'ideological', and the second 'sociological'. Both may produce instructive forms of intelligibility, and they can be defined as follows. A literary approach is characterized by a close attention to ideas *as* ideas, to subtle levels of linguistic innovation in the text being studied and by a greater or lesser bracketing of (social) context in order to examine (literary) content. In a sociological analysis, by contrast, documents and ideas are not examined for their own sake, on their own terms, but as passive signs of something else. They

are read and quantified as symptoms of larger movements (the prevalence of a particular 'mentality', the extent of dechristianization, the localization of superstitious or folkloric 'residue', the spread of literacy as such, etc.).[19] The former approach treats knowledge as knowledge, so to speak, while the latter uses it to make social classifications. At an initial level, they constitute simply two distinct interpretative techniques.

Certeau, however, questioned the concrete applications which historians were making of these procedures. He noted that in the historical analysis of dechristianization over the seventeenth and eighteenth centuries, each distinct method tended to correspond to a different section of society. A 'literary' analysis was used to interpret the ideological productions of a cultural elite, and a 'sociological' analysis to read off the traces remaining of the mainly rural 'masses' (*WH* 118–19/125). He explores the implications of this interpretative dichotomy.

Certeau argues that historians and literary critics were employing 'literary' procedures to interpret those texts which in sociological terms most resembled their own – in other words those of a cultural elite. Other texts and documents were reduced by contrast to the status of statistical information. To some extent this division is still inevitable today given the nature of the documents now available.[20] More fundamentally, however, Certeau suggests that such a methodological bifurcation works to separate the society under consideration into two extremely unequal parts. On the one hand, it presents a small section of society which is mentally and linguistically proficient, and whose productions are worthy of serious consideration. On the other hand, it presupposes that the 'productions' of the vast majority of the population are hardly worth the name, and that their mental, linguistic and practical activity is inevitably derivative, inculcated, superstitious, recalcitrant or passive. Certeau emphasizes that this representation is not a direct reflection of historical reality. Rather, he shows it to be the product of a diverging set of formal procedures, which are themselves largely determined by the place of historians in contemporary society.

Of course, there had already been attempts to move beyond the interpretative dead-end set out above, and to apply a 'sociological' model of interpretation to the ideological productions of an elite. An emblematic example here would be Lucien Goldmann's *The Hidden God*.[21] Yet Certeau can in many ways be seen as a pioneer in his repeated and varied advocacy of the opposite inversion. His work shows how one can 'read' in what might provisionally be called a 'literary' way those productions which are not obviously (or at all) 'literary'. This development is rendered possible by the way in which Certeau delimits or denaturalizes the conventional operations of historiographical interpretation. We will see in subsequent chapters how it allows him to uncover creativity or difference where a standard interpretation might see only uniformity. Equally, it permits him to discern sociohistorical mutations at a level beneath that of explicit ideological proclamations. If this approach can initially be labelled 'literary' in so far as it seeks to uncover creative twists and turns which had hitherto escaped interpreters' attention, it is important to note that it does not do this by bracketing off what is distinctively historical about such moves. Certeau shows rather how these moves are constituted in their turn precisely by active operations within and upon the elements of a historical context. In effect, Certeau's work serves to reconfigure prevailing oppositions between the 'literary' and the 'historical', by fostering a close attention to the textual historicity of overlooked operations.[22]

(3) The 'writing up' of historical or literary research is reducible neither to the transparent presentation of an object, nor to a simple exposition of results, but represents rather for Certeau an operation in its own right. I shall introduce here just one key aspect of this operation. Certeau shows how a practice of 'citation' enables the historian to construct what he calls a 'layered text' (*un texte feuilleté*). Certeau uses this term to designate a form of writing which combines in a single text both the language of the interpreter and the fragmented language of his or her object. The end-product of this process is a 'discourse which "contains" [*comprend*] its other', and which 'attributes to itself the power of stating what the other unknowingly signifies. Through "citations", references, notes, and the whole apparatus of permanent referral to a language which precedes it . . . historiographical discourse sets itself up as a *knowledge of the other*' (WH 94/111). The construction of the historiographical text is no mere transcription, but represents rather a form of 'staging'. Certeau foregrounds the peculiar textual operation to which the interpreter subjects his or her material. He plays on the ambivalence of the 'citation' which ostensibly closes the interpretative process. Like a judge, in a position of authority, the interpreter 'summons' others to appear, assigns to them their place

and 'cites' them before other judges. This (inevitable) technique of 'citation' both confirms the historian's own place, and constitutes a linchpin of the process through which historiographical texts are put together: 'the split [*dédoublée*] structure of such discourse functions like a machinery which extracts from citation a narrative verisimilitude and a validation of knowledge' (*WH* 94/111). The practice of 'citation' represents in Certeau's analysis the culmination of a series of operations. These allow the historian to 'tame' the fragmentary traces which had initially figured as a disarming or perplexing lacuna in a body of knowledge. The historian circumscribes these traces, and thereby converts them into the very proof of epistemic mastery.

Certeau seeks in his own interpretative practice to problematize such a conversion. I will show in chapter 3 how he focuses on the points of articulation between interpreting and interpreted language. He suggests how processes of citation may backfire to put in question the very interpretative edifices which they are designed to support. He himself experiments with other uses of citation. This supplementary work, however, is again predicated on a prior delimitation. Certeau analyses interpretative discourses as the products of particular strategic and literary operations. He is able thereby to expose certain limits of these operations, and to suggest both what they reveal of the human subjects who propose them, and also how these subjects 'miss', in various senses of the word, the objects of their interpretation.

The illustrations above have revolved around questions of writing and textualization. They have also demonstrated what one might call the 'delimitative' function of Certeau's analyses. By breaking down interpretative activity into a series of formal operations, Certeau is able to push this activity up against its borders. This is not to say that he can simply overstep these borders. His work produces rather what he himself in a different context calls a 'vibration of limits' (*WH* 38/50). He constantly unsettles pre-established frontiers between inside and outside, self and other. One could perhaps see in this practice the reason for the 'permanent anticipation' which characterized Certeau's position in diverse intellectual fields.[23] His work exemplifies what it is tempting to describe as a basic 'heterological' law: the operation which draws up a limit to familiar space insinuates by the same movement foreignness into that space.

Interpretative operations as real activity

The preceding discussion of the formal or irreducibly 'artificial' nature of interpretative operations may have raised understandable reservations in the mind of the reader. If all interpretations inevitably 'miss' their mark – or at least the mark of the other – does this mean that they float in some abstract sphere forever detached from the reality they aspire to comprehend? To adopt such a position would in effect be no less problematic than asserting that the historical interpreter can have direct and intuitive access to the object of his or her interpretation. Moreover, the examples above were designed to demonstrate precisely that the interpreter cannot operate in an entirely abstract or detached sphere. The interpreter's enterprise is structured through and through by – though by no means reducible to – social and institutional presuppositions and constraints. These are not generally explicated as such in interpretative discourse. They tend to work rather as what Pierre Bourdieu might call a cultural 'unconscious'. For Certeau, they inevitably *implicate* interpretative activity in a social reality which it cannot necessarily master.

By analysing historiographical work as a series of operations, Certeau aims to underline that it should not be reduced simply to the artefacts which it finally turns out (books, papers, programmes). He envisages it rather as an ongoing form of social practice. He argues that we should take seriously 'expressions which are loaded with meaning – "doing history", "doing theology" – whereas we are all too liable to erase the verb (the productive act) in order to privilege its complement (the object produced)' (*WH* 20/28). Hence, by turning historiography back upon its own place and procedures, Certeau does not divert it from the 'real'. Rather, he confronts historiographical discourse with its concrete and finite (real) conditions of possibility:

> The situation of historiography makes the question of the real appear in two quite different positions within the scientific process: the real as that which is *known* (what the historian studies, understands or 'brings to life' of a past society) and the real as that which is *implicated* in the scientific operation (the present society to which the problematic of the historian, his procedures, his modes of comprehension and finally a practice of meaning all refer). (*WH* 35/46–7)

Certeau thus conceives what he designates as the 'real' both in terms of the intended historical object of interpretation, and also as a function of the 'implicit' social forces and technical apparatuses which organize interpretative activity. Furthermore, he argues that it is only by explicating the latter that the interpreter can come to a lucid conception of his or her relation with the former.

Certeau's use of the word 'real' (*réel*) needs at least a brief comment. Tom Conley notes that we cannot always equate this term with 'reality' (*réalité*). In Certeau's usage, 'reality' tends to constitute instead 'what the subject strategically chooses it to be'.[24] It represents an effect of historiographical discourse, analogous to the 'reality effect' (*effet de réel*) which Barthes analyses in realist fiction.[25] The 'real', by contrast, – a term which in Conley's view Certeau often uses in a similar way to Lacan – refers to that which resists direct symbolization, and which strains all representations and systems of knowledge.[26] Certeau does not therefore in his analyses seek simply to substitute one conception of reality (the present) for another (the past). He traces rather how the 'effects' of the 'real' not only surface in the elusive object of historical research, which inevitably breaks away from the systems of intelligibility governing this research, but also emerge in historiographical production as symptoms of the interpreter's own contemporary position and project. For Certeau, historiographical discourse is not so much detached from 'reality' (it produces 'reality' through processes of interpretation) as *involved* in a 'real' which it can alter but cannot fully contain.

These considerations could take us back to the tropes of trace and finitude which I discussed at the beginning of this chapter. However, I would like for now to concentrate on the more specifically social and epistemic aspects of the reversal outlined above. Firstly, Certeau turns interpretative procedures and discourses away from their intended objects and towards their own localized conditions of possibility. He then shows how these procedures are implicated as concrete modes of productive practice in the societies and scientific communities to which they belong.

Certeau argues that any historical interpretation must be understood in terms of the social organization which enabled, shaped and constrained its production. More specifically, it is indissociable from the contemporary state of those sectors of society – the 'scientific community' – which most directly provide it with its status and rationale. He underlines as a 'fundamental' fact that 'a "historical" text (that is to say, a new interpretation, the application of distinctive methods, the elaboration of other criteria of relevance, a displacement in the definition and use of documents, a

characteristic mode of organization, etc.) expresses an operation
which is situated within a larger body of practices' (*WH* 64/73).
Certeau provisionally brackets off the relation of an interpretation
to the real which it professes to interpret, in order to foreground
the question of the yield which any particular historiographical
work must produce in the terms of a contemporary intellectual
community. Certainly, the question of the historical real cannot be
erased, and I will suggest below how Certeau considers that it
must indeed, through historiography, return (like the repressed) in
order to haunt and disquiet contemporary organizations of meaning. Equally, the 'contribution' which historiography makes to
knowledge will be shown to be somewhat paradoxical. Nevertheless, the question of its interest and pertinence must for Certeau
be referred in the first instance to a contemporary organization of
knowledge. This problematizes the more traditional imperative
assigned to historical interpretation of corresponding 'adequately'
to the past. Certeau argues that it is through the effects which
controlled historiographical operations can exert on contemporary
understanding that they can themselves be conceived as a concrete
practice in the present.

Yet Certeau does not analyse historiographical practice with
reference purely to the preoccupations of the strictly scientific or
intellectual sectors of society. For these preoccupations are themselves caught up in larger social processes. Indeed, intellectual
labour may also for Certeau be characterized as a form of controlled work on more general configurations of knowledge, sites of
concern, or 'common sense': 'what is "scientific", in history as in
other disciplines, is the operation which changes the "environment"
– or which makes a social, literary or other kind of *organization*
into the condition and site of a *transformation*' (*WH* 72/83). Historiography in Certeau's account, like other forms of 'scientific' practice, denaturalizes (or historicizes) what is considered as 'natural'
in order to produce something different or 'useful'. In the case of
historiography, this operation has an inescapably literary dimension. I have referred already to the 'defamiliarizing' effect of
Certeau's historiographical analyses. This can also be placed in a
wider perspective. Certeau argues that his task as a professional
historian is to work upon the generally circulating narratives
(*histoires*) which he reads and hears around him.[27] Ordinary men
and women tell each other familiar stories about the development
of society, the history of sexuality, the truths of nature, the 1960s,
the demise of religion, etc. They articulate their social, historical
and personal identities by exchanging these stories. Historians

operate on the symbolic 'environment' which others constitute. It is their job to provide other (scientifically controlled if not definitively true) stories. These may be used either to create, to discredit or to 'make strange' diverse forms of interlocutory exchange. Effective historians may, in a limited way, reorganize the way others think. For Certeau, they work on the borderlines between what is socially and naturally given and what may be produced through an activity of epistemic and poetic transformation. Certeau suggests how this work may operate as a form of social praxis.

The theoretical reflections above have, I hope, prised open a breach in the interpretative process which I do not intend to repair. They indicate the sort of space in which Certeau works. He envisages interpretations of the past as localized fabrications (or 'stories') of the present, and problematizes the relation which these interpretative fabrications hold with the traces of history which they manipulate/comprehend. I shall now go on to examine Certeau's reflection on the structural organization and mutation of meaning. This will serve to show more clearly how historical interpretation constitutes for Certeau a properly paradoxical form of contemporary operation. I will also illustrate how his recourse to a concept of 're-employment' (*réemploi*) brings into new relief both historiography and other forms of historical practice.

Systems and Re-employments

It is already clear that the significations produced through interpretative acts cannot be isolated for Certeau from the situations in which they take place. Certeau thus presents the historian's work as a function of a larger set-up in which he or she is implicated. This set-up may be conceived as that of a circumscribed intellectual community, or be analysed in terms of more general social and linguistic orders. The sort of operations considered above are not seen as free-floating, self-sufficient acts of volition. Certeau supposes them on the contrary to be enmeshed through and through in an organization of elements and forces which can be called a 'structure', a 'system', or an 'economy'. Facts, inscriptions and interpretations can only *make sense* in terms of such organized (if shifting) wholes. This is no doubt a commonplace of the 'structural' conception of meaning which has become widely disseminated over the last few decades.[28]

Certeau bases his theory and practice of historiography on broadly structural postulates. He traces the processes and conditions which make intelligibility, belief and meaningful action possible in different sets of historical circumstances. As Philippe Boutry helpfully observes, 'what really seems to have been for Michel de Certeau the least elusive object of history . . . is a certain type of "formality" in the order of discourses and practices, a certain arrangement, a certain articulation of the fields of belief and those of culture, of society and of power.'[29] Such formal organizations (or 'articulations') do not provide for Certeau the underlying truth of history. They constitute rather a series of necessary and shifting frameworks through which to read dispersed textual clusters. It will become apparent in the following discussion to what degree the resolutely historical orientation of Certeau's thought develops, complicates and delimits basic structural premises in interesting ways.

One should note, nevertheless, that it is unhelpful in approaching Certeau's work to become too fixated on words such as 'structure' and 'system'. He finds other terms equally useful. He examines for example Foucault's focus on 'mode(s) of being of order' (*H* 176/*HP* 23), and integrates the latter's notion of *dispositifs* into his own analyses (*PE* 45–9/75–81, *MF* 14/26).[30] I will introduce in chapter 2 his conception of an 'economy' of writing. Other expressions such as 'organization of meaning' and 'social network' are common. One should emphasize likewise that the function of these terms in Certeau's work is not simply to isolate and to 'freeze' fixed structures. They serve on the contrary to set thought in motion. They uncover its partiality by setting it incessantly into larger configurations, and by bringing it up against its limits. Moreover, the strictly technical aspects of this interpretative apparatus cannot be separated from a more general figurative force. As Jacques Revel writes, 'the metaphorical system which he held dear – crossroads, networks, places of transit, limit markers – has more than simply a descriptive value. It has a heuristic function: it spatializes and dynamizes the operation of knowledge.'[31] Certeau's habitual conceptual tools should be read as an integral part of what Revel calls a 'poetics of transition and displacement'.[32]

Historical and historiographical systems

Certeau does not set out to uncover 'the' formal structure of a society, past or present. History (the 'real') is more complicated and less graspable than this. Its mutations and shifts exceed any single point of view. Certeau deliberately proposes therefore a multiplicity of perspectives. He performs a series of what Philippe Boutry calls 'plural readings',[33] conceived in terms of a 'plurality' of logics.[34] He analyses history in terms of a multitude of combined and distinct, evolving and dissolving, composed and decomposed systems, in which he himself as a historian is necessarily also caught up. He is particularly interested in the relations between and hence the limits of such systems. He explores their modes of respective resistance and the thresholds of their mutual compatibility. By concentrating on the interstices and interferences between different configurations of meaning, Certeau both works at the limit of structural conceptions and also probes the blind-spots of contemporary thought as such.

One can isolate here two related foci of Certeau's attention. I will begin by presenting these at the necessarily abstract level of structures or systems, before going on to examine Certeau's treatment of the 'elements' without which these are nothing.[35] Firstly, Certeau is repeatedly drawn as a historian to moments of historical transition or rupture. Secondly, his work throws into particular relief the problematic relation between the interpretative systems deployed by historians and the effective reality of other historical systems.

Questions of historical rupture and transition are central to Certeau's work. How do social orders (and the human subjects who live within them) cease to be organized in certain ways and come to be organized in others? Such breaks often assume the form of inexplicable lacunae encountered in historical research and covered over by the operation of writing up which follows. In Michel Foucault's *The Order of Things*, to take a hyperbolic example, the substitutions of one 'episteme' for another seem to be hidden in the subterranean depths of history.[36] For Certeau, the passage from a 'religiously' conceived world to a politically ordered society over the early modern period constitutes a fecund testing ground for what might be termed second-order models of structural transformation and slippage:

> The socio-cultural shifts at work in the seventeenth and eighteenth centuries concern frames of reference. They operate a transition from a *religious* organization to a political or economic *ethic*. They provide a privileged terrain for the analysis of the mutations which touch both upon the structures and upon the 'believable' in a society. (*WH* 148/153)

Certeau returns repeatedly to these questions, experimenting with different approaches and perspectives. Indeed, it would be misleading to present Certeau's work on early modern religious history as what one could call after Pascal a purely 'geometrical' exercise. The transitions and ruptures which he discerns are not merely pretexts for elaborate theoretical constructions. The dissolution of a religious cosmos and the possibilities for 'belief' in a secularized society were for Certeau objects of visceral concern.[37] His affective 'implication' in such questions is itself an important element in the configuration of his historical analyses.

This concern also invests the second focus of attention evoked above with a peculiar intensity in Certeau's writing. What is the relation between contemporary systems of intelligibility and the historical systems on whose traces they are set to work? Or: what kind of meanings do we produce when we (inevitably) explain or 'present' a past social and symbolic order according to models of comprehension which would have been foreign to it?

Again, Certeau's specialized terrain of early modern religious history provides for this problem a significantly 'charged' field of inquiry. Certeau argues that the criteria which modern thought prioritizes in accounting for past (or 'primitive') societies tend to be narrowly socioeconomic. The criteria in terms of which, say, French society around the beginning of the early modern period would have accounted for its organization would have been 'religious'. At this time, the organization of society had to be read through reference to (*inter-lectum*) a transcendent principle (God, the Christian revelation, etc.). Today, the representations of this transcendent principle must themselves be rendered intelligible through reference to social and economic reality. Certeau notes, for example, how modern historiography detects in successive conceptions of the Christian Trinity reflections of corresponding mutations in socioeconomic structures.[38] He certainly does not want to undo the scientifically controlled work of demystification which this interpretative chiasmus has produced for contemporary society. His work is exempt from what Jacques Le Brun calls the 'restorationist temptations' to be found in much religious historiography.[39] However, Certeau does ask to what extent the interpretative procedure outlined above can give us anything approaching the 'real' otherness of past societies, or whether our interpretative techniques can only ever isolate us in our own way of seeing, or 'structure of perception'.[40] Certeau's attempt to pursue this question does not consist simply in confronting two monolithically conceived 'periods of consciousness or . . . historical types of intelligibility' (*WH* 138/149). As I have already suggested, this would represent rather an abstract and sterile procedure. Instead, he examines both this problem and that of historical transition at the concrete level of the 'operations' which take place within – and in a sense between – systems. He traces how different elements of different systems are variously appropriated (recombined, reinterpreted, converted and distorted) in different historical practices. This line of inquiry brings us to Certeau's pivotal notion of 're-employment'.

Re-employments: forms of practice

The category of 're-employment' in Certeau's work can be conceived initially as a conceptual tool which enables him to organize and to interpret the material he collects. I will also suggest below how it involves a conception of human history as such, in which the historian is also implicated.

How does Certeau (re)constitute a series of structural breaks and developments on the basis of the documentary evidence before him? Turning again to his specialized inquiry into early modern religious history, we can see how he operates at the level of the mutating elements 'within' different systems, and from which alone the effective reality of these systems can be induced. Certeau traces, by focusing on certain 'marks' or 'indices', how what are nominally the same elements begin to function differently. The different functioning of formally identical elements points to the fact that they are actually being 're-employed' (reappropriated, resituated, redefined) in terms of another organizing system. Certeau analyses such processes at a supplementary formal level, which he designates as that of the 'formality' of practices (*la formalité des pratiques*). This concept is designed to direct attention to the 'forms' of heterogeneous practices, and to how these affect and alter the 'forms' of the various objects, writings and images on which they operate. Beyond the level of manifest representation or 'content', Certeau seeks to grasp something of the specific uses and trajectories of formal elements as they are taken up and trans-formed in different practices.

One can see this interpretative technique at work in Certeau's analysis of the passage over the early modern period from a religiously conceived cosmos to an explicitly politically ordered society. Indeed, the expression 'formality of practices' seems itself to

have its origin in this analysis.[41] I have isolated three instances of
re-employment which Certeau detects, and which all point to the
latent mutations which were reorganizing early modern societies
at a level beneath that of explicit ideological discourse.

(1) Between the break-up of European Christendom in the sixteenth
century and the development of increasingly secular authorities by
the eighteenth century, Certeau sees the church(es) as implicated
in – and subjugated by – a process of political transformation.
Whereas they had once been seen to organize and to guarantee the
nation, they became increasingly organized and defined by the
nation.[42] Through an extensive interim period, Certeau traces how
the rulers of French society ceased to relate their enterprises to the
interests and dictates of the Church, but rather used the authority
and credibility supplied by the Church in order to advance projects
and designs conceived more and more in terms determined by the
concept of the 'state'. At first this transition passed through the
intermediary figure of the king, a divinely guaranteed secular ruler,
under whose representative authority 'religious structures were
taken up again, but as part of another system. Christian organizations were re-employed as a function of an order which they
no longer determined. . . . The weakened Christian "system"
was transformed into a sacred "theatre" of the system which was
taking its place' (*WH* 156–7/165–6). Certeau detects a striking
instance of such theatricalization in Richelieu's intervention as a
function of political strategy in the possession of Loudun.[43] He places
this spectacular but 'metonymic' detail in the context of the more
generalized use of Catholicism to cement and consolidate a centralized national unity. A more conventional indicator of this process would be the revocation of the Edict of Nantes in 1685.

(2) At the same time as religions became defined and used increasingly in terms of state policy (*raison d'état*), Certeau detects another,
inverse movement crossing both national frontiers and internal doctrinal disputes (for example between the Jansenists and the Jesuits). This constitutes the 'mystic' treatment (or re-employment) of
the Christian tradition. As the pronouncements and practices of
official Christian institutions began to seem ever more 'opaque'
(that is, political), believers in different nations and orders began
to turn towards a 'hidden' interiority.[44] They invoked an 'experience' which, defining itself by its 'foreignness' with regard to institutional structures, was strikingly familiar in its expression across

its different national and institutional localizations. The mystics effectively combed Scripture and Christian authorities as a function of this experience. They extracted and appropriated particularly those passages which suggested how a transcendent God might make Himself directly accessible to the soul, without the mediation of institutions. Certeau traces how 'the social use of religious criteria became dislocated, as it were, from a mystic reinterpretation of the same religious structures' (*WH* 128/134). It is striking that he does not, as many studies do, interpret the mystic texts in a 'purely' literary way. Rather, through the conceptual tool of re-employments, he is able both to provide a close linguistic analysis of the ways in which the mystics constructed their texts, beginning with the material at their disposal, and also to show how their reinstrumentation of this material points to a general sociohistorical set of circumstances – specifically to the deterioration of Christian frames of reference and the transition towards politically organized national states. Furthermore, the structuration of mystic practices is conceived in his account both as a function of, and as a reaction to, the larger system outlined above imposed by state policy. In the interstices created by generalized transitions and mutations, Certeau discerns a proliferation of operations combining and recombining redistributed elements in unpredictable ways. Certainly, general structures determine the conditions of such practices. Nevertheless, Certeau's attention to the re-employments whose traces can be reconstituted at the limits of these structures, and which form their own transitory microstructures, reminds us that the Brownian movement of history (a multiplicity of erratically interacting particles) cannot be reduced to a few geometrical shapes or reassuringly linear narratives.

(3) The idea of re-employment informs finally Certeau's reading of the sharp rise in witchcraft trials in rural areas of France towards the end of the sixteenth century and at the beginning of the seventeenth century. Once more, I want here simply to abstract a scheme from his treatment in order to demonstrate his interpretative technique. Certeau points again to a series of reinterpretations set within and against the general disarticulation of the doctrinal structures of Christianity. He detects in the traces left by witchcraft trials – and later, in cases of diabolic possession – a process by which 'the collective symbols of religious belonging are detached from the churches so as to form the imaginary lexicon of an anti-society' (*WH* 153/161). Elements were removed from their place in an

orthodox edifice and reconfigured so as to alter or even invert their meaning. Obviously, there is a problem concerning the extent to which one can interpret such appropriations as meaningful instances of 'resistance' or as unwitting lapses from the codified rigours of post-tridentine Catholicism. Nevertheless, Certeau argues in his critique of Robert Mandrou's work on magistrates and sorcerers in seventeenth-century France that these destabilizations of the Christian order can be conceived at one level to have been in advance (*avant la lettre*) of the more learned sections of contemporary society. When the judiciary of the seventeenth century moved towards a more rational attitude with regard to witchcraft, they were effectively acting upon a deterioration of Christian frames of reference which had already taken place.[45]

The preceding examples demonstrate in a summary manner Certeau's conception of the formality of practices. They show how he reads human history as a multiple and mobile series of re-employments. He interprets discursive and symbolic formations at the level of 'use' rather than of manifest sense, arguing that 'in order to discern the new order being inscribed in traditional forms of behaviour, it is not sufficient simply to analyse their contents: the same ideas or the same institutions can be perpetuated at the very time when their social signification is changing' (*WH* 157/166). Certeau displaces a more conventional preoccupation with representations as such in order to foreground the question of practices. He approaches representations both as the products of strategical and tactical practices proper to specific social groups, and also as forms which are appropriated by other types of social practice. Hence, he does not interpret representations as holding their own truth, but instead sets them off from this truth, and configures them as more or less contingent moments and precipitates of the practices in which they were implicated:

> The formality [of practices] is more or less in accord with official or theoretical discourses; it calls them into question since it also organizes a practice of reading or hearing; in other words, a practice *of* these discourses, not to mention the practices which they forget or exclude. One of the tasks of history consists in measuring the distance or the relations between the formality of practices and that of representations. (*WH* 157–8/167)

The project of elucidating the relations between representations and practices is one which runs through Certeau's work.[46] It is a distinctively 'historical' as opposed to a purely 'literary' approach to interpretation in so far as it does not dissociate textual documentation from its relation to a series of heterogeneous human operations without which it could not exist.

One can usefully extrapolate from the preceding analyses in order to show how the practice of the historian can equally be conceived for Certeau as a series of re-employments. The historian carries across (trans-lates) elements from one system (that of the past in which they were embedded, or that of their current conservation) and restages them so that they figure in his or her own interpretative system. As indicated above, the 'citation' involved in this enterprise does not directly resurrect the past. Nor are glittering relics simply displayed in the transparent showcase of the historian's text. On the contrary, the historian *reuses* these relics and thereby becomes caught up in the series of re-employments which he or she aspires to present. This must affect the process of interpretation, as Certeau implies when he comments on the religious historian's position with regard to a historical series of re-employments of the term 'religion'. These re-employments effectively splinter this term into a scattered multiplicity of differing meanings, including the meaning which it will assume in the historian's own interpretation:

> we must differentiate the modes according to which religious 'facts' *function* (even supposing that these facts are in any way identical), that is to say, we have to distinguish the orders which determine the re-employments of these facts and hence their successive significations; all this before – and with the purpose of – being able to grasp what historical relation exists between these modes, and therefore our means of 'understanding' them or interpreting them 'faithfully'. (WH 141/152)

The possibility of a faithful interpretation must, as I have said, remain an open question, a breach in our understanding. Nevertheless, by examining the 'resuscitations' effected by the historical interpreter as re-employments of organized fragments from other historical orders, we can advance beyond the unwieldy confrontation between opposing monolithic systems which I outlined above. This move will also allow me to describe in more detail the ambivalent mode of productivity which defines for Certeau both the principal task of his historical research, and the nature of its relation to other forms of contemporary knowledge.

Working on Limits

I have shown how the writing of history problematizes for Certeau the relations between fabrication and the 'real'. To borrow a traditional metaphor, such truth as historiography yields should be considered to 'limp'. Yet the fabrications of historiography cannot be reduced to pure fictions: to do so would be to disregard the reality of the criteria and controls which govern its production, and which distinguish it from what can be designated as literature. Historiography is scientifically 'bound' in a way in which literature is not. It must show its evidence, regulate its procedures, expose its assertions to the criticism of a scientific community. Despite his work on the extreme precariousness of any absolute distinction between historiography and literature, Certeau never loses sight of these constraints which limit and define the historian's practice. He resists Paul Veyne's erstwhile claim that historiography operates in another sphere to that of science.[47] For Certeau, historiography is defined by a particular *relation* to science (understood roughly as a contemporary body of knowledge, working hypotheses, interpretative models, rules and disciplines). He argues, however, that this relation should consist in a practice of 'falsification'.

We have already seen how the approach of historians to the past is in Certeau's analysis always informed by contemporary models of intelligibility. One might provisionally group these models together as a scientific or social orthodoxy. In this respect, one could say that Certeau presents the case for a strictly speaking heterodox practice of historiography. He argues that the task of historians is not simply to consolidate the interpretative models which they use, and thereby to confirm and extend their mastery of reality. On the contrary, historians should in Certeau's view seek to disarm these models and to expose their irreducible locality and limits (what in rather archaic English one might call their 'idiotisms'). Historical research should demonstrate that such models cannot be used to interpret and to account for the whole of the 'real'. Historiography as Certeau conceives it

> intervenes in the mode of a critical experimentation of sociological, economic, psychological or cultural models. It is said, to quote Pierre Vilar, that it uses 'borrowed tools'. This is true. But the point is precisely that it *tests* these tools by transferring them to different terrains, in the same way that a touring car is 'tested' by being driven on

racetracks, at speeds and in conditions which exceed its norms. History becomes a site of 'control'. In it a 'function of falsification' is put to work. (*WH* 80/93)

The notion of falsification is taken from Karl Popper's theory of scientific discovery,[48] but is distinctly ambivalent as Certeau (re)employs it. On the one hand, exposing instances where scientific and interpretative models malfunction or break down, such a strategy provides the means of adjusting these models to make them more appropriate, and thus refines scientific analysis. On the other hand, at least as Certeau tends sometimes to use it, it becomes a tactic by which iconic and textual fragments from other historical orders are re-employed precisely as lacunae, blind spots, or active *tears* in a contemporary scientific or social order.[49] For Certeau, it seems, such a method is alternately scientific and anti-scientific. It oscillates between interpretation and something like anti-interpretation. Sometimes he presents collections of historical material as a field of experimentation for contemporary inquiry, in the manner suggested by the figure of the 'test-drive' cited above.[50] Sometimes he insinuates clusters of this material like grains of sand or ground glass into the smoothly working machinery of scientific and interpretative production.

Certeau notes how the recent practice of the human sciences, at least in France, has been characterized by a renewed confidence in 'abstractions', and particularly in formal 'structures' and 'artificial' languages. We have already seen how Certeau himself is implicated in this development. In the wake of this, however, historiography as Certeau conceives it receives a specifically critical contemporary role, for even as it 'applies' such abstractions, 'history tends to manifest the limits beyond which these models or languages cannot produce valid meaning' (*WH* 76/88). In other words, historiography operates for Certeau by running such models and languages up against the 'real' and (their) death, just as it does with regard to the vagaries and intuitions produced by a more romanticist style of interpretation. This is not to say that historiography in Certeau's view counters formal analysis with the earthy and reassuring reality of solid 'facts'. Certeau remains sceptical with regard to Paul Veyne's apology for historical 'detail' as opposed to the abstraction of structural models. Certeau argues that these 'facts' only receive their aesthetic and hence effective reality for the observer through their (dissonant) *relation* with internalized formal models, whose predominant place in the

intellectual field 'endow(s) the exceptional detail with a new kind
of pertinence' (*WH* 80/93). Thus Certeau reads the details which a
historian like Veyne orchestrates so artfully in terms of the strategy
of falsification outlined above. He does not by contrast attribute to
them any privileged ontological solidity, as 'the "fact" in question
is henceforth not of the kind which offered up for the knowledge
of the observer the emergence of a reality. Combined with a constructed model, it assumes the form of a *difference*' (*WH* 80/94).
Historiography cannot sever its ties to a limping truth. It can,
however, by working upon the margins and blind spots of contemporary thought, point to the way in which other truths are also
condemned to limp. No doubt, it cannot provide 'faithful' interpretations. Instead, Certeau proposes the possibility of a different
kind of fidelity, according to which historiography might remain
'faithful to its fundamental purpose, which doubtless remains to
be defined, but of which we can already say that it links history
simultaneously to the real and to death' (*WH* 76/88).

The writing of history as Certeau presents it is a contemporary
practice defined by controlled operations which take place at the
limits of contemporary systems and organizations of meaning. The
ambivalent 'interpretations' which it produces are related to and
distinct from both the 'real' whose traces constitute the historian's primary material and the 'real' in which contemporary scientific procedures are enmeshed. Certeau points to something like
a reversal in the historiographical project, as compared, say, with
the grand schemes of the nineteenth century. Its aim is no longer
to present and to comprehend the totality of history – such an
undertaking could in any case end only in a mirage. The historian
becomes rather a liminal figure, a textual poacher on the territories
of others:

> The historian no longer sets out to construct an empire. He no longer
> sets his sights on the paradise of a global history. He comes to circu-
> late *around* acquired forms of rationality. . . . In this respect he becomes
> a prowler. In a society which is adept at generalization and endowed
> with powerful means of centralization, he advances towards the fron-
> tiers of the great regions which have already been exploited. He devi-
> ates [*fait un écart*], moving in the direction of sorcery, madness, festival,
> popular literature . . . etc., all zones of silence. (*WH* 79/91–2)

Certeau's own treatment of some of these 'silent zones' (for
example those of the 'popular' or of diabolic possession) will be

examined in later chapters. In so far as the figures who inhabit them have traditionally been introduced only *in absentia* into the archives of written history, they pose acute problems for learned interpretation. Nevertheless, the essential move described above is particularly striking in Certeau's work. It consists in turning scientific and interpretative operations towards an 'other' for which they cannot account, or to which their very proficiency makes them blind. As Certeau writes with reference to Foucault's *History of Madness*, 'scientific "reason" is indissolubly wedded to the reality that it meets again as its shadow and its other at the very moment when it excludes it' (*WH* 40/52–3). In Certeau's writing, history represents for reason the limit of the 'real'. By virtue of its object, historical interpretation can therefore work at the borders of (contemporary) interpretative models. This does not mean that it can itself transcend the existential limit by which it is separated from this object. The historical interpreter is for Certeau simultaneously bound to and separated from the past in ways that he or she cannot fully control.

2

Interpretation and its Archaeology

The Concept of an 'Archaeology'

I have already explored the move through which Certeau disconnects as it were historical interpretation from its intended object in order to confront it with the contemporary determinants and limits of its production. He substitutes for a more intuitive diachronic perspective on the work of the historian a particularly abrupt form of synchronic analysis. Like Aron, Foucault, Veyne and others before him, Certeau questions the capacity of contemporary interpretative procedures to produce adequate representations of past reality. He brackets such aspirations, and delimits interpretative procedures in a distinctive manner as 'operations' which he shows to be functions of present social forces and epistemic configurations. These forces, he suggests, are implicit in the historian's work, whether they correspond to tacit presuppositions or to a form of social 'unconscious'. They need to be uncovered and analysed if historical interpretation is to become a more lucid activity. Equally, we have seen how he sets up a second-order model for the work of historical interpretation. He argues that this work is not reducible to the contemporary conditions which both limit it and render it possible. Rather, its task is to take contemporary interpretative models precisely in order to 'falsify' them, or to expose them in their turn to their historical limits.

These moves have been read by French historians as powerful

theoretical interventions in their intellectual field.[1] Taken in themselves, however, they risk becoming overly schematic or programmatic. They need to be read in the context of other aspects of
Certeau's thought. I shall therefore bring together in this chapter a
set of interpretative moves in which Certeau appeals to the notion
of an 'archaeology'. He himself does not dwell on his use of the
term, but I will argue that it leads to interesting developments
of the conceptions outlined in chapter 1. Firstly, it reintroduces
a diachronic fault-line into the inevitably artificial construction of
a 'synchronic' system governing the work of interpretation. The
interpretative models through which the interpreter organizes and
comprehends the traces of the past are themselves shown to be the
products of a particular history, which must in turn be analysed.
This history corresponds to the 'archaeology' of the interpreter's
present practice (we will see below how Certeau's use of the term
differs significantly from that proposed by Michel Foucault). Such
'archaeologies' add a historical dimension to the forms of alterity
which we can conceive as being 'implicit' in the practice of interpretation. This supplements the sociological and institutional considerations discussed above. Secondly, these analyses correct the
slightly instrumentalist conception of interpretative models contained in the second-order model of falsification outlined above.
Interpreters cannot necessarily always 'take' a model from elsewhere and 'apply' it, for their own structures of perception are
themselves informed by models of interpretation which cannot
necessarily be discerned precisely *as* models. They correspond
rather to incorporated schemes which define for the interpreter
what seems natural or self-evident. Interpreters are not in control
of these schemes as they might be of an intellectual tool-kit: the
schemes determine instead a way of being and a particular relation to the world and to others. To recognize and to 'falsify' these
schemes, which are inextricably linked to the identity of the interpreter, requires a more intimate work of reflexivity.

Certeau's theorization of 'the historiographical operation' is
founded on the idea of a radical separation between the present of
the historian and the past which he or she studies. He presents the
historian's object as a collection of traces – a kind of raw material
– on which to set to work a contemporary interpretative apparatus.
Yet his work also problematizes this separation in so far as it might
serve to guarantee the autonomy of the present and its progression
from a superstitious or archaic past. Historical traces will not necessarily remain in the position to which the theoretical operation

outlined above appeared to have consigned them. The inert corpus set up for treatment in an economy of intellectual production may itself 'work' upon that production. The overall effect of Certeau's analyses is to present a highly complex and mobile conception of the interpretative process. Far from constituting the means by which the historian could tame the traces of the past, the historian's interpretative apparatus is itself the product of a particular past. The historian becomes in an important sense 'subject' to this past, and his or her productions can themselves be interpreted as after-effects of an implicit history:

> The historian is in an unstable position. If he awards priority to an 'objective' result, if he aims to introduce into his discourse the reality of a past society and to bring a forgotten figure back to life, he nonetheless recognizes in this reconstitution the order and the effect of his own work. The discourse designed to express what is other remains his own discourse and the mirror of his own operation. Inversely, when he returns to his own practices and examines their postulates in order to innovate, the historian discovers in them constraints originating well before his own present, dating back to former organizations of which his work is a symptom, not a source. (WH 36/47–8)

Certeau's intricate syntax follows here as elsewhere the incessant displacement of alterity as it emerges in his reflection. One thing is always being taken for/by another, producing an indefinite series of quid pro quo's. One cannot read Certeau's work in terms of a simple opposition between 'self' and 'other'. The interpreter's representation of others is contaminated by his own intrusive identity. This identity is itself, however, organized for Certeau from within by the unanalysed work of other ('implicit') instances of social or historical alterity.

The 'archaeologies' analysed in Certeau's thought may be defined initially as residual structurations which organize interpretative practice. These structurations are the result of historical formations which precede the interpreter, but whose effects continue to inform the interpreter's work. They induce forms of unconscious repetition, through which the past returns, so to speak, to haunt the present which seems to have taken its place. These repetitions require for Certeau a diagnosis which brings his historical work close to a form of psychoanalysis. Indeed, it is worth quoting in full Certeau's presentation of two different 'strategies of time' which for him distinguish a historiographical from a psychoanalytical treatment of temporality:

Psychoanalysis and historiography have two different ways of distributing the space of memory. They conceive of the relation between the past and present differently. Psychoanalysis recognizes the past *in* the present; historiography places them one *beside* the other. Psychoanalysis treats the relation as one of imbrication (one in the place of the other), of repetition (one reproduces the other in another form), of the equivocal and of the quid pro quo (what is 'in the place' of what? Everywhere there are games of masking, reversal and ambiguity). Historiography conceives the relation as one of succession (one after the other), correlation (greater or lesser proximities), cause and effect (one follows from the other), and disjunction (either one or the other, but not both at the same time). (*H* 4/*HP* 99)

Certeau himself introduces into historical interpretation a psychoanalytically inspired model of temporality. This in effect belies the clear distinctions laid out above (one strategy starts in his writing to work 'in the place' of the other). Likewise it complicates the conception of a sociologically based economy of intellectual production outlined in the previous chapter. The distinct contours of the place which the interpreter is assigned in a contemporary intellectual field are blurred by diverse instances of residual historical alterity which only an archaeological analysis can uncover. Certeau's work does not rely on a single (sociological) model to provide an exhaustive description of interpretative practice.[2]

Certeau's notion of an 'archaeology' differs significantly from the extensive use which Michel Foucault made of the term in his work in the 1960s.[3] One could even say that the 'psychoanalytic' model of temporality guiding Certeau's thought leads him to carry out a partial misreading of the intentions governing Foucault's recourse to such a figure. Interestingly, this misreading means that the idea of an 'archaeology' in Certeau's work escapes the dead-end to which Foucault's systematic employment of the term was leading him.[4] Put bluntly, Foucault used what he called an archaeological method of description in order to petrify the discourses of the past, to turn them to stone. Studying past thought as an archaeologist studies buried cities, he sought to bracket questions both of meaning and reference, to lay aside the serious truth-claims made by thinkers of the past, and to uncover the impersonal regularities and structures which governed their discourse. To take a programmatic passage from *The Archaeology of Knowledge*, where Foucault endeavours to provide a theory which would encompass his previous work:

In our time, history is that which transforms *documents* into *monuments*. In that area where, in the past, history deciphered the traces left by men, it now deploys a mass of elements that have to be grouped, made relevant, placed in relation to one another to form totalities. There was a time when archaeology, as a discipline devoted to silent monuments, inert traces, objects without context, and things left by the past, aspired to the condition of history, and attained meaning only through the restitution of a historical discourse; it might be said, to play on words a little, that in our time history aspires to the condition of archaeology, to the intrinsic description of the monument.[5]

Certainly, there are interesting points of convergence between the theory mapped out in *The Archaeology of Knowledge* and Certeau's own theory and practice of historiography. In particular, the two thinkers both show how the historian must operate on what Foucault calls a 'documentary materiality' in order to isolate pertinent structures and sets of correlations.[6] Yet we have already seen how Certeau is far from ready simply to 'bracket' the lost human presences implied by residual, petrified traces.[7] Equally, he would see the very metaphor of petrification as problematic. In a review of Foucault's earlier work (after the publication of *The Order of Things* and before that of *The Archaeology of Knowledge*), Certeau gives a slightly different twist to the idea of an 'archaeological' analysis:

> The subtitle of the *The Order of Things* ('An Archaeology of the Human Sciences') already announces the movement which, according to the book, propelled Western thought of the Classical Age towards the formation of the human sciences. . . . Primitive scenes, in the psychoanalytic sense of the term, lurk within and determine this development. Beneath the cultural displacements there survive original wounds and organizing impulsions [*poussées organisatrices*] still discernible in thoughts that have forgotten them. (*H* 179/*HP* 28)[8]

Foucault saw his own work as leading to and predicated upon an archaeological detachment from the inert mass of past discourses which it analyses.[9] Certeau by contrast sees Foucault's work as giving an unsettling new pertinence to the past precisely in so far as it is not reducible to an inert set of documents/monuments, but rather continues to inhabit and to inform the present. His own practice of archaeological diagnosis seems to be based on this fruitful psychoanalytically based appropriation of Foucault's work.

For Certeau, the historical past will not necessarily stay in its place. It returns in differing modes to haunt and partially to organize the present. In this sense, the present cannot be radically distinguished from the 'archaeologies' which it carries within itself. Indeed, the figure of an 'archaeology' is strictly speaking not fully adequate for the description of such a process. It connotes primarily static remains and forsaken relics. Hence no doubt Certeau's attraction to the intriguing and 'fabulous' archaeology proposed by Freud in *Civilization and its Discontents*:

> I dream of the fantastic representation that Freud gave of Rome one day by supposing an 'a-topic' image where incompatible sites would coincide, 'where nothing that has ever come into existence would be lost, and where all the recent phases of its development would continue to exist alongside the ancient phases'. . . . Different histories 'subsist' in the same place, as in the Rome fantasized by Freud. . . . The Freudian fiction does not lend itself to that spatial distinction of historiography in which the subject of knowledge gives himself a site, the 'present', separated from the site of his object, defined as 'past'. Here, past and present are moving upon the same polyvalent site. (*WH* 312/317)

Freud's image is of course impossible, or at least spatially incoherent: it figures the disruptive, irrepressible work of time in a spatial order.[10] The examples I shall give of Certeau's 'archaeological' analyses bring him closer to this Freudian model than to the Foucauldian programme discussed above. These analyses take his work beyond a narrowly historicist approach to historical interpretation, according to which it would be enough simply to inscribe and enclose historical traces in a stable 'context'. I showed in chapter 1 how the traces of the past cannot necessarily be submitted to a historiographical or chronological ordering, but are liable to return in Certeau's account as unassimilable fragments of alterity to unsettle and/or to alter a contemporary interpretative apparatus. In this chapter I shall explore how for Certeau this apparatus itself also carries with it forms of 'implicit' historical alterity which organize its interpretative operations as it were from within.

Archaeological Diagnoses

Historiography and the computer

Certeau's study of the role of the computer in historiography provides an emblematic illustration of his 'archaeological' analyses.[11]

Certainly, Certeau saw the use of computers in historical research
as a necessary and quintessentially 'modern' ground-breaking venture. He nevertheless distanced himself from the more euphoric
claims made in the late 1960s and early 1970s concerning the scientific potential of quantitative history,[12] just as he did with regard
to the anti-scientific theses of Paul Veyne discussed in the previous chapter. Roger Chartier has noted that Certeau's work could
be identified with neither of these opposing and finally self-
reinforcing orthodoxies which at one time tended to define the
practical and theoretical options open to historians. It was for this
reason, according to Chartier, that Certeau's work was initially
perceived as difficult to situate.[13] I have already discussed Certeau's
emphasis on the technical reductions which quantitative historians
must impose on their material in order to construct a limited number
of homogeneous series. I want here to show how Certeau exposes
the properly symbolic power of the computer in the field of historiographical production.

Certeau presents a complex picture of the initial interdisciplinary encounter between historiography and computer studies. For
him, the computer did not simply represent a neutral technique
which historians could unreflectingly incorporate into their practice. He argues that the effective use of this technique produces a
series of formal transformations in the interpretative operations of
historians.[14] Indeed, one should note how these transformations
(which combine with more general epistemic shifts) reverberate in
Certeau's own analyses. These did not themselves emerge directly
from strictly quantitative studies. Certeau suggests, nevertheless,
how the organizing presence of the computer in the contemporary intellectual field has revolutionized our apprehension of archival textual material. It has facilitated the working separation of
epistemological 'moments' (conceptualization, documentation, treatment, interpretation) which previously remained undifferentiated
or confused in interpretative practice (*WH* 74–7/86–9). At the same
time, however, the computer had also become in Certeau's view
the object of problematic symbolic investments in the economy
of intellectual production. It represented a new capacity for the
technical control and ordering of the environment, and any work
which could invoke its name was liable to win for itself an added
authority among its readership.[15] This interdisciplinary prestige
was not necessarily dependent on a respect for the procedural logic
of computer-based research. Certeau mischievously compared
these 'invocations' of the computer to the tributes once paid to

another kind of ruling authority – the Prince (*H* 213/*HP* 84). More fundamentally, he saw at work in the 'appeal' of contemporary historians to the computer the age-old ghost of discredited interpretative ambitions. The archival circuits opened up by the computer had for Certeau reawakened something of a grandiose and 'archaic' desire to master the historical process:

> In order to come into being, a science must resign itself to the loss of both totality and reality. But whatever it has to exclude or give up in order to establish itself returns under the figure of the other, from which it continues to expect a guarantee against the lack which is at the origin of all our knowledge. The spectre of a totalizing and ontological science reappears in the form of a belief in the other. . . . It is not surprising that historiography – which is undoubtedly the most ancient of all disciplines and the most haunted by the past – should be a privileged field for the return of this spectre. . . . So it is that in its very relation to scientificity, to mathematics, to the computer, historiography is 'historical' – no longer in the sense that it produces an interpretation of previous epochs, but in the sense that the past . . . re-emerges in it and expresses itself. (*H* 214/*HP* 86)

Certeau argued that the unspoken presence of this fantasm overdetermined the technical function of the computer in contemporary historiography. The ingrained 'archaeology' (*H* 217/*HP* 90) at work in the writing of history converted the computer into the vehicle of a 'fiction'. It became a metaphor or 'carrier' for the historian's desire for interpretative control. The ease with which the computer enabled historians to manipulate a set of formal data had led, in Certeau's experience, exponents of quantitative history to forget the limits both of this data and of their own interpretative practice. Certeau suggests that these researchers had been seduced through their nostalgia for more substantial forms of epistemic mastery. One might contrast Certeau's own symbolic recourse to a lexis of technical fabrication (or 'bricolage'), which, combined with figures of the trace and transcendence, is designed precisely to return interpreters to the irreducible limits of their production.

This archaeological analysis gives an interesting twist to Certeau's concept of re-employment. Generally Certeau uses this concept in order to uncover conditional freedom where other interpreters had seen only constraint and determination. In the case of early modern mystics or popular religious practices, for example, he aims to show that agents are not necessarily identifiable with a standardized set of religious representations. He contends that they creatively re-employ these representations in such a way as to transform them.[16] In the case above, however, the historian's appropriation of the computer does not represent a case of creative re-employment. Certeau argues rather that this apparatus reactivates deep-rooted desires for interpretative authority, and thereby induces forms of unconscious repetition. The valorization of 'active' re-employments which is often regarded as characterizing Certeau's thought is offset in his work by the discernment of such unconscious repetitions, or of what one might call 'passive' re-employments. The latter component of his reflection, although it is not made explicit in these terms, needs to be emphasized in order to guard against the slightly fetichistic investment in the possibility of creative re-employment which his work seems sometimes to elicit.

Conceptions of practice

Far from providing a convenient interpretative key, Certeau's work repeatedly problematizes the interpretation of practices. He uncovers forms of interpretative distortion due to the workings of different instances of alterity implicit in the interpreter's 'own' operations. His treatment of mutations in early modern religious practice brings this move into striking relief. He confronts a peculiar limit-situation, where the object of contemporary inquiry also works in this very inquiry as a residual 'archaeology'.

Certeau argues in chapter 1 of *The Writing of History* (first published as an article in 1970) that in interpreting the sociopolitical and cultural transitions which can be traced over the early modern period, modern historians were continuing to employ a conceptual apparatus whose formation was itself rooted in this period. This apparatus had its origin moreover in the ecclesiastical and administrative elite of the societies in question, and corresponded to clear ideological and political imperatives. Its transportation into modern historiography (albeit with important modifications or reversals) necessarily produced forms of interpretative partiality. Certeau saw this process at work in sociological analyses of the spread or decline of religious belief in early modern France.[17] These analyses worked on records of concrete religious practice, as these seemed to provide a basis for the objective measurement of the spiritual state of different parishes and regions. The interpretative concern of historians had become directed primarily towards attendance figures at mass or Easter communion, towards rises or falls in the number of baptisms, and so forth. Certeau, however, pointed out the uncanny resemblance which this concern bore to the 'concern' shown by the ecclesiastical and political authorities of the time. Certeau discerns over the seventeenth century an intensified pre-occupation on the part of these authorities with the visible or tangible reality of religious practices. The Catholic church had become deeply worried by the degree of 'ignorance' which was being discovered among the rural masses. It needed a set of objective criteria through which to measure and to impose the programmes of the Counter-Reformation.[18] This development should be read in the context of the deterioration of Catholic (and then Christian) frames of reference, during which the internal, 'spiritual' realities of religion began to seem less stable or probable. As a consequence, official attention became fixed on the apparently more solid and above all more controllable reality of prescribed religious practices. This fixation was reinforced as religious institutions came to function more and more according to 'political' structures, and as Catholicism came to operate under Louis XIV as an instrument of a primarily national unity.[19] For various reasons, therefore, religious practices were set up at the time as strategic objects of knowledge. They were actively objectified in such a manner that they could be integrated into an enterprise designed to organize and to discipline French society. The ecclesiastical administration, by registering the names of those who did not come to mass or communion, facilitated the construction of an orthodox, cohesive nation.[20] These registers enabled administrative authorities to locate pockets of resistance or indifference. They constituted an essential tool in the elaboration of a campaign to conform French society to a set of models drawn up by political and ecclesiastical authorities.

For Certeau, contemporary interpretative practice becomes problematic when it takes over without sufficient reflection such 'preconstituted' objects of knowledge. He stresses that they were too closely linked to the social and political programmes of a social elite to be able to provide contemporary interpreters with an adequate representation of the effective beliefs held by the population of seventeenth-century France. They constitute indispensable evidence, but he emphasizes that they are the result of overdetermined strategies of objectification on the part of those charged with propagating their own model of orthodoxy. What was important for the latter was less the 'private' beliefs of their subjects than the degree of their 'effective' conformity to required modes of

behaviour. Certeau considered that contemporary interpreters were
in danger of simply taking over this notion of effectivity:

> Today, when it takes practice as the basis for a quantitative measure-
> ment of religion, sociology transports a historical organization of
> Christian consciousness back into science. . . . It also accentuates a
> presupposition which was already latent in these origins dating from
> four centuries ago: that is, a rift between objective gestures and sub-
> jective belief. . . . At present, in the studies which count gestures, inter-
> est is drawn to practices because they represent a *social reality*, and the
> obverse of this is a scientific devalorization of their *signification as
> expressions of opinion*. . . . The logic of a sociological investigation thus
> widens the schism between social religious facts and the doctrines
> which claim to explain their significance. (WH 25–6/34–5)

Certeau does not want to suggest that there is a direct causal relation between the interest of early modern 'agencies of control' in the
counting of objectified religious practices and the re-employment
of these counts in modern quantitative historiography. He points
also, for example, to a more recent archaeology. Historians such as
Le Bras were drawn to concrete sociological research as a reaction
against the abstraction of typologies and against the impressionism
of a purely literary or doctrinal historiography. Nor does Certeau
want simply to invalidate the findings of such statistical inquiries.
He seeks rather to expose the limits of this contemporary practice
of interpretation in so far as it is founded on a peculiar kind of
historical 'complicity' – by which I mean, in the etymological sense,
a particular 'folding together' of apparently discrete historical
agents. Certeau's diagnosis of this archaeological complicity forms
part of a more general strategy to be discerned in his work. He
problematizes the programmes drawn up by representatives of
political and cultural power in so far as these are designed to inform
and to mould the social body. He foregrounds the gap between the
representations of these representatives and the people whom they
are supposed to represent. In so far as they cannot necessarily
command the belief of their subjects, these representatives cannot
provide us in our turn with fully credible historical material.

We have already seen in chapter 1 how Certeau devises an alternative approach which focuses on the 'formality' of practices. He
explores how practices operate on the objective forms of standard cultural or religious representations, and appropriate them in
such a way as to transform them. The immense, silent work of this
appropriation casts a fantasmatic shadow in Certeau's writing over

epistemically more consumable forms of cultural and religious history. I want here simply to suggest that the innovations which emerge from this shadow in Certeau's analyses were themselves not conjured up out of thin air. Their 'archaeology' may be discerned precisely in his own previous study of early modern religious history. In the introduction to his critical edition of Jean-Joseph Surin's *Guide spirituel*, published in 1963, Certeau draws attention to Surin's distinction between the 'formal' (*formel*) and the 'material' (*matériel*). Surin used this distinction to prevent those under his spiritual direction from identifying the truth of a given exercise or practice with its objective content. Certeau's exposition of Surin's thought here constitutes a striking prefiguration of his own later distinction, re-employed in a range of widely diverging contexts, between the objective form of a cultural artefact or practice and the 'formality' of its appropriation:

> Surin often repeats that spiritual life cannot be measured by examining the material nature of an action. . . . The true criterion of action is situated at the 'formal' level: its 'intention' or its 'motive'. . . . It is a question of a 'principle of purity which renders our actions perfect not in their material aspect but in their form'. . . . Not identifiable with any particular charitable enterprise, or with a specific mode of prayer, none the less inseparable from effective works undertaken through faith, [this 'direct intention'] determines their organizing movement and internal dynamic. . . . By the 'formal' aspect of spiritual life . . . Surin understands that which orients from within the activities of the Christian.[21]

Certeau's influential concept of the 'formality' of practices bears the mark of his immersion in the writings of early modern mystics, and thereby also of an earlier 'organization' of a Christian consciousness (and conscience). Certainly, his contemporary redeployment of the notion subjects Surin's distinction to a kind of chiasmus which is not without its dangers. Surin insists that one cannot remain satisfied with the reassuring content or manifest form of objectively 'good' actions because these are liable to mask baser intentions. Certeau, particularly in his work on contemporary cultural practices, wants to insist that apparently 'base' cultural forms may be subject to more interesting formalities of appropriation. I will discuss in due course the excesses to which such a 'charitable' reading may lead. For the moment it is enough to note that Certeau's own diagnoses of the work of historical alterity in the interpretative operations of others are themselves informed by (indebted to) an implicit archaeology.

Uses of knowledge

Certeau seeks not only to reconfigure our conceptions of practice, but also to defamiliarize through historicization our understanding of 'knowledge'. He produces this defamiliarization once more by working on the limit-case where a field of historical inquiry also constitutes an 'archaeology' of the interpretative models which govern this inquiry. He shows again how our understanding of the past cannot be dissociated from 'the influence which it still exercises over our methods of inquiry' (*WH* 26/35). The influence in question concerns here the sociopolitical 'uses' of knowledge.

Certeau argues that knowledge began over the course of the seventeenth century to function in a new way. Like religious practices, it became the object of a distorted and amplified concern on the part of ecclesiastical and political authorities. Its new role emerged with the demise of the cosmic framework which had been supplied by orthodox theology, and with the discovery of the disturbing ignorance or resistance confronting the projects of the Counter-Reformation. To an unprecedented degree, knowledge became the operative instrument for ordering and classifying a fragmented society, and also the means for measuring the success of this operation. The Catholic Church and the nation were to be preserved from disintegration and cemented by the dissemination of catechisms, by common elementary education and by a great campaign against ignorance. The population were to be judged and treated (somewhat as raw material is treated in industry) according to the degree of their conformity to this knowledge. We shall see in chapter 5 how Certeau discerns analogous strategies at work over the time of the French Revolution, which retained the form of these techniques of propagation and insemination, while substituting a patriotic, secularized orthodoxy for the disparaged contents of Catholic doctrine.

Although Certeau is not always as clear about this as one might wish, it is not a case of denying the enormous benefits eventually brought by the spread of elementary education. Rather, Certeau wishes to show that such educational strategies were powerfully overdetermined, and that they were designed to impose and to facilitate the rule of political and ecclesiastical authorities.[22] These authorities had particular conceptions of what constituted 'knowledge' and of what constituted 'ignorance' with regard to the societies they were trying to organize. In the light of this, it becomes problematic for interpreters today simply to take over these classifications, and to use divisions between 'knowledge' and 'ignorance' as though they were neutral markers through which to construct an objective representation of the social order. Certeau's work emphasizes that these divisions are always a function of socially and politically defined practices of objectification, which must themselves be analysed as such.[23] He notes how archaeologically determined models of knowledge and ignorance were continuing to govern modern interpretations of deviant historical phenomena such as sorcery:

> Historians today willingly place sorcery under the rubric of ignorance; but they thereby adopt precisely the interpretation already carried out by the missionaries and judges of the seventeenth century. In this way, do not all these groups attest together to the social *a priori* (new, I believe, in the seventeenth century) which makes *participation in knowledge* (as defined by an elite) the prerequisite for belonging to a society, and makes this very knowledge the means by which a society hierarchizes its members or eliminates the 'deviants' [*errants*] who do not conform to common reason? (*WH* 142/136)

The purpose of Certeau's 'archaeological' diagnosis in this instance is to drive a wedge between the models (catechisms, programmes, etc.) drawn up and deployed in the past to order societies in prescribed manners and the contemporary interpretative models used to analyse such societies. His work repeatedly problematizes the capacity of written programmes drafted in places of authority to inform and fully to mould society. He thereby also frees a space for differently conceived interpretative approaches (to the past and to the present). These are not generated by a process of simple inversion. They do not set out to deride all accepted forms of intelligibility in order to project the compensatory fantasm of a privileged, more or less folkloric enlightenment where once there was ignorance. They are designed instead firstly to articulate the ways in which people may enter into different kinds of relation with regard to apparently stable forms of knowledge. Secondly, they propose new forms of division and interference between what can be conceived as 'knowledge' and what can be conceived as 'ignorance'. I shall explore in the chapters which follow how Certeau

traces in domains of supposed ignorance social and symbolic practices which are not reducible to an empty position in relation to the
contrasting 'fullness' of Knowledge.

We saw in chapter 1 how for Certeau the interpreter is not engaged
in a one-to-one relation with the historical 'other' encountered in
the archives. Interpretative practice is instead organized through
and through by the generally unspoken presence of contemporary
social, institutional and epistemic configurations and conflicts. We
can conceive these as a first form of 'implicit' alterity interposing
itself for Certeau between the interpreter and his or her intended
'other'. So far in this chapter, we have seen how Certeau detects at
work in contemporary interpretative operations another form of
implicit alterity, in the guise of residual historical structurations.
Extrapolating from his recurrent but untheorized recourse to the
term, we may call this second form of 'implicit' alterity an 'archaeology'. Of course, it is problematic to make clear-cut distinctions
such as that between an 'implicit' alterity and an 'other' defined as
'outside' or 'external' in some sense to the interpreter. The category of the fantasmatic *other* to be discussed in chapter 3 will
highlight a disturbing in-between zone in such a schematization.
Likewise a strict distinction between a 'social unconscious' and a
more historical 'archaeology' of interpretation would not survive
sustained analysis. To dismiss such distinctions on these grounds,
however, would be to miss their point. They are designed not to
supply a definitive nomenclature for alterity, but rather to help
clarify our reading of Certeau's work 'on' otherness. In order to
follow his thought in all its rigour, we must differentiate just what
Certeau is *doing* in particular analyses of or appeals to alterity. Such
considerations will also allow us, in due course, to assess the significance of certain 'lapses'.

Economies of Writing

The discussion of practices and knowledge above questioned the
faith of political and cultural elites in the power of written programmes and models to construct the social body. The place and
function of writing as such in the organization of the social order
represents a key component of Certeau's thought. I outlined in
chapter 1 his conception of a tautological 'circle' of writing which

encloses, as it were, the operations of learned interpretation. Certeau also traces the history of such circles. He does not consider writing to constitute simply a neutral technique which remains fundamentally constant in its successive employments throughout history. Rather, he analyses European history in terms of a series of differing 'economies' of writing. His use of the term 'economy' in this context should not be understood in the now common sense of a strictly industrial and financial political economy. One should bear in mind the wider sense of the term defined by the *Oxford English Dictionary* as 'the organization, internal constitution, apportionment of functions, of any complex unity'. Certeau considers techniques of writing to be of fundamental importance in determining the ways in which a society orders, manages and distributes its material and intellectual resources. These techniques comprise for example operations of recording, transcription, registering, stocking and standardization, as well as the propagation and dissemination of information. The resulting 'economies' of writing work to organize and divide social space, instituting forms of hierarchy and engaging different sections of society in diversely prescribed relations with each other.[24]

Writing and history: a transition

Economies of writing are not conceived by Certeau in a purely synchronic manner. He argues that the ways in which modern Western societies have employed techniques of writing are caught up in a long history (or 'archaeology'), and discerns in modern social and intellectual programmes the marks of prior organizations of meaning. He explores both the manifest ruptures and the latent continuities which govern the changing relations between writing and the social body. He tells us that his book *The Writing of History*

> is born of the relation which discourse holds with the real which it takes as its object. What alliance is there between *writing* and *history*? It was already fundamental to the Judeo-Christian conception of Scripture. Whence the role played by this religious archaeology in the modern elaboration of historiography, which has transformed the terms and the very nature of this past relation, ascribing to it the figure of fabrication and no longer that of reading or of interpretation. (*WH* xxvii/5)

History, Certeau suggests, is no longer what is 'read' or 'interpreted' – as Christian theologians once used the corpus of writings called Scripture to read the unfolding of God's design in the world. Instead, history has become for modernity what can be 'written' or 'fabricated' – in the sense that human history can be actively made through the implementation of programmes designed to construct preconceived orders. This transition ascribes in principle a new status to modern historiography. It becomes charged so to speak with interpreting the fabrications of humankind. It must write the history of the way history has been 'written'. Needless to say, historians have seldom based their work on such clear-cut directives.[25] Certeau examines for example in his own historiography the ways in which those who aspire to 'write' history have for one reason or another not been able to do so. To begin with, however, I would like in an unavoidably schematic manner to expand on the basic historical transition outlined above. This scheme is important precisely as a scheme in Certeau's thought. Sometimes he fleshes it out with impressive historical detail and nuance,[26] at other times it is put forward peremptorily or with self-conscious irony – he refers in *The Practice of Everyday Life* to 'a vast programme for which I shall substitute a mere cartoon' (*PE* 132/197). It may be that the broad brush-strokes with which Certeau lays out the history of succeeding 'scriptural economies' reintroduce into his writing part of what he had sought to expel as the panoramic or totalizing 'delusions' of an older form of historiography. This would suggest that historical reflection, even or especially a reflection so aware of its intrinsic finitude as that of Certeau, cannot do without a larger backdrop or horizon which gives direction to its thought.

The scheme in question begins with Certeau's conception of the 'Middle Ages'. This period is characterized for Certeau by a perception of the world as an integrated whole (or 'cosmos'), in which each human being is assigned a place in a divinely sanctioned hierarchy. The supposed order of this whole, and the corresponding place and destiny of humankind, could be read through the unified institutional mediation of Holy Scripture. There is even something oddly prelapsarian about Certeau's presentation of this world where human conduct and conscience are embraced and held together in a larger unity:

> All through the Middle Ages and up to the sixteenth century it remains accepted that morality and religion have the same source: reference to a single God organizes at once a historical revelation and an

order of the cosmos; it supposes Christian institutions to constitute the legible form of a law of the world. Society is built in terms of an integrative belief. At the level of the practices which unfold on the visible surface of society (putting to one side for the moment the rural 'depths' which seem to have escaped Christianity), private life as well as professional and public life moves within a Christian framework: religion envelops forms of conduct. (*WH* 148–9/155)

In this strangely readable and 'enveloped' world, the writing which ordered society (that is, Scripture) could still for Certeau be considered as a form of 'voice'. It was inseparable from the divine presence which it guaranteed. What was transcendent or separate by definition was also held to be readable through these writings as immanent in the world. Certeau sees the advent of 'modernity' in terms of a progressive loss of confidence in the possibility of such a 'voice'. It began to seem less and less probable that the corpus of sacralized writings could carry with it through its institutional mediation the presence which it promised. As God ceased to 'speak in the world', attention became directed away from the deciphering of his 'mysteries', and began to search for 'substitute' speakers and languages (*PE* 138/204). I will take up below Certeau's approach to this emergent problem of 'speech'. The collapse of the scripturally sanctioned cosmos, however, also ascribed in Certeau's account a new function to writing. He argues that it was in this way that the old metaphysically conceived order was gradually displaced by explicitly political programmes. Indeed, Certeau suggests that the productive work of writing overrode to a considerable extent the more fragile endeavours to establish new conditions for interlocutory exchange.[27]

Modernity thus begins for Certeau with the loss of a unitary order and with a process of separation. This separation – like a historiographical myth for other forms of exile – figures ambivalently in his writing. It is presented at one level as a predicament which had to be suffered. Certeau looks for example in *The Mystic Fable* at those who felt that they were living among the 'ruins' of the older cosmos. Yet at the same time he shows how this cosmos was destroyed precisely through volitional operations of severance. Modern Western history came into being through the active 'differentiation between the *present* and the *past*. In this way, it also distinguishes itself from (religious) *tradition*, though it never succeeds in separating itself completely, maintaining with this archaeology a relation of both indebtedness and rejection' (*WH* 2/9). A religiously conceived world was forcefully converted through the disenchantment of Scripture into an archaic tradition. Writing, in Certeau's account, ceased to be organized around a stable corpus which allowed the world to be 'read'. It became rather an instrument which permitted its practitioners to detach themselves from this world and thereby to design and to construct their own environment:

> In place of the metaphysician's and theologian's discourse, which once deciphered the order of all things and the will of their author, a slow revolution constitutive of our 'modernity' has substituted those writings capable of establishing forms of coherent interconnection which can be used to produce an order, a progress, a history. (*H* 201/ *HP* 68).

The unprecedented possibilities opened up for writing allowed those in a position to exploit them to move beyond their allotted place as 'scribes' and to assume that authorial privilege which had hitherto been the exclusive preserve of the divinity. They now seemed able to become the creators of their own world. Indeed, Certeau suggests that one of the most important factors in this modern economy was precisely the new mythical status of writing as such. This status was not reducible to what modern forms of writing were able actually to achieve. For the practice of writing acted in itself as a 'symbol'. It represented for a multiplicity of 'authors' the nature of their own power – that of bringing into existence a new social order:

> Writing replaces the traditional representations which once authorized the organization of the present with a representative form of *labour* which combines upon the same site both absence and productivity. . . . Little by little, writing has replaced all of yesterday's myths with a practice designed to produce meaning. As a practice . . . writing symbolizes a society capable of managing the space which it sets up for itself, . . . of changing the tradition which it receives into a text which it produces, in short, of constituting itself as a blank page upon which it can itself write. (*WH* 5–6/12)

Much of Certeau's work is designed to expose this myth of writing, together with its technocratic avatars, precisely as a myth. He shows in detailed case-studies how the enterprises set up as functions of modern economies of writing do not have the power to 'bring the alterity of the universe into conformity with [their] models' (*PE* 135/201). He problematizes the position of 'author-ship' which the dominant agents of such economies seem to have taken over from the God which preceded them.

One should note that Certeau's analyses in this respect are them-selves not entirely unproblematic. In particular, one can ask whether his writing does not serve on occasion to reinforce the very myth which he sets out to dismantle. His model of a modern 'scriptural economy' appears intermittently to take on a life of its own, and to become a quasi-autonomous motor of history. It slips across the line separating a descriptive model from a substantial and strangely demonic entity. Like the mutating protagonist of some fanzine science-fiction scenario, 'the scriptural enterprise transforms or retains within itself what it receives from its outside, and creates internally the instruments for an appropriation of external space' (*PE* 135/200). Of course, Certeau's work sets out to demonstrate that this image can only be a myth, that the 'scriptural enterprise', to use his term, can never assimilate all that it aspires to devour. Nevertheless, his work manifests a tendency to assign a greater degree of coherence and substance to successive economies of writ-ing than is feasible. This leads occasionally to a peculiar dramati-zation of such economies, which can thereby function as a kind of homogeneous foil for Certeau's own work on orality and on the heterodox ways in which writings may be appropriated. Such con-ceptual dramatization is hardly exclusive to Certeau as a thinker, and it does not invalidate the analyses for which it sets up a space (an intellectual work without plot, peripeteias and what Ricoeur might call 'quasi-characters' would indeed be a strange affair). It can, however, facilitate problematic investments in figures of alterity, and readers should thus be alerted to it.

Certeau questions the act of separation which he sees as found-ing modern practices of writing. These practices may be defined as 'modern' by virtue of their voluntaristic detachment from what they thereby constitute as 'tradition'. Certeau, however, interprets this ideal of historical detachment as a further myth attached to modern conceptions of writing. He argues that these conceptions in effect carry with them residual structurations which bind them to a more archaic history. He bases his argument in particular on the continuing confidence which social elites have placed in the capacity of writing to explain and control the processes of history. He suggests that this deep-rooted faith derives from an erstwhile belief in the power of Scripture. It is in order to preserve the con-notations of this implicit archaeology that I occasionally render

Certeau's *économie scripturaire* as 'scriptural economy' (rather than simply as 'economy of writing'). He also argues that many key components of Enlightenment ideology were informed by a disavowed 'Christian' archaeology. These comprise for example the explicitly political conception of national organization which Certeau suggests took up (and radically transformed) those projects once characteristic of ecclesiology; a notion of individual 'conscience' which became implanted, so to speak, in the vacant interior space produced by forms of spirituality and pietism; the myth of 'progress' whose form seems to be derived from traditional 'messianic' themes to be found in Christianity.[28] One must emphasize that Certeau's objective in uncovering such implicit filiations does not constitute part of an apologetic hidden agenda.[29] Nor is it simply a case of demonstrating that, despite everything, modern society owes a debt, Nietzschean or otherwise, to Christianity. Rather, Certeau's analyses are designed to expose the modern productivist myth of absolute detachment. Certeau shows how the work of separation, necessary and unavoidable as it is, cannot sever itself from or recognize fully the historical alterity which it carries within itself.

Indeed, the idea of an authorial separation from the social body seems itself to repeat the older theological scheme of God's *ex nihilo* creation of the world. The very mark of distinction which characterizes the representation of writing in a modern 'economy' can for Certeau be read as a derived myth. Certeau repeatedly challenges what he sees as the inveterate ambition of political and administrative elites to organize the social order on the basis of blueprints drawn up on a 'blank page'. He shows this ambition to be contaminated by forms of historical alterity which it cannot fully control, and to be implicated in the social body from which it aspires to distance itself. The practice of writing is enmeshed through and through in a complex distribution of social, historical, institutional and epistemic configurations. Certeau reads authoritative sociopolitical programmes as localized fabrications within such distributions. They do not provide an ab-solute (unbound) view of the social order which they are designed to master (see also below pp. 148–50, 176–9). Moreover, the relations between the dominant practitioners of writing and the social 'body' are, as Certeau sees them, fraught also with other kinds of complication. I have shown so far how Certeau considers the work of 'productive' social elites to be inhabited by forms of otherness which members of this elite carry as it were within them. I shall now go on to explore the relation of such elites to what one might provisionally call external forms of alterity. Certeau shows how, in their position precisely as an elite, they may be subject to unexpected forms of seduction or alteration in their exchanges with that which they place 'outside' themselves – namely the general 'mass' of the population, more 'primitive' forms of culture and orality.

Productivity and fable

Interpretative labour is always situated for Certeau in larger economies of writing, which are themselves partially governed by multifarious archaeological determinations. These instances of 'implicit' alterity work to prescribe the relations between socially authorized interpreters and that which falls outside sites of learned, scientific or technical competence. Certeau suggests how modern economies of writing organize not only social space but also the linguistic exchanges which take place within that space. The linguistic practice of the interpreter is positioned as a function of larger sociohistorical divisions, and the relation of this practice to other practices of language which it sets out to interpret thereby becomes problematic.

I have discussed Certeau's account of the transition in early modern French society towards explicitly political and national forms of social organization. Certeau argues that the new imperative to 'make' society led productive and efficacious modes of rationality to be privileged over mere representation, superstition or devotion. He traces the spread of an ethic of 'utility' over the eighteenth century,[30] finding evidence for this development in the distribution and unprecedented dichotomization of linguistic practices:

A *passive* sector of language shifts in the direction of areas where opinions, ideologies and superstitions will find themselves gathered together, forming a pocket isolated from politics and science (two domains indissolubly united, despite their frictions, through the marriage of rationality and efficiency). From all the outward signs, religious expressions are the most important element of this inert sector (this place will be filled later by folklore and popular literature). (WH 170/185)

A group of technically productive or 'operative' uses of language gradually became set apart from what could differentially be defined as a zone of linguistic 'passivity' or 'passion'. The latter comprised the vast body of utterances or representations which were denigrated as merely expressive or derivative, and which did not appear to 'do' anything. These constitute for Certeau a privileged object of study. He focuses on the changing forms of the 'inert' sector mapped out above. His original preoccupation with the fate of religious belief is diffracted into a concern with questions of folklore, popular, marginal and 'ordinary' cultures.

We will see in subsequent chapters how Certeau's treatment of these objects serves to problematize the opposition adumbrated above between the socially operative and the socially passive. I want here, however, simply to pursue his analysis of the process through which dominant forms of rationality have constructed for themselves a series of 'others'. Certeau argues that over the early modern period 'a rift was cut between reason and its "remainder" – or between the discourses of action and the more or less exploitable mass of mere utterances without "force"' (*WH* 170–1/185). The 'others' in question came into existence as a kind of residue in relation to more directly productive types of linguistic competence. I should mention here that in discussing such figures of the 'other', I will generally place the term either in inverted commas, or, for particular purposes, in italic. These devices are designed to foreground the 'artificiality' of the figures in question. They are to be conceived in these instances as projections, residues or by-products of certified interpretative operations rather than as references to the effective existence of other people or practices. These distinctions themselves cannot but carry a measure of artificiality. They also enable us, however, to introduce important nuances into our reading of Certeau.

As Certeau sees it, the residues produced by modern economies of writing have generally been assigned the subaltern status of a set of 'fables'. This term is of strategic importance in Certeau's work. It connotes both fictionality (fables have been set off from authorized regimes of truth) and also orality (they have been set aside by official economies of writing). Certeau binds these connotations together through etymology, arguing that 'to define the position of the other (primitive, religious, mad, childish or popular) as a "fable" is not merely to identify it with "what speaks" (*fari*), but with a speech that "does not know" what it is saying' (*PE* 160/233). Nevertheless, modern forms of rationality have not in Certeau's account simply abandoned the mass of 'fables' from which they have distinguished themselves. Rather, their representatives have sought to manifest their intellectual control of this mass through scripturally organized practices of interpretation.

Serious interpreters have, for Certeau, supposed that there are important truths to be found in these 'fables'. Yet they have seen their task to consist in extracting this truth rather as one extracts a mineral from its ore, or energy from raw material. They have assumed that the technically incompetent speakers who provide them with this material are unable to accede in any meaningful way to the truth of their own speech. Instead, their essential truth remains untapped until the competent interpreter arrives with the correct set of interpretative keys:

> The 'fable' is a word full of meaning [*parole pleine*], but what it says 'implicitly' becomes 'explicit' only after learned exegesis. Through this ruse, learned inquiry sets up for itself in advance, within its very object, a justifying rationale and a place. It is sure of always being able to insert its interpretation into the lack of knowledge which undermines the speech of the fable. (*PE* 160/233)

One can see a similar if inverted ruse at work in Certeau's own writing. I have foregrounded in these first two chapters how he himself seeks to diagnose forms of alterity which he supposes to be 'implicit' in the operations of learned or scientific interpretation. The unanalysed constraints thus posited in other interpretative practices assign a particular 'rationale' to his own work of elucidation. Certeau, however, in contrast to the exegetes of the fable evoked above, focuses on that which remains unthought in epistemically competent interpretation. He thereby problematizes the manner in which this interpretation itself endeavours to extract that which remains unthought in 'incompetent' modes of expression. He shows how the learned interpretative concern with what remains 'implicit' as a hidden kernel of truth in its uninformed 'other' is directed from within by forces and dispositions which themselves have not been fully explicated. This raises supplementary problems for a hermeneutics of the other from which Certeau himself cannot simply escape.

Certeau confronts these problems in his analysis of the linguistic dichotomization outlined above. He slips, interestingly, from the register of historical description (itself couched for the most part in his writing in. the 'historical present') to the direct implication of the first person plural present:

> What do our interpretative methods bring back to us when they are applied to 'expressions' which function in other ways to our

'productions'? . . . Two different functionings of language require different kinds of interpretation, since in reality, in each respective instance, the signs are not spoken in the same manner, even when they are saying the same thing. The statements are played out according to heterogeneous modes of utterance. (*WH* 182/199–200)

The questions put in play by different attitudes to language, together with Certeau's recourse to the problematic of 'utterance' (*énonciation*), will be taken up in the next chapter. One should note here simply how for Certeau a sociohistorically produced linguistic 'disposition' may institute an unbridgeable separation between the interpreter and his or her intended object.[31] This separation is complex because it does not coincide with the intellectual detachment which for some would ideally govern the work of interpretation. The interpreter is separated from a full understanding of his or her 'other', but is not for Certeau located in a free-floating position of neutrality. Certeau does not seek to erase such a 'non-detached separation', but endeavours rather to set it up as a mobile object of analysis in its own right. He looks for ambivalent instances of somatic and cerebral 'interference' in the interpreter's relation to figures of alterity. He detects such interferences in the relation between eighteenth-century 'enlightened' culture and its 'other':

> Having constructed itself in relation to its 'brutish' (*sauvage*) other, culture sets up a double language: that of 'enlightened' reason, avowable and productive, organized by an axiomatic of social utility; and that of beliefs which are disavowed although they are still there, and which, denied in the present, take on the figure of an obscure origin, an 'obscurantist' past of the systems which have taken their place. (*WH* 171/186)

Certeau suggests – sifting no doubt through the archaic strata of his own analytic practice – that trained interpreters are exposed to unsettling forms of seduction or 'alteration' in their confrontation with uninformed (or extradisciplinary) 'fables'. His work traces how these alterations overdetermine their representations of alterity, and lead them to produce, under the guise of interpretation, variants of what we shall explore in the next chapter as a fantasmatic *other*.

Part II

Fables

3

Voices in the Text

Certeau looks in his work at the ways in which successive representatives of written knowledge have cut themselves off from what
he calls 'orality'. They have based their social and epistemic distinction on the distance between their writings and the lapses of
undisciplined hearsay. Certeau argues that they have inscribed their
conceptions of truth in opposition to the rumour of 'fables'.[1] We
have already seen how Certeau conceives his own historiography
as performing an analogous though essentially critical role, 'falsifying' the confabulations of ordinary discourse or the schemes of
contemporary social science. Certeau does not suppose, however,
that the rumour of history (his story) ends with this process of
disciplined substraction. He considers that the 'fables' which practitioners of writing set out to eliminate or to control are not fully
amenable to such operations. He suggests instead that they work
like the Freudian repressed. Their exclusion from the sites of written production is followed by their return – in another form – to
unsettle the interpretative fabrications which proceed from these
sites. Such returns are the objects of the case-studies by Certeau
presented in this chapter.

Jean de Léry: Heterology and Myth

Jean de Léry's *Histoire d'un voyage faict en la terre du Brésil* (*History
of a Voyage to the Land of Brazil*), published in 1578, tells the story

of the author's experiences in the bay of Rio between 1556 and 1558.[2] He originally left Europe to join a Calvinist retreat established on a small island in the bay, but was soon forced to leave this retreat due to the doctrinal inconstancy or duplicity of its leader, Admiral Nicolas de Villegagnon. As a consequence he was forced to spend some three months on the shore with the indigenous Tupinambou tribe before finding a ship to take him back to France. The result of this stay is an engaging account of Léry's encounter with the alterity of Tupinambou culture, which Claude Lévi-Strauss has called the 'breviary of the ethnologist'.[3] One should, however, be wary of seeing in Léry's exceptional presentation an anachronistic, prophetic example of ethnology *avant la lettre*, let alone a transparent window on the reality of Tupinambou society. Anne-Marie Chartier has analysed the fortuitous concourse of material, doctrinal and social conditions which permitted Léry to enter into a comparatively disengaged relationship with the Tupinambou: the singular nature of a Protestant venture which was less a mission than a retreat; the remoteness of any significant economic or territorial interest; the defencelessness of Léry and his companions, the transitoriness of their stay, etc.[4] The 'surprised and attentive gaze'[5] of Léry, surprising as it is in its turn, was not formed in a utopian space isolated from the constraining forces of European history and what Foucault would call their concomitant 'structures of perception'. Indeed for Certeau a text like that of Léry constitutes a precious trace of such structures of perception, precisely in so far as they were put into relief and problematized when they were applied to a foreign culture. They both altered (distorted) this culture in the representations which they produced, and were altered or transformed by it. To begin with, Certeau seeks to follow the moves through which Léry's writing converts alterity into something assimilable to the prevailing configuration of European knowledge. He then shows how this very operation produces an unassimilable residue which returns in Léry's text to upset the fabrications of interpretation.

Certeau's analysis uncovers various implicit devices by which Léry's text produces representations of the New World and the Savage which could be transported, so to speak, with their author across the ocean and circulated in a European culture. He looks for example at narrative structure, at the presentation of the natural world, at various transitions between 'savagery' and 'civilization', and at the question of a common humanity. I want here to concentrate primarily on one episode which Certeau examines, and to trace in his analysis the interplay and tension between interpretation and alteration.

Interpretation and translation: a tautological apparatus?

Léry's account as analysed by Certeau is split between a controlled 'comprehension' of alterity and an excess which is a function of this very act of comprehension. It oscillates also between a heterology (the introduction of alterity into familiar space) and a tautology (the repetition and confirmation of a prescribed identity). Léry endeavours to weave, as it were, the perplexing otherness of Tupinambou culture into the continuous text of European knowledge. Characteristically, Certeau focuses his attention on those points where the effects of this operation seem most precarious. He shows how the textual seam produced by Léry's interpretative practice is intermittently torn by ambivalent moments of rapture.

I shall begin by citing after Certeau Léry's account of one such moment of rapture. Léry is describing his response to a ritual chant of the Tupinambou at a scene where he was present as a semi-illicit voyeur. He experienced

> such a joy that not only, when I heard the beautifully measured harmonies of such a multitude – especially the cadence and refrain of the ballad, all of them together raising their voices at each couplet, and going: *heu, heuaüre, heüra, heüraüre, heüra, oueh* – did I remain totally ravished; but also, every time the memory comes back to me, my heart thrills, and it seems as though their music is still ringing in my ears.[6]

Léry is 'ravished'. Literally, he is taken out of himself. At the moment of hearing, the faculties of his understanding were, so to speak, suspended. At the time of writing (a considerable number of years later) the chronological succession of instants which for Certeau constitute 'productive time' are in turn suspended. The orthodox unfolding of history is disrupted. In Certeau's interpretation, 'an absence of meaning opens a rift in time. Here the song chants *heu, heuaüre*, or, later on, *Hé, hua, hua*, like a voice going *re re*, or *tralala*. Nothing of it can be transmitted, brought back and preserved' (WH 213/221–2).

I should perhaps gloss what may appear as an inconsistency in Certeau's reading. On the one hand, Certeau argues that the chant

of the Tupinambou had for Léry no 'meaning' (*sens*). On the other
hand, Certeau himself obligingly translates for us the sort of impression which this 'meaningless' chant seems to have made on
Léry ('like a voice going *re re*, or *tralala*'). It may be helpful to distinguish for our present purposes between two broad meanings of
'meaning', or 'sense'. To begin with, the chant can be ascribed no
positive meaning by Léry. He cannot abstract from the sounds he
hears a set of forms which signify by virtue of their position in a
scripturally based European nomenclature or epistemic system.
Nevertheless, the chant acquires a (differential) 'sense' for Léry. It
breaks open, so to speak, a path into the organization of his psyche
and 'impresses' itself therein.[7] One might say that Certeau is
working on the divide between these two conceptions of sense.
He suggests that Léry's text cannot tolerate for long the breach
which this divide seems to have opened in a controlled configuration of knowledge. It is for this reason that Léry must turn to an
'interpreter':

> Immediately afterwards, Léry appeals to his interpreter [*truchement*]
> for a translation of several things that he was unable to 'comprehend'.
> Now comes the task which, through this passage to 'meaning', trans-
> forms the ballad into a utilizable product. From these voices, the deft
> interpreter extracts the story of an originary flood 'which is', Léry
> notes, 'the closest thing they have to Holy Scripture': a return is
> accomplished, to the West and to writing, to which the gift of this
> confirmation is brought back from the distant Tupi shores, a return to
> the Christian and French text through the combined efforts of the
> exegete and the voyager. The fabric of productive time is repaired,
> the production of history begins again, after the break precipitated by
> a thrill in the heart which drew the observer back across the sea,
> towards the moment when, 'totally ravished', seized by the voice of
> the other, he forgot himself. (*WH* 213–4/222)

Certeau grasps the moment of transition in which the fleeting
resurgence of a 'voice' is about to be lost. He interrupts the movement of the text as it passes over the hiatus between rapture and
orthodox signification, and attempts to prise open again what had
been covered over by the work of interpretation. Writing is arrested,
as it were, as the traces of the scribe's dispossession or ravishment
are reintegrated into the cohesion of Scripture (that which took
Léry out of himself turns out after all to be merely a degraded
version of the familiar biblical story of the flood). Certeau isolates

the series of operations through which Léry's fantasmatic recall of what for him were quasi-palpable voices is set aside by the artifice of interpretative fabrication. I will discuss below the ambiguity involved in thus reactivating a desire for lost voices. It is enough to note here how Certeau turns a 'senseless' fragment of memory (*'heu, heuaüre, heüra . . .'*) against the hermeneutical process through which it is forgotten even that something has been forgotten – both in the order of meaning (an irreducible moment of incomprehension) and in the order of pleasure (Léry's ravishment).

Certeau breaks down Léry's interpretative operation into a number of formal components. Its precondition consists for Certeau in the institution of a fundamental separation between the interpreter/translator and his object (in Léry's case this separation can be symbolized by the Atlantic Ocean). Far from undermining any possible comprehension, this line of separation was converted by a European hermeneutical apparatus into an instrument of interpretative mastery. Certeau shows how in Léry's writing, 'the narrative plays on the relation between the structure which posits a separation, and the operation which overcomes it, creating in this way effects of meaning. A break is presupposed throughout the text, which itself works as a form of suturing' (*WH* 218/227). Thus the story recited in the Tupinambou chant was assigned the position of a 'fable' – the natives spoke, but for their European observers they did not know what they were really speaking about. The line drawn between them and their European counterparts was that between ignorance and knowledge. It was the implicit existence of this line which allowed the interpreter then to step in and to fill the empty song of the Tupinambou with the plenitude of scriptural knowledge. The line of separation between self and other, old and new world, Scripture and fable functioned precisely to permit the distinction and then transportation on to the field of alterity of an exegetical machinery which would turn this field into a confirmation and support of a European identity.

Léry was implicated in a particular scriptural economy, and Certeau underlines the special position of the written word for a sixteenth-century Calvinist. Scripture constituted the privileged element through which the truth of historico-religious origins was preserved and transmitted. Certeau notes, moreover, in Léry's text the traces of an ongoing transition between this numinous status of Holy Writ and the privileging of writing in terms of efficacy. Writing was becoming a primarily technical means for the advancement of a European/Christian enterprise. The status of orality became

redefined as a function of this development in the organizational
capacity of writing as such:

> Speech is now placed in a very different position. It does not 'pre-
> serve' things. . . . In respect to a Tupi oral tradition concerning the
> flood which allegedly drowned 'everyone in the world, except for
> their grandfathers who took refuge in the highest trees of their coun-
> try,' Léry notes that 'being deprived of all kinds of writing, they find
> it difficult to retain things in their purity; like poets, they added this
> fable about their grandfathers taking refuge in the treetops.' Thanks
> to his scriptural standard, Léry can measure what orality adds to
> things, and he knows exactly how things have been. He is a historian.
> Speech, by contrast, belongs to custom, which 'turns truth into false-
> hood'. More fundamentally, it is a fable (from *fari*, to speak). Now the
> fable is a kind of *drift* – an adjunction, a deviation and a diversion, a
> heresy and a poetry of the present in relation to the 'purity' of prim-
> itive law. (WH 217/225–6)

Certeau argues that speech in this emergent scriptural economy
was constituted as unreliable and unproductive. Its manifestations
had to be measured against the controls (*contre-rôles*) produced by
writing. In Léry's case, an unsettling moment of drift is checked
and integrated into a prescribed hermeneutical order.

Such scripturally based enterprises have not, of course, limited
themselves to gauging the deviations of orality. They have worked
since to eliminate these and to turn fields of orality/alterity into
passive matter on which to inscribe their programmes. Certeau
evokes a series of operations which began to impose the directives
of European centres of power. Writing as a technical instrument
became divested of its Christian determinants and was re-employed
as a function of new strategies of reproduction and capitalization.
To pursue these historical developments would take us beyond the
events circumscribed by Léry's text. Certeau discusses elsewhere
the resistance of native communities in South America to colonial
devastation.[8] I shall restrict myself here to examining how Léry's
text suggests for Certeau that the effective dissemination of European scriptural prototypes was neither one-directional nor univocal.

Residue and excess: the seduction of the voice

Certeau does not simply explicate the functioning of Léry's exegetical apparatus. He looks also at the points where this interpretative

machinery seems to break down. It is clear that 'something of Léry himself does not return from across the sea' (*WH* 227/237). His experience of alterity was not entirely absorbed by the production of intelligibility. There remains in his text the trace of something which falls outside language's 'operative capacity to bring what lies outside back into "sameness"' (*WH* 227/237). Certeau reads in this manner Léry's 'senseless' and sensual citation of the Tupinambou chant. Yet this 'ravishing' and opaque fragment of memory is not equivalent, any more than the interpretation designed to take its place, to the indigenous meaning of the chant. Instead, it seems retroactively to work as a dysfunctional corollary of the interpretative operations discussed above. It corresponds for Certeau to a residue which they themselves create in separating, so to speak, a kernel of scriptural truth from its contingent oral husk:

> The 'residue' I mean is . . . like a fallout, a side-effect of this operation, a waste which it produces through its very success but which it did not intend. This waste product of constructional thought – its fallout and its repressed – will ultimately become the other. (*WH* 227/237–8)

We can make here a further heuristic distinction between different figures of alterity. A series of scripturally based operations produce in Certeau's reading an 'other' which serves to confirm and indeed to reinforce a European sense of identity. They also produce, however, a residue which returns insistently as a fantasmatic *other* to put in question stable figures of the 'other' (and therefore also of the self). I should emphasize again that this typographical distinction between 'otherness' and *otherness* is intrinsically unstable. Its function is precisely to set up somewhat heavy-handedly a symbolic limit transgressed in Certeau's analysis by a quicksilver play of inversions and substitutions. Speaking again in general terms, one might say that the 'other' corresponds to the pole of prescribed, putatively stable meaning, and the *other* to the pole of *frayage*.[9]

Léry's hermeneutical apparatus does not emerge unscathed from its confrontation with Tupinambou reality. The discarded material husk which it produces as residue returns as excess. Certeau discerns in Léry's text an 'eroticization' of Tupinambou voices, oscillating for the European eavesdropper between sense and nonsense. Certeau's analysis of Léry's tentative intrusion, heavy with a sense of danger and transgression, into the space of the Tupinambou ritual, evokes powerfully the quasi-sexual seduction which these 'uninformed' voices exert on the representative of the written word. These voices blur and transgress the boundaries on which an operative exegetical apparatus is founded:

> The voice moves through an intermediary zone between body and language, but in a moment of transition from one to the other and as though *in* the space of their least perceptible difference. . . . The body, which represents a thickening and an opacification of phonemes, is not yet the death of language. The articulation of signifiers is disrupted and effaced; there nonetheless remains vocal modulation, almost lost but not absorbed in the rumours of the body. A strange interval, where the voice gives a speech without 'truths', and proximity a presence without possession. (*WH* 230/240–1)

One should note here that the 'ex-voto . . . to absent speech' (*WH* 212/218) produced by Certeau's writing does not work to reactivate the Rousseauist myth of speech as deconstructed by Jacques Derrida. This myth, which privileges the supposed transparency, plenitude and authenticity of speech over the inauthenticity or alienation of writing, is based for Derrida on the fantasm of a voice which would be 'closest to the signified'[10] – a fantasm which Derrida sees as fundamental in the history of Western philosophy. In Certeau's analyses, by contrast, the voice is that which constitutes an irreparable breach in the process of orthodox signification; it signifies the 'derision of the signifier';[11] it 'ravishes', it takes the self-possessed agent of a scriptural economy out of himself and dispossesses him; it figures in his text as opaque and ephemeral.

At a general level, one could say that the operations of exegesis correspond in Certeau's analysis to the *action* which the European interpreter carries out on an American alterity. This action alters the culture which it confronts by converting this culture into its 'other'. It takes a series of what it presupposes to be degraded, deviant or ignorant semantic propositions and assigns to them their 'proper' sense. By contrast, certain irrepressible voices seem for Certeau to mark the interpreter like a *passion*. The interpreter is himself altered by an alterity which he cannot control. His being is modified at the most intimate level. He is removed from his own 'proper' place, which he finds to be inhabited and redirected by an impossible desire for what lies outside. 'Echoes' of other voices enter into and alter his text in a series of metaphorizations. His words in this perspective can only ever stand for something else (a definition of metaphor). In a brusque reversal, his means of interpretative control come to seem nothing but a derisory substitute for lost voices. These voices *now* work as 'an alteration, an abduction, but also a calling of [his] discourse' (*WH* 236/248). They interrupt for Certeau the autonomous, linear unfolding of discursive presentation. They reintroduce the forgotten questions of loss and death into the deceptive plenitude of a text.

'For what dream or lure is my writing a metaphor?'

Does Certeau's text, with its forceful mobilization of a desire for absent voices, lead to a problematic aestheticization of Europe's 'New World'?[12] If such were the case one could apply to it Derrida's critique of the Lévi-Straussian idealization of savage orality.[13] Such an idealization would function as a hunter's decoy (*leurre*), substituting for a disturbing alterity a dazzling representation which works finally to bring this alterity back to a place defined by a configuration of Western knowledge. I have already argued that Certeau's conception of orality cannot be directly mapped on to the binary opposition between voice and writing which constitutes the object of Derrida's deconstruction. I want now to show how Certeau's analysis, while it is clearly concerned with aesthesis in the sense of perception and response to perception, nevertheless does not itself produce an 'aestheticization' in the standard sense of reassuring or edifying idealization.

Many of the representations of the Tupinambou which Certeau extracts from Léry's text (nudity, festivity, seductive chants and so forth) tend to the status of myth, if one defines a myth again as an altered reality which exists effectively in the place of its poetic figuration. They are u-topian figures. Certeau is, however, careful to present them as such. They correspond initially to the way in which Léry's interpretative practice 'stages' what it constitutes as its 'other' (*WH* 211/217). Yet Certeau demonstrates how, like dream fragments, they are not necessarily docile to the effects of this staging. Voices return, for example, like the Freudian repressed to upset an aesthetic construction and to blur the 'proper' distance between observer and observed. The onlooker is not secure in a detached position of contemplation. He is shown instead to inhabit an ambivalent, violent realm of seduction and fascination.

One should note that this violence is presented by Certeau (more perhaps than by Léry himself) as a violence directed against the onlooker/eavesdropper's own culture, the marks of his own 'distinction':

Through these metaphorical irruptions of fable and these lapses of meaning, the voice exiled on the borders of discourse might flow back, and, with it, the murmur and the 'noises' from which the process of scriptural reproduction distinguishes itself. In this way an exteriority without beginning or truth might return to visit discourse. (*WH* 236/248)

Léry's writing is for Certeau intermittently carried towards a space outside its own discursive order, towards a derision of the textual edifice of which it forms a part. No doubt one should say that this space, in the very movement of its fantasmatic irruption, always figures as relative to the particular scriptural order which it unsettles. In this perspective the 'savage' voices might be conceived as pretexts for a violence which is desired as much as it is feared. Nevertheless, these voices do not reassure, or even 'edify', the interpreter. Rather, they break him down and expose the fragility of his identity.

The 'violence' which sends cracks running through the self-assurance of the interpreter need not substantially affect another more direct type of violence. The programmatic strategies of socio-economic exploitation may function without regard to the permutations of desire. Nevertheless, the relegation of the figures discussed above to the status of mere aesthetic diversion would itself represent a problematic operation of repression. Such an operation would neglect the force of the questions which these figures return against cultural and economic orders which produce them as side-effects or residue. Luce Giard argues that

underneath the sound and fury of [the *destructive violence* that Europe inflicted on the American Indian societies], de Certeau heard the rumor of another one, more secret but equally important, a *transformative violence* of the meeting with the Other whose shock waves had finally reached Europe to undermine its old certainties. He often remarked that 'no one returns unchanged' from an encounter with the Other.[14]

Certeau shows how the human subject may be profoundly transformed, and the systems of knowledge which he transports with him significantly altered, by the confrontation with an alterity which at another level they control and explain.

In Certeau's account, the Tupinambou represent for Léry both a ravishing figure and a phenomenon to be understood. Certeau's

writing traces – and in an important sense reduplicates – a perpetual oscillation between these poles. Together they symbolize for
Certeau the essentially dual nature of the 'fable'. He argues that
the voices of the Tupinambou both exceeded what could be written by Léry, yet were also integrated, as 'fiction', into the scripturally
based system of truth which he represented. They were 'cited' by
the interpreter who also 'missed' them. The meaning of the fable
for learned interpretation (notwithstanding Certeau's suggestions
that it always irrupts as that which in one sense is senseless) seems
to lie in this very tension:

> The savage becomes the senseless speech which ravishes Western
> discourse, but which, because of that very fact, forces the science that
> produces meanings and objects to continue indefinitely to write. *The
> place of the other*, represented by the savage, is hence 'fabulous' on two
> counts: firstly by virtue of a metaphorical rupture (*fari*, the act of
> speaking which has no nameable subject), and then through its status
> as an object for comprehension (the fiction which has to be translated
> into the terms of knowledge). An utterance *arrests* what has already
> been said – it erases what has been written – and yet compels further
> linguistic production – it generates writing. (*WH* 236/248)

The 'fable' as Certeau understands it both induces and threatens
to nullify a proliferation of written discourse. 'It speaks' (*ça parle*):
irrepressibly but unintelligibly something speaks (or echoes) and
in so doing violates the distinctions which constitute knowledge.
For this very reason it produces a continual work of reintegration
which aspires to recover (at the cost of altering) the same distinctions of knowledge. The fable 'takes in' (*fait marcher*) for Certeau
the interpretation which it provokes. Something is touched within
the interpreter which suspends a prescribed order of rationality,
and which can only figure as a breach or interference in the continuity of his thought. The subsequent work of interpretation
corresponds in Certeau's analysis to so many fabrications designed
to cover over a more fundamental fable.

The Possession of Loudun

'Normally, strange things circulate discreetly under our streets.
But it requires only a crisis to bring them swirling up everywhere

from under the ground, and, as if swollen in the flood, for them to lift up the covers which sealed up the drains and to invade our cellars, then our towns' (*PL* 7). So begins Certeau's 1970 presentation of the famous case of multiple diabolic possession which began at Loudun in 1632. Readers are warned about what they are not going to find in Certeau's account: history is never 'sure', what took place was, in one way or another, 'strange', and Certeau does not set out to absorb and resolve this strangeness by means of a convenient contemporary interpretative apparatus – whether psychoanalytic, semiotic, historical or sociological. Certainly, Certeau tries out such tools in his attempt to organize the archival traces which remain of the possession.[15] Yet he never loses sight of their limits, despite or perhaps because of the very virtuosity with which he manipulates them. If anything Certeau's analyses serve finally to exacerbate our consciousness of such limits.

None the less, 'we must first try to understand' (*PL* 18). The nuns in the recently founded Ursuline convent at Loudun manifested the first declared symptoms of what would soon be diagnosed as their 'possession' in September 1632. Certeau draws attention to various factors which must take interpretation beyond the level of elementary explanations based on the mortal *ennui* of life in a convent and the sexual frustration of the nuns.[16] A plague, experienced as a metaphysical calamity, had just ravaged the town (its last effects were being recorded at the same time as the first symptoms of possession). Loudun itself was a town uneasily divided between Protestants and Catholics: such coexistence and a history of conflict had led, despite official hardenings of doctrinal principles, to a gradual disintegration of the institution of shared meaning represented by the Catholic church. It was becoming less clear what sort of power it exerted, while the Protestant heretic was an omnipresent reminder of diabolic deviation.[17] The lives of the nuns, at the forefront of the educational strategies of the Counter-Reformation, were inevitably caught up in these larger historical processes.

Certeau reads the possession to begin with through the framework of these general shifts and mutations. He argues that it is only in this way that one can reconstitute the conditions in which the nuns could give expression to what possessed them. In order to voice something which was perhaps without a ready name (anxiety? panic? desire? despair?), they had only the languages of their place and time. Moreover, this nameless 'something' should not for Certeau be hypostasized as some kind of archetypal essence beneath the superficial play of language. Certeau detects rather in the events at Loudun the symptoms precisely of a crisis of 'nomination'. He suggests that the very disintegration of a common historical language itself served to provoke a collapse into the seemingly ahistorical, sublinguistic symptoms of panic and possession:

> The well-established practice of examining their conscience, the requirement for an indubitable religious faith nevertheless subjected to such examination, a general discredit of those institutions which could be invested with meaning and which could guarantee their conformity to the Christian spirit – all these factors constantly lead the nuns to place their real experience behind the 'theatre' of regular religious life. The dark seething of unavowable intentions – wasn't *that* reality? . . . Many Ursulines . . . fall at this point into despair, pulled down by the indubitable but unreliable experience of doubts and impulses which are intolerable in the language of orthodox fidelity. According to received theological schemes, the nuns can do nothing else except attribute all of this reality to the devil, and recognize him in the infernal shadow spreading over and dividing their interior landscape. (*PL* 147–8)

The language of the nuns developed through a series of encounters with confessors, priests, demonological and spiritual writings, rumour and gossip. Yet this language (and its break-up) could serve both to interpret a disturbing interior strangeness and to 'produce' it. Indeed, one could say that Certeau's interpretation itself works precisely in the gap between a standard seventeenth-century French sense of 'produce' (to bring to light what exists already) and its more usual contemporary definition (to fabricate something which previously did not exist).[18] He shows how the diabolic artifice manifested by the nuns sent fissures through stable conceptions of nature and truth. One should cite in this respect Certeau's commentary on Jacques Callot's *Temptation of Saint Anthony*. Rather like Brueghel in his more famous painting, Callot shows the saint as a minor bodily presence lost in the monstrous landscape of his 'temptation' as it is 'produced' before him. Certeau notes how

> horrific visions are inscribed in the landscape just as they are in learned literature. The imaginary forms part of history. Like the architectural structures of Callot, writing is haunted by the unstable *vision* which is both a *spirit* within the spectator and an *object* in front of him: there is a dangerous ambiguity between what the subject produces himself and what he perceives of the world.[19]

We have already seen in chapter 1 how Certeau problematized in the early 1970s the question of 'reality' in historiography. It is striking that he had already taken as the object of his own historiography a set of phenomena which produced, precisely, an obsessive concern with what could be considered as 'real'.[20]

The conflict of interpretations

The nuns were not alone in wanting to interpret or to 'produce' the motions possessing their bodies and minds. For reasons whose intricate implications are patiently drawn out by Certeau, it suited many peoples' interests (from the local apothecary to Cardinal Richelieu) to have Urbain Grandier, an ambitious and philandering local priest, convicted as a scapegoat for the obscene delirium of the nuns. In due course he was burnt at the stake as a magician. Yet before this could happen the strange occurrences reported at the Ursuline convent had to be certified and treated as an orthodox possession. There were models for this, based on accounts of other possessions,[21] and Certeau traces how the initial interpretations of confessors and exorcists led the nuns into the 'magic circle' or 'prison' of a pre-established system of demonological knowledge. No doubt this operation required a fair amount of willing or unwilling complicity on the part of the supposed demoniacs, although the extent of such complicity is problematized by Certeau's analysis of the textual records of the exorcisms. Furthermore, given the strangely compulsive logic of exorcism, saturated with techniques of suggestion and induction, the concept of 'compliance' in its standard sense comes to constitute a rather unwieldy tool of analysis. One could instead see in the bizarre scenes played out between exorcists and possessed an archaic antecedent of the 'mechanism(s) of incitement and multiplication' and the 'perpetual spirals of power and pleasure' which Michel Foucault was to see at work in the more recent 'production' of sexuality.[22]

With time, the magic circle drawn up at Loudun would serve as the field of conflict in which multiple positions would be taken up according to a multiplicity of religious, political and personal interests and desires. Moreover, this conflict worked to displace, break apart and finally disperse the elements which had initially been grouped together by the traditional discourse of diabolic possession. Certeau traces the process through which nominally religious elements were taken up and re-employed as functions of essentially political strategies: in particular Richelieu's campaign against provincial autonomy and the Protestants in the name of state policy (*raison d'état*). The possession became a state-supported 'theatre' where the cohesive power of royalty over the forces of hell and subversion could be demonstrated. Certeau interprets in this way the spectacular and finally monotonous scenes at Loudun as both an emblem and an integral part of the more general socio-historical transition from an older religious cosmos to an explicitly political state. These mutations in the functioning of superficially identical elements come once again under the rubric of the 'formality' of practices. They are alterations, so to speak, in the forms of forms. Certain religious forms, in this case, changed their form as they were integrated into new strategies and tactics. Exorcisms thus became effectively an instrument of political authority. Certeau shows how, in the words of the Capuchin Father Tranquille (one of the more violent exorcists), 'the demons [could] only be chased away using blows of the royal sceptre – the cross alone [was] not enough to split the skull of this dragon.'[23]

For Certeau, such mutations themselves work to produce a more general 'strangeness' of history, an ongoing process of 'alteration' as successive orders collapse and are constituted, exposing each time the subjects who inhabit them to new forms of (dis)possession:

> Tied to a particular historical moment, that is to the transition from a set of religious criteria to a set of political criteria, from a cosmological and celestial anthropology to a scientific organization of natural objects arranged under the scrutiny of man, the possession of Loudun opens out also on to the strangeness of history, on to the reflexes triggered off by its alterations, and on to the question raised from the moment there emerge the new social figures of the other, different from the devilries of times past but disturbing just as they were. (*PL* 328)

Successive historical arrangements never cease to be put in question as apparently identical elements are 'taken' differently. Certeau does not set against the axiological instability and flux which he diagnoses in seventeenth-century Loudun the illusory solidity of a contemporary set of values. He refuses the historian's task of 'exorcizing' the danger and alterity/alteration of history, the operation of sealing it off and circumscribing it in another place. The interpretation of the possession challenges our own suppositions about what is real, reliable or permanent.

Certeau's analysis of the manifold shifts discernible over the course of the possession goes far beyond the rather monolithic distinction between a religious order and a political and scientific organization. Hervé Martin talks of his impression in reading *La possession de Loudun* of 'a vast structure in which all the elements are constantly evolving, while remaining in perpetual relation with each other'.[24] This complexity is particularly striking in Certeau's presentation of the conflict of interpretations which arose at Loudun. One could contrast Certeau's analysis with that of Jules Michelet, who saw in the struggle for the interpretation of the events at Loudun a fairly straightforward conflict between the forces of medical enlightenment and the obfuscations and bad faith of the Church.[25] Certeau investigates instead both the manner in which apparently incompatible positions shared a constraining if increasingly unstable epistemological framework, and the aporias which confronted even those observers who in retrospect might seem to have been the most 'advanced'.[26] It is worth quoting in full the following passage from the chapter entitled 'The gaze of the doctors':

> The abnormality of the facts and the contradictory nature of the different interpretations introduce into vision the fissure of doubt. In this way, the doctors are touched in their turn by the social disquiet of which the possession is a symptom. In the prevailing scepticism, they experience it in the form of an epistemological uncertainty: some kind of *deception* is going on. But where precisely? The question borders on that which consisted in assigning a place somewhere in knowledge for the unknown. For some, it is knowledge itself which is mistaken, and one must return to fideism, blindly trusting in truths received from elsewhere. For others, the lure lies in experience: *Experimentum fallax*, said Patin. Perception leads us astray. Or, as Dr Duncan will say, 'the imagination is mistaken, it is false, it is damaged,' and it deceives the senses. Unless one could attribute the illusion to the actors themselves, repress it by supposing it to lie in the artifices and simulations allegedly producing the observed facts, and get rid of the problem like that. This is by far the most tempting hypothesis, but it remains difficult to accept. The doctors as a body are not convinced by it, any more than they are by the 'explanation' through miracles, even if they do accept it as an element which should not be neglected. (*PL* 174–5)

The modern reader is perhaps caught in the labyrinthine detours of Certeau's erudite reconstruction of the interpretative options available to seventeenth-century observers. It is as though one were presented with a series of pre-emptive allegories of interpretation. Certeau stages throughout *La possession de Loudun* the repeated failures, hesitations or dubious precipitation of diverse medical, theological, philosophical and juridical interpretative acts, and deliberately holds the phenomena presented in intermediary zones, beyond the range of any specific interpretation. The very heterogeneity of explanations proffered in this uncertainly ironic and distorting historical mirror obliquely discourages the reader from trusting in his or her own contemporary 'competence'. One could see here a variant of what Tzvetan Todorov analyses as the principal device of 'fantastic' literature: a more or less prolonged hesitation between conflicting interpretations produces an uncanny breach in a system of meaning.[27]

Nomination

The company of politically, ecclesiastically, medically and legally authorized interpreters shared despite their differences a common function. They had to attribute to the irruption of alterity a name through which it could be integrated into the prevailing sociolinguistic order. Against the evanescent doubts or compulsions of the possessed, they set the apparatus of social classification:

> On the one hand, the possessed speak from a site which is undetermined and which declares itself always as 'somewhere else' speaking in me. . . . On the other hand, the exorcists or the doctors respond by a labour of nomination or designation which represents a characteristic feature of possession in any traditional society. Therapy in cases of possession . . . consists essentially in naming, in giving a name to what manifests itself as speech, but as an uncertain speech inseparable from disturbances, bodily gestures and cries. (WH 246–7/251–2)

The symptoms of the possessed bore witness to an 'alteration' of the human subject, which threatened in turn to contaminate the propriety of the social order. The diverse representatives of this order turned in response to the authorized nomenclatorial lists prescribed for such eventualities. Certeau cites the catalogue of demons' names (Asmodeus, Iscaron, Leviathan, Aman, Balam, Behemoth . . .) which, applied to the inchoate utterances and gesticulations of the energumens, enabled the exorcists to produce working simulacra of comprehension and order. Qualified observers assigned a theoretically stable set of such names to the profusion of symptoms/

manifestations which confronted them. When the Prioress, for example, showed signs of 'impurity', then she was possessed by Iscaron; when she was subject to uncontrollable fits of blasphemy, and treated her exorcists with scorn and derision, then she was possessed by Behemoth.

Certeau underlines the centrality of 'confession' in this process: if the energumen could be brought to say that she 'was' the demon in question ('I am Behemoth,' etc.), then the human subject could be returned to her place in a linguistic order. Certeau argues that the exorcists endeavoured through such confessions to 'restore the postulate of all language, that is, a stable relation between the speaking 'I' and a social signifier, the proper name' (*WH* 256/261). This position of the *I* – both place of siege and a turning or vanishing point – brings us up against Certeau's problematization of 'utterance' (*énonciation*). Before examining this in more detail, however, I shall briefly indicate in the work of nomination two points of tension which Certeau's study brings into particular relief.

Firstly, Certeau draws out what one can call, after Derrida, the impropriety of the proper. As Lévi-Strauss puts it, one never names, one classifies.[28] The 'proper name' never fully belongs to the subject as such. Instead, it introduces him or her into the sociolinguistic order of which it is a function. The 'propriety' of the subject has always already been eroded by his or her 'own' proper name, imposed by others or by the Other represented by language. There is an irreducible violence in this process – again, an ongoing alteration – which fissures any possible identity. This violence is in retrospect all too manifest in the workings of the demonological and medical machinery of nomination at Loudun. Certeau, however, does not seek to replace this deleterious machinery with the myth of a fully adequate and transparent practice of nomination. He insists that the distortions generated by the 'impropriety of the proper' are inescapable. In this way he seeks to avoid the lure of attempting, from another time and place, to restitute the authentic propriety/alterity of possessed speech.

Secondly, as I have already suggested, the classificatory systems at Loudun were themselves in a state of conflict and flux. One should not think in terms of a simple opposition between nomination and aphasia or delirium. Certeau presents rather a set of interpenetrating linguistic spaces – which the possessed seem both to inhabit and to elude – comprised of incompatible and antagonistic terms, disaffected debris of older systems and emergent neologisms:

At Loudun ... there exist several dictionaries of proper names: the demonological, the medical, and also the political. ... The possession is played out here upon a plurality of historically stratified and non-synchronized onomastic tables. The capacity for speech of the possessed woman is hence not bound solely to the possibilities offered to her by the proper names of the demonologists. The list of the 'strongest' party will triumph, that of the doctors and politicians. (WH 262/269)

Certeau places the linguistic enterprise of the demonologists in the larger framework of a 'will to power' involving heterogeneous and mutually determining interpretative and denominative forces. The discussion of a more circumscribed scene of interpretation which follows should be read in the context of this general development.

Duplicitous citation

The documentary traces which remain of the possession are largely a result of the work of nomination outlined above.[29] Thus for Certeau they must from the very beginning be considered as 'altered documents' (WH 252/257). As such they constitute a point of no return. One cannot accede to the 'proper' voice of the possessed. The marks of the demoniacs' speech in diverse medical, ecclesiastical, juridical and epistolary reports are the result of the questions or demands put to them by representatives of institutional knowledge and power. The utterances of the nuns have always already been integrated into 'alienating' taxonomies. In this sense perhaps, scriptural systems may possess orality. Of the latter they give us only cited fragments.

We have already seen in chapter 1 how Certeau exposes the ambivalence of citation as an interpretative technique. Interpreters introduce into their texts extracts from the languages they want to explain. They strategically manipulate these 'citations' – and the term should be understood in both a literary and juridical sense – in order to confirm positions of interpretative mastery. At Loudun, exegetes and doctors cited the utterances of ignorant and possessed speech in order to assign to them their true place in the orders of knowledge. Yet Certeau sees such instances of citation as precarious. A fragment of alterity inserted into a text may itself turn against this text. The excerpts of 'ignorant' speech designed to consolidate a scriptural edifice can be compared to the echo of a Tupinambou chant recalled in Léry's narrative. Such excerpts may invert their sign and come to represent a dangerous breach in that edifice:

> Something different returns in . . . discourse with the citation of the other: it remains ambivalent; it maintains the danger of a strangeness which alters the knowledge of the translator or commentator. Citation represents for discourse the menace and the suspense of a *lapsus*. The alterity mastered – or possessed – by discourse retains the latent power of returning as a fantastic ghost – or indeed as a 'possessor'. (*WH* 251/256)

At a fairly direct level, one might think of the 'irreverence' and 'insolence' of the nuns, cited as evidence that they must surely be possessed by evil and mendacious spirits. Claire de Sazilly, for example, in the role of a demoniac, protests to a Father Elisha that 'You're taking me for a Bohemian. Truly you're abusing the patience of these gentlemen. What will they say to the King and the Cardinal?', and to no less a person than Laubardemont, the ambitious royal intendant in charge of the proceedings, 'And you, Sir, you've been caught. Up to now you've deceived so many people, but now you've been found out' (*PL* 155).

It is not that such reinterpretable slights necessarily posed a serious problem to such as Laubardemont, immured against doubt and derision by what Michelet saw as an 'unlimited power . . . the whole force of the kingdom, a horrible bludgeon'.[30] Nor do they present us with a grain of truth uncontaminated by the ubiquitous effects of deception or 'alteration'. Rather Certeau sees in the ephemeral inversions operated by such citations – they can be 'taken' in opposing ways – a fundamental question addressed to the all-too-imposing notion of an 'unlimited power':

> Certainly, the citation is not a chink in the ethnographical text through which we could see another landscape or another discourse. What is cited is fragmented, re-employed and patched together [*bricolé*] in a text; it is altered therein. Yet in this position where it keeps nothing of its own, it remains capable, as in a dream, of bringing back something uncanny [*une inquiétante étrangeté*]: it retains the surreptitious and altering power of the repressed. (*WH* 251/256)

As he does in a rather different manner in his interpretation of mystic texts (see chapter 4 below), Certeau detects in the necessarily 'alienated' utterances of the possessed the mark or 'wound' of an alterity which threatens to undo the linguistic fabric in which it is cited. The 'other' breaks away from its prescribed place in an official catalogue, and takes on the unsettling force of the *other*.

Possessed utterance

No amount of citation could enable the modern interpreter to resurrect the true voice of the possessed. As a result of this a priori impossibility, Certeau displaces his objective, and traces instead the disruptions effected by possessed speech in the contemporary systems of knowledge which set out to classify it. He defines as the object of his analysis 'the nature of this speech which is *interdicted by* discourse and *returns within* discourse, or, to put it another way, which is "inter-jected" (*entre-dite*) through the alteration of the same discourse' (*WH* 249/254). The questions raised by his approach can initially be articulated in terms of the linguistic problematic of 'utterance'.

The concept of 'utterance' (*énonciation*) has been developed by a number of French linguisticians over the last twenty or thirty years.[31] It addresses what for Certeau was a point of fundamental concern – namely the manners in which linguistic subjects appropriate the languages available to them. One might note that two years before the publication in 1970 of *La possession de Loudun*, Certeau had produced an influential interpretation of the events of May 1968 entitled, precisely, *La prise de parole* [Starting to speak]. Émile Benveniste argues that the operation through which the speaking subject appropriates language may be broken down into a fourfold 'formal apparatus'. This consists of: (1) the present, individual act by which a speaker turns the mere possibility of language into a concrete instance of discourse; (2) the process through which the speaker 'positions' himself or herself in language by means of a series of specific 'indices' or marks; (3) the implied positioning in relation to the speaker of an other; (4) the expression of a certain relation to the world, as a pragmatic condition of communication.[32] Certeau repeatedly uses analogous criteria of analysis in order to direct the readings he proposes of a variety of operations. As he himself suggests, it is more helpful to treat the problematic of utterance in his work as a 'theoretical marker'[33] rather than as a fully-fledged, self-contained theory. It indicates the sorts of borders or margins to which Certeau's attention seems to gravitate: the disjunctions between socially and institutionally authorized linguistic systems and the distinctive ways in which different subjects inhabit or move through these systems; the gaps between representations and the ways in which those who are represented appropriate these representations; the sorts of operations which both depend on and also displace or unsettle a pre-established set of sociolinguistic classifications. In his analysis of possessed speech, Certeau focuses on the relation of present, individual utterances to a set of interpretative systems, and on the 'marks' by which the possessed are called to position themselves in these systems.

Certeau explores in particular the function – or dysfunction – of the pronoun 'I' in the theatricalized duels played out between exorcists and possessed. I have already drawn attention to its strategic importance in the process by which the exorcists extracted a 'confession' – 'I am Behemoth', etc. – which enabled them to integrate the troubled and troubling alterity before them into the reassuring solidity of their prescribed classifications. Certeau notes, however, that this process did not really seem to work. The machinery of interpretation was perpetually strained by an incessant movement and flight of its objects. The exorcists might succeed in securing a confession – 'I am Leviathan' – but this would be rendered worthless the next moment when the same energumen would protest another identity: 'I am Iscaron.' The succeeding utterances of the possessed – 'I am X', 'I am Y', 'I am B' – fissured the identities which they were supposed to secure, and disrupted the classificatory grids which were supposed to contain them. Moreover the nuns began to insinuate anomalous elements into the classical demonological lists of the exorcists. Low-life demons such as *Queue de chien* ['Dog's Dick'] or *Souvillon* ['Sooty Pussy'] started to appear (WH 261/267). Certeau compares such interjections to the act of suddenly introducing a 'duke of clubs' into an ordinary game of cards. He traces how the possessed shuffled the terms of the interpretative taxonomies drawn up for them, but could not be assigned *a* term. The apparatus designed to bring the 'ignorant' or delirious speech of the nuns into conformity with a demonological configuration of knowledge was for Certeau itself set in motion and altered by this same speech.

By producing a proposition of the type 'I am X', the exorcists aimed to insert the speaking subject before them into a prescribed order of words and things. Their strategy represents in one sense an inversion of the formal analysis of utterance outlined above. That analysis addresses the ways in which the speaking subject may actively appropriate and position herself within a linguistic system. The exorcists, by contrast, sought to demonstrate how a sociolinguistic system could itself appropriate the subject. Their hermeneutic apparatus was designed, through the extraction of a confession, to immobilize the speaking subject. Certeau's interpretation can therefore at one level be conceived also as an anti-interpretation. He analyses how the speech of the possessed, even before the kind of onomastic improvisations evoked above, incessantly transgressed the limits ascribed to it by the exorcists' systematic interpretative enterprise:

> The endless rotation of the *I* within a closed list of fixed proper names generates demonological discourse, but prevents it from functioning smoothly, obliging it to repeat the denominative operation indefinitely. This procedure of perversion is in the discourse of possession the equivalent of what Rimbaud expressed in the form of a commentary on his poetry: 'It is false to say: I think. We ought to say: it thinks me [*on me pense*].' What is this *it*? This is precisely the question introduced by the possessed: '*it* speaks me.' (*WH* 257/262)

The nuns substituted for the single required proposition which would give them a stable place in an interpretative field a series of utterances which yield only superficially to the form 'I am X'. In effect their very succession, incessantly altering and effacing one another, brings them closer to the (anti-)grammatical form of the Rimbaldian 'I is another'. The possessed 'slip incessantly from place to place' (*WH* 257/263): they have no proper name, each new name is manifested in Certeau's reading for what it was – another alteration. For Certeau, the nuns did not so much position themselves in the tables of the demonologists as move across these tables in a series of 'altering traverses' (*traversées altérantes*) (*WH* 249/254). Certeau's interpretation does not work by delving 'beneath' the apparent superficiality of these linguistic contracts, games and transgressions. He does not suppose that a single deep and hidden truth of the possession remains to be found. Nor does he want to sift through the variety of interpretative systems deployed at Loudun in order to separate truth from fable and modern insight from archaic delusion. Instead, he focuses his attention both on the complicated historicity and on the vestigial 'voicing' of the documents which he has before him. He seeks to follow (as one can 'follow' a musical score, perhaps) the marks and the alterations which the aberrant voices of the possessed left on the scriptural systems which also subjugated them.

Impertinent voices and irrelevant interpretations

> Interrogated: *Quis es tu, mendax, pater mendacii? Quod est nomen tuum?* [the demon] said, after a long silence: 'I've forgotten my name. I can't find it . . .'
>
> And ordered again to say its name, it said: 'I've lost my name in the wash.'[34]

The problem of utterance displaces in Certeau's work the conventional objectives of interpretation. In his analysis of the events at Loudun, he argues that a set of questions concerning the place of the speaker threatened to override a more traditional hermeneutical concern with the content of discourse:

> What proves problematic and surreptitiously stirs up an entire semantic organization is the suspicion which weighs upon the speaker of this language and hence on the status of discourse as a whole. In this way traditional hermeneutics is inverted. It presupposed an unchanging locus and a stable speaker, God, communicating through a language whose secrets, as yet unknown, had to be deciphered. Here, however, the content is known, and the speaker is unknown: we have in the texts of the possession the mark of this disappearance of the subject. (*WH* 264/271)

The interpretative task of the retrieval of meaning is complicated by the question of the relation which the speaking subject may or may not hold with regard to this meaning. Certeau discerns a passage from what Louis Marin calls one 'economy of the secret' to another. The secret of (possessed) language is no longer to be sought in the manifest contents of this language – as Certeau notes, these tend often to be indistinguishable from the orthodox catechisms of the time. It becomes instead an attribute of the speaking subject who withdraws from these contents even as she utters them ('I am Behemoth' > 'I am Dog's Dick' > 'I have lost my name' > . . . : every proposition is always on the point of being effaced, altered or derided). The only linguistic traces which remain of this withdrawing subject are those indices evoked above which mark or 'personalize' her utterance (personal pronouns and other deictics). Moreover these indices do not manifest this secret: they 'secrete' it.[35] A series of blind spots paradoxically marked as such (secreted) upon an interpretative field put in question an entire edifice of language. They point outside this language towards what one might call the 'virtual' alterity of its appropriation.

For these indices of a speaker's utterance do not yield a positive semantic content. They are rather what destabilize the semblances of such contents. How are we to read the proposition 'I am X' if a series of other utterances indicate that 'I is (always) another'? The *I*, far from working as a discursive support, functions here as a principle of substraction or negativity. The possession in Certeau's reading 'does not give rise to another discourse, as if the alterity to which it bears witness came endowed with a different and recognizable semantic positivity. It produces the alteration of demonological discourse' (*WH* 265/271). A standard interpretation of the nuns' speech would aspire to translate it into a 'positive' semantic form. It would, for example, endeavour to substitute for her ignorant proposition that 'I am X' a theological, legal or scientific translation to the effect that 'she is (you are) in fact Y.' For Certeau, it is precisely such a hermeneutical operation which is put in question by the incessant alterations produced by possessed utterances. They 'inhabit' a series of positive interpretative forms – but only so as to 'pervert' them.

To substitute, say, a new set of modern interpretative forms for the more archaic discourses which set up the scene of the possession at Loudun would be to miss the point of Certeau's analysis. He notes that today's psychiatric patients inevitably face similar problems with regard to the psychiatric discourses within which they must position themselves or be positioned. Certeau endeavours instead to elucidate a disturbing vanishing point of a classificatory enterprise, the result of a peculiar indifference or distance of hermeneutically incompetent subjects with regard to expert games of interpretation:

> The possessed woman insinuates her silence into the system that she 'disquiets' and which nevertheless allows her to speak. Her 'perversion' does not consist in herself giving an interpretation of her difference, but rather in altering the ways in which the internal relations that once defined this system now play upon each other. Hence she leaves the other with the responsibility of interpreting her. She hides what is moving in her simply because she has no discourse except that provided by the interpretation of the exorcist, the doctor or the scholar. She escapes thanks to the explanation of her given by the other. (*WH* 265/272)

The proliferation of interpretations set in motion by the speech of the possessed do not set up an asymptotical progression towards elucidation. They work rather for Certeau as a series of alibis and quid pro quo's. The subject is never really *there*. The possessed repeatedly transgress the contractual rule by which they should accept their social identity as produced by a certified interpretation. This is not to deny either the overwhelming and finally self-confirming power of such interpretations, or the varying degrees of 'complicity' which they produce in those subjects for whom they provide a language. Rather, Certeau focuses his attention on the recurrent distortions which are introduced into the deceptive stability of dominant classificatory systems. He shows how these systems may be both appropriated and dispossessed by the withdrawing presence of a virtual other.

Reflections and Interruptions

Archaic scenes

What are we to make of these case-studies? Certeau presents the 'scenes of interpretation' produced by Léry's encounter with the Tupinambou and by the possession of Loudun as 'archaic' variants of the scenes constituted by modern interpretative practices. Monique Schneider notes Certeau's own recourse to a psychoanalytic interpretative terminology. Certeau proposes that Léry's text may be analysed as 'the equivalent of a "primitive scene"' (*WH* 211/218). Yet this move is double-edged. Schneider records how it also serves to put in question (her own) contemporary psychoanalytic practice:

> Is the reference to psychoanalysis introduced as a means of interpreting scenes which are situated elsewhere – the exoticism of savage speech or the archaism of the relation between energumens and exorcists – or can the apparatus of writing be turned upon itself so as to uncover the ways in which these scenes from elsewhere themselves 'regard' (both 'view' and bear upon) what happens in a present situation, when a psychoanalyst listens to a patient.[36]

In Certeau's presentation of these remote events, the contemporary interpreter is seized by certain uncanny resemblances. She expected to 'reflect' on the past, and finds rather that the past 'reflects' her. Certeau's writings here seem to work like an anamorphotic mirror.

The strangeness for which they provide a textual space is suddenly put into perspective as a disturbing familiarity. They point up by implication the 'original wounds' and the 'organizing impulsions' (*H* 179 / *HP* 28) which inhabit contemporary interpretative practice.

Certeau's analyses both of Léry's narrative and of the possession at Loudun show how an interpretative force may be used to eliminate or to 'exorcize' the fragility or threat of others' 'voices'. In both cases, the interpreters are dominant agents in an economy of writing, while the 'voices' are necessarily (albeit problematically) associated with a field of orality. In Certeau's reading, the utterances which emerge from this field (songs, outbursts, cries, murmurs) both 'wound' a scriptural order, and are organized by it according to persistent structures.

One can define this structural organization in terms of three intermeshing operations. Firstly, a line of separation is posited between a learned expertise and its 'other'. Secondly, this 'other' is thereby placed in a space of 'ignorance': it is by *definition* uninformed, naive or unconscious. Thus speech not founded on a set of written authorities is seen to be talking but without knowing what it is talking about. Finally, this inchoate mass of ignorant 'fables' is brought under the official control of certified knowledge through various techniques of interpretative 'stitching', such as exegesis, translation, citation and nomination. These techniques enable interpreters both to preserve the separation initially set up as a mark of their distinction and repeatedly to transgress it in order to prove – or test – their mastery.

Such operations of separation and 'stitching' may seem evident – some would ask whether experts can do anything else. Yet the effect of Certeau's historical (allegorical?) accounts is precisely to defamiliarize what seems evident and hence to permit us to isolate it as such. The superficially detached modern interpreter inherits certain organizing principles as an unconscious 'archaeology'. In so far as it is passively received, this archaeology corresponds to a form of 'passion'. By demonstrating how this passion can be broken down into a series of formal operations, Certeau insinuates into deep-rooted intellectual habits the fissure of a critical distance. He shows, moreover, how these operations of learned interpretation may themselves be subjected to forms of 'alteration'. They may be confronted by the disruptive force of the *other* or dispossessed by the withdrawn 'virtuality' of an other. In the analyses discussed above, as in the Rabelaisian fable, the voices which a given scriptural organization of people and things appeared to have stilled begin to stir again.[37] A perennial compulsion to interpret is unsettled by an exposure to what might be heard.

From interpretation to alteration

Certeau shows a marked tendency at strategical points in his work to interrupt the development of an argument with an appeal to another 'voice'. This 'voice' figures always as an absence and potential breach in the organization of his text. It is worth examining the function of these invocations in the studies discussed above.

Firstly in the analysis of Léry's text:

> What ex-voto does my writing address to absent speech? For what dream or lure is my writing a metaphor? There is no answer. Self-analysis has lost its prerogative, and I cannot substitute a text for what only another voice could reveal about the place from where I write. (*WH* 212/218)

I have already indicated how the mythical figure of a full, authentic and transparent speech can operate as a surreptitious 'decoy', serving to keep the alterity which it idealizes in a predefined place. I have sought to demonstrate the remoteness of Certeau's conception of orality from the facility of this myth. This does not necessarily render unproblematic the appeals which Certeau makes to other 'voices' in the course of his writing. Yet one should note that Certeau does not in the passage above invoke another's voice in order to support his text. On the contrary, he expects that this voice will disrupt or interrupt his writing in ways that can be neither anticipated nor pre-empted. His text exposes itself to a forceful displacement. Certainly, at one level Certeau's analyses may sharpen a desire for lost or absent voices. But these voices are not fetichized by Certeau as the symbol of some prelapsarian pastoral idyll. Rather, his work frees a space for a different kind of relation between a written text and the sea of voices from which it emerges. Or: he deliberately distorts the way in which we read a text by invoking the possibility of hearing a (different) voice.

There is a similar invocation in his study of the possession at Loudun:

> An analysis which might specify today how a text (the one I am writing) relates to demoniac speech of the seventeenth century might

represent a way of reformulating the question which this speech poses without falling into folklore or scientism. It would lead us to think through the strange remark that Freud picked up from Goethe: 'So muss denn doch die Hexe dran' – we must therefore appeal to the sorceress – and hope that she brings us an elucidation (or a change?) of our discourse. (*WH* 255/260)

Again, Certeau is displacing his position as an interpreter. I should begin by glossing certain elements in this rather condensed passage. The illusion of 'folklorism' would consist in conceiving the energumens' speech in terms of a mythical plenitude or force which would in turn support the text of their idealizing interpreter. The hubris of scientificity would be to suppose that one could explain this speech by means of a technical terminology and apparatus. The relation which Certeau assumes with regard to this speech is by contrast both more complex and more unstable. On the one hand, like his seventeenth-century equivalents, he is attempting to understand the enigma of the possessed, and, within defined limits, to give a better interpretation than others of the utterances of the nuns in so far as they can be made intelligible. In so doing, as he himself is the first to stress, he is evidently altering these utterances. On the other hand, however, he is, like the speech of the possessed, posing a 'question' to the process of interpretation as such. Like this speech, he aspires to alter – if not tear – the discourses of knowledge. He 'appeals' to the voice of the possessed precisely to turn it against these discourses. This appeal appears to originate as much in the desire for a 'change' (in terms of communicative contracts and structurally defined positions) as in the search for a convincing 'explanation' (a contribution to scientific capital). Yet Certeau's appeal also provides the analytic focus for his elucidation of the relations between interpretative discourse and its object. It facilitates the isolation of the constraining structures which inform the interpretative machinery at Loudun. It allows him to supplement (both add to and destabilize) the analysis of these structures by 'following' the disruptions which incompetent speech operates in them.[38]

Certeau's writing repeatedly expresses the desire to move beyond what he presents as the charmed (or demonic) circle of written and authorized interpretation. This involves less a movement 'against' interpretation in any programmatic sense than a series of tactical attempts to confront it with disconcerting forms of otherness. In the analyses discussed above, this implies an exposure to other 'voices' which have apparently been ordered and stilled by a set of interpretative operations. Certeau traces how, like the repressed, these voices return in differing forms to unsettle the sociolinguistic contracts through which certified interpreters assign to speaking subjects identities and places. His historical analyses serve to shake our assurances about the contemporary set-up of such contracts. They problematize the divisions we draw both between authorized knowledge and ignorance, and also between pertinent and impertinent or insignificant utterances. Certeau's texts work to disarm the 'professionals of meaning'. They point to a mobile conception of 'learning' whereby 'instead of expertise or ideas piling up in a site from which knowledge itself is always deemed to be speaking, the very forms of utterance might let themselves be altered so as to change, along with knowledge, the site where it is established' (*AH* 172). Certeau urges that the holders of official interpreterships expose their learning repeatedly to a change of 'place'. The experience of (interlocutory, textual, geographical, spiritual) 'travel' constitutes itself for Certeau a crucial facet of learning (and unlearning), through which the speaking subject discovers that his or her voice can only ever be one of many, his or her expertise a form of 'idiotism'. In this way, interpreters are for (by?) Certeau dispossessed of their mastery of alterity and implicated in a process of alteration.

4

Mystics

The Mystic Fable represents, in Jacques Revel's words, 'the provisional result of a very long journey'.[1] It was conceived not as a monumental *summa magna*, but as a deliberately 'flawed' vessel, a passing review of the landscapes which had emerged in twenty-five years of travel through the writings of early modern mystics. Certeau was working on a second volume at the time of his death.[2] I cannot myself propose here an exhaustive analysis of Certeau's work on the mystics, which would require a full-length study in its own right. I should begin, moreover, by underlining a further restriction. Certeau's study is not, as has sometimes been supposed, a study of 'mysticism' in general, whatever one might define that to be.[3] He sets out rather to trace how a sociohistorically situated 'discipline', 'la mystique', was constituted over the early modern period, and how it subsequently broke apart. The American translator of *The Mystic Fable* explicitly demarcates the work for his readers from more generalizing or initiatory works on 'mysticism':

> The theme of . . . *The Mystic Fable* is *la mystique*. This term cannot be rendered accurately by the English word 'mysticism', which would correspond rather to the French *le mysticisme*, and be far too generic and essentialist a term to convey the historical specificity of the object of this study. There is no need here to retrace the steps by which *la mystique*, the noun, emerged from the prior adjective, *mystique*. But it may be of some interest to note that this grammatical promotion has its parallel in English, in the development of such terms as 'mathematics' or 'physics', fields of inquiry of increasing autonomy, also

taking their names from an adjectival forerunner. I have, therefore, *in extremis*, adopted the bold solution of introducing a made-up English term, *mystics* (always in italics, to distinguish it from the plural of 'a mystic'), to render *la mystique*, a field that might have won (but never did, in English) a name alongside metaphysics, say, or optics.[4]

Michael Smith's lexical innovation has given me the title of my chapter. Yet one must also bear in mind two initial points concerning the status of this mystic 'science', as it was called by its early modern theoreticians. Firstly, one should not identify this status with that of those forms of science since constituted over the course of modernity.[5] Secondly, it figures in Certeau's analyses as a form of learning which develops through a reflection on its own status as a 'fable'.

Absence, Difference, Repetition

Prefatory strategies

As we have seen in chapter 1, Certeau emphasizes the irreducible existential separation which divides him as a historian from the object of his study. He supposes the apprehension of his documentation to be informed by two fundamental conditions: absence (we are given only traces of what will never return) and difference (these traces were produced by social orders and organizations of meaning radically different from our own). These conditions do not simply work against his interpretative practice: they set up the space in which it operates.

Certeau retraces in *L'Absent de l'histoire* [The absent of history] the itinerary of his research into early modern spiritual writings.[6] He notes how these writings accentuated his consciousness of absence and difference. The more he worked on them, the more they seemed to withdraw from him:

> I had to renounce the proximity which I had initially presupposed between these spiritual believers of the seventeenth century and our-selves when I had set out to rediscover them. As I got to know them better, they revealed themselves as strangers. . . . This approach un-covered their distance – a *difference* which concerned not only ideas or feelings, but also modes of perception, systems of reference, a type of

experience whose 'christianity' I could not impugn, but which I could
not recognize as mine. (*AH* 155–6)

One should stress that the 'difference' in question was not simply
that of a quasi-exotic stimulus to desire and interpretation. Certeau's
texts evince rather at certain points the traces of a painfully negotiated severance. Beneath what Jean Louis Schefer has called the
'vivacity of his thought, running in vigorous zigzags through this
work full of "wonderment", of truly jubilatory flashes of intelligence',[7] there emerges at intervals a palimpsest of scar-tissue. Luce
Giard has suggested that the 'profound humiliation' which is intermittently discernible in Certeau's writing may be associated with
the contemporary 'humiliation' and discredit of that Christian tradition with which he had once identified (and which he did not
simply disown).[8] Certeau underlines that these historical figures,
contrary to the claims of a spiritual tradition, cannot provide a set
of identificatory exempla for the elucidation of contemporary
problems.[9] They are separated from us by the screens of multiple
political, cultural and religious upheavals. Why, then, does Certeau
recollect them from the folds of historical oblivion? What does he
suppose that these 'fables' can still say?

The introduction to *The Mystic Fable*, written some ten years
later, intensifies the sense of absence which it seems that Certeau
had as a historian to 'suffer' before he could begin to 'operate'. Yet
this absence reverberates here with the force of a mortifying passion. The mystics 'show' him what he cannot possess. Luce Giard
has drawn attention to the violence of these 'abrupt' and 'cutting'
opening sentences:[10]

> This book can claim no special authorization. It stands exiled from its
> subject matter. My writing is devoted to the mystic discourses of (or
> on) presence (of God), but does not itself belong with them. It emerges
> from a mourning, an unaccepted mourning that has become the
> malady of bereavement. (*MF* 1/9)

The mystics work to produce in Certeau a redoubled form of severance. Historically and culturally, these texts belong to another
world. Yet they also withdraw from him in another sense. They
provide their modern historian with no real access to the unbound
presence which they figure. They manifest this presence to him
only in the form of a thwarted desire.

Certeau's reading of mystic writings reveals, however, that they

are themselves informed and generated by a thematization of their
own exilic condition. The fantasmatic or recalled plenitude of divine
presence returns incessantly to figure in them as a painfully assumed
absence. Certeau cites for example John of the Cross:

> Whither hast thou hidden thyself,
> And hast thou left me,
> O Beloved, to my sighing?[11]

Certeau reorganizes the structure of compounded absence outlined above, through which the interpreter is separated both from
the mystics and from their Object. He points to a mode of formal
reduplication binding the interpreter to those texts which also
evade him. Certeau is, albeit problematically, drawn into the
writings before him, precisely through the repeated work of
separation:

> The historian of the mystics, summoned, as they are, to *say the other*,
> repeats their experience in studying it: an exercise of absence defines
> at once the operation through which he produces his text and that
> which constructed theirs. A mirrorlike structure: like Narcissus, the
> historian-actor observes his double, which the movement of another
> element makes it impossible for him to grasp. He seeks one who has
> vanished, who in turn sought one who had vanished, and so on. (*MF*
> 11/21)

Again, history functions in Certeau's reading as a peculiar kind of
anamorphotic mirror. It does not yield by virtue of the historian's
treatment a stable set of contents. Rather, a series of strangely familiar forms come intermittently into focus in the course of his textual
peregrinations. Both the historian and the mystic are engaged in
a work 'upon' absence. Nevertheless, the reference to Narcissus
warns the reader that one cannot 'rest' with this image (to borrow
another term from the mystics). It risks degenerating into intellectual artifice. We have already seen how the importance of formal
models in Certeau's work lies above all in the differences which
they put into play.

Certeau's presentation of his relation to mystic writings can be
compared with his interpretation of a text by Jean-Joseph Surin.
This interpretation is again based on the discernment of a formal
reduplication. It addresses once more questions of historical rupture and continuity (or difference and repetition). It allows us,

however, to point up by contrast a textual strategy in Certeau's own work. This strategy is in a strong sense of the word 'prefatory': it concerns what must be said before speaking (*fari*).

In his analysis of the preface to Surin's *Science expérimentale des choses de l'autre vie* [Experimental science of the things of the other life],[12] Certeau notes how Surin authorizes his written testimony through an appeal to biblical predecessors. Surin begins by citing Saint John: 'What we have seen, what we have heard, what our hands have touched of the word of life we announce to you' and 'We speak of what we know, we testify to what we have seen.'[13] Surin wanted to impart to his readers the spiritual insights which he felt he had gained as a result of his travails at Loudun over the time of the diabolic possession.[14] They were for him an important sign that God's presence ('operation') could be discerned in contemporary life and was not confined to a circumscribed corpus of biblical revelation. Yet in order to carry off the transition from the 'dangerous logic'[15] of his precarious, uncertain experience to its scriptural 'production', Surin derived from this same corpus a repeatable formal sequence. Certeau demonstrates how this led broadly from a palpable 'experience' to a 'knowledge' which had to be 'testified' in order to reinforce the 'faith' of others.

As we shall see, the actual effectuation of this sequence was problematic – not least because the agent of the revelation in question seemed now to have shifted from the realm of the divine to that of the diabolic (of the *pater mendacii*), and was hence by definition deceptive. Yet Certeau reads Surin's textual strategy as the historically altered repetition of an essentially evangelical form as it continued to determine the way in which heterogeneous experiences were organized. One should note here how Certeau does not direct his own interpretative enterprise towards the reverential exhumation of edifying contents. Instead, he seeks to follow the vicissitudes of such formal re-employments:

> It is through form, not content, that there is continuity, and even identity, between the past and the present. . . . To interpret . . . is not to go back to a past moment and an authorized content in order to make them produce (dogmatic or historical) truth-effects but to recognize the same form in the element of different events. (*MF* 184/252)

Certeau shows the texts of Surin and of his evangelical predecessors to exhibit the same form in their manners of treating very different historical material. One should contrast this mode of formal repetition with that analysed above. Both concern the strategies through which authors (Certeau and Surin) produce their work for their contemporaries. Surin cites biblical predecessors in order to establish his testimony under the aegis of a common presence. Certeau invokes the mystics (including Surin) in so far as they partake of a shared suffering of absence. Surin legitimates the publication of his text through a forceful appeal to scriptural authority (which, as we shall see, occults a more essential fragility). Certeau sets up a working space by a paradoxical tactic of negation. He rejects the jurisdiction which he might have claimed over his domain. This no doubt constitutes the ambivalent appeal of his book. Certeau writes under the sign of a contemporary 'separation' – or melancholia. He holds out a seductive emptiness which to begin with could draw in anybody's memory.

'Mystic historicities'

Certeau moves beyond the formal repetition (a common exercise upon absence) which precariously binds him as an interpreter to the texts before him. This partial analogy puts into play a series of significant differences. These revolve around the tensions between historiographical and mystic (or poetic) practices of time.

For Certeau, the historian uses time primarily as an ordering principle. Certainly, historical objects are 'absent' and 'different'. Yet this is precisely what allows the historian retrospectively to distinguish them and to assign to them their respective places and limits. The historian's job is, as Certeau puts it, to 'calm the dead' (*MF* 11/21). Dispersed traces are correlated in order to construct an intelligible whole. The historian brackets the possibility of an absolute beginning, and shows how each event may be read as a function of another preceding event and of a larger structure. The mystics, by contrast, take up for Certeau certain questions with regard to the passing of time which the historian tends necessarily to occlude. Above all, these are questions of rupture and instauration. The writings of the mystics place in dramatic relief the relation of the mortal subject to time. They are driven by the belief that the subject may be brought to life or broken down by what comes to pass. The structure of anticipation which sustains their thought clashes for Certeau with that required for the usual work of historical interpretation:

The mystic is seized by time as by that which irrupts and transforms; hence time is for him the question of the subject seized by his other, in a present which is incessantly the surprise of a birth and a death. The endlessness of instants that are beginnings creates therefore a historicity in which continuities lose their relevance, just as institutions do. These events . . . continually contradict the time produced by historiography. (*MF* 11/22)

Certeau emphasizes that the mystics were engaged in a form of 'historicity'. They did not speak from a site outside the vicissitudes of history. Indeed, Certeau argues that their aberrant graphical and biographical itineraries, converted since into devotional relics, were the products precisely of a historical crisis. They inhabited the 'ruins' of the old cosmos. Yet their relation to history was also paradoxical. Thrown outside the new forms of power which emerged with modernity, they testify to what Certeau calls so many 'lapses of history' (*lapsus de l'histoire*) (MF 174/239). Indeed there may be, to a greater degree than Certeau is willing to admit in this respect, something which is intrinsically 'hyper-bolic' about the mystics' enterprise. *The Mystic Fable* shows forcefully how the mystics worked at the limits of the historical configurations which they inhabited. They sought to throw themselves beyond these limits.[16] This is not to say that they could efface these limits, and certainly not to say that their writings should be conceived 'ahistorically'. What emerges rather in Certeau's readings is the *passionate* (suffering) relation of the mystics to history. He notes how their writings constitute strange mixtures of archaic and radically modern elements. They were perhaps 'counterhistorical' in a broadly Nietzschean sense (*unhistorisch*, or *unzeitgemäss*). Certeau discerns in their writings a movement of excess (*dépassement*) whose form he sees as persisting today under other names. He cites René Char on the final page of *The Mystic Fable*: 'in poetry, we dwell only in the place we are leaving, we create only works from which we break away, we open spaces in time only by destroying it.'[17] The 'archaic' *poeisis* of the mystics serves in Certeau's work to challenge the writing of history.

Certeau has little time for mysticism conceived as a supposedly ahistorical phenomenon. Indeed, he suggests that such an approach is itself a function of a recent historical genealogy, produced by the splintering of human knowledge into diverse 'human sciences', an ensuing 'crisis' of philosophy, and the need to find a common 'ground' (designated for example as 'mystic') beneath the putatively 'superficial' fragmentation of history and knowledge.[18] This image of mysticism is for Certeau falsified by his inquiry into *mystics*. He stresses that his investigation is based on an inescapably social collection of documents.

To begin with what one might call the 'negative' pole of *mystics*, there were, Certeau asserts, no early modern mystics without institutional trials.[19] The fourth part of *The Mystic Fable* uncovers a constant, largely concealed and subterranean conflict between established authorities and those designated as 'mystic'.[20] The mystics problematized the cohesion between institutional formalities and effective belief. Even when their objective behaviour remained docile, they pointed to cracks in the administrative machinery of their orders. They threw open unsettling questions concerning a 'politics of the believable'. The 'mystic resistance' (*MF* 242/331) both disquieted and provoked. It set in motion numerous processes of investigation and exclusion. It was the latter which have provided modern historians with the bulk of their material. Certeau evokes, on the threshold of his own investigation into a case of mystic unrest at Bordeaux around 1630,

> many other 'minor prophets' and 'inspired women' whose passing has left scarcely a trace in the archives and whom history, acquiescent to the logic of the documents produced by the past, knows only through the censures, trials or banishments to which they have been subjected. These 'small to middling figures', far more numerous than one might think, and tending to form networks . . . proliferated in Bordeaux. (*MF* 254/350)

This passage also gives an idea of what one could call the 'positive' social dimension of *mystics*. Certeau finds not only the marks left by forms of social exclusion. He retraces in addition the existence of multiple social networks, groups of interlocutors and correspondents. Certeau argues that the mystics were endeavouring to recreate sites for effective communication (with an Other or with others). This task was rendered both necessary and deeply problematic by a set of deteriorating frames of reference, the contemporary collapse of confidence in the ontological grounding of language and the ensuing climate of linguistic 'duplicity'.

Certeau looks for ways of interpreting early modern mystic texts which do not reduce them to the expression of an always identical 'mystical experience' (a night where all cows are black). He employs an approach which we have already seen at work in his interpretation of possessed speech. He diagnoses a mystic 'style', constituted by particular ways of treating and mistreating language. He argues that the mystics played on and 'tormented' the verbal forms and configurations which set the conditions of their historical existence. He compares the formal demonstrations which he generates to 'musical' interpretations in so far as they maintain an irreducible distance between the interpreter and his object, while trying at the same time to 'repeat' (to practice?) the procedures through which this object was produced:

> To look at processes in this way, to 'interpret', in the musical sense of the term, this mystic writing as a different utterance, is to consider it a past from which we are cut off and not to presume ourselves to be in the same place it was; it is the attempt to execute its movement for ourselves, to retrace the steps of a labour but from afar. . . . To do this is to remain within a scriptural experience and to retain that sense of modesty which respects distances. (*MF* 17/29)

It is worth pausing over the implications of this 'musical' figure. The modern reader is 'removed' from the experience of the mystics. Certeau historicizes their writings by analysing them as formal moves within and upon the elements of a historical 'context'. Yet the way in which Certeau does this produces also a powerful 'dehistoricization' (the term as I am using it here must be distinguished both from oblivious ahistoricism and wilful anachronism). The effect of his own operation is to abstract these texts from their historical context and to reintroduce them as seductive 'tunes', fragmentary melodies, 'airs' into another (our own) historical environment.[21] Certeau's historical interpretation is not simply a device for immobilizing the past as past. It insinuates, rather, through a consummate series of poetic 'repetitions', foreign tones into familiar space, and hence alters contemporary aesthetic experience.

Certeau argues that mystic texts act(ed) as 'fables'. He means by this that they shook up the languages of their time. They re-employed the verbal matter available to them in order to open linguistic spaces for that which had previously been unable to speak:

> The fable . . . is discourse in its capacity to institute afresh. The mystic labour within language consists in transforming it or turning it upside down so that it inaugurates through speech, and hence in metamorphosing it into myriad 'manners of speaking'. This is the mystic science: an alteration of all existent discourses so as to turn them into

'fables'. This linguistic alchemy forged for itself a set of extremely subtle rules and procedures, but these should not lead us to forget the concern which animates them and which aims to bring into language the presence of a founding speech act.[22]

We have seen over the previous two chapters how the category of the 'fable' is produced in Certeau's account through the disqualified positions of fictionality and orality in early modern and modern economies of writing. He analyses both the relegation of scripturally unauthorized speech to the status of a fable, and also the unsolicited returns of such speech into the orders of written knowledge which had excluded it. His work on the mystics uncovers a further facet of the 'fable'. It is a 'mobilizing fiction' (*une fiction qui fait marcher*) (*MF* 196/268). Certeau contrasts its operation to the forms of standardization and consolidation which have characterized in his eyes systems of written production. A 'fabulous' use of language authorizes without being authorized. It opens up possibilities in the instituted order of things. It corresponds to a form of *poeisis* (cf. the Greek, *poiein*, to create, generate, invent). Certeau writes the history of a set of fables. He sets out to repeat/ practise the forms of their invention and to inscribe them in contemporary memory.

Manners of Speaking

Certeau argues that the 'passing figure of *mystics*' may be organized around the question of 'speech' in a transitional economy of writing. He focuses on the forms of mystic speech – or phraseology – in so far as it marks the texts of mystic writers. He analyses how these scriptural artefacts are 'voiced' – they bear the marks of particular speakers – and how they are 'addressed' – they are organized through and through by the presence or absence of implicit and explicit addressees.

Certeau's linguistic analyses also follow in the traces of early modern mystic theoreticians. It was precisely through their strange 'ways of speaking' (a particular *modus loquendi*) that the mystics were characterized and generally denigrated by their contemporaries.[23] Certeau traces how these manners of speaking were disseminated from the beginning of the early modern period together with a set of diverse and proliferating re-employments of the adjective 'mystic'. The term was removed from its technical applications in theology and in biblical hermeneutics, and was taken up as a necessary poetic resource in order to describe a number of more intimate and exorbitant 'psychological' itineraries. Certeau retraces the process by which this series of re-employments came, by the middle of the seventeenth century, to be grouped together to form a single 'science'. This was known as 'the mystic science' (*la science mystique*), or, as the adjective assumed substantive status, simply as 'mystics' (*la mystique*). Certeau shows how this unity proved to be precarious, and how it fell apart as the orthodox religious postulates which it both needed and eroded continued to disintegrate. It is in this sense that *mystics* constituted for Certeau a 'passing' historical figure, bound to the conditions of a specific historical epoch (and notwithstanding the effects of its fragmentary, altered returns as outlined above). He argues that for the duration of its relatively brief historical existence as a besieged unity, both its defenders and censors drew up their battle-lines around the emergence of 'strange' or 'new' linguistic procedures. These now archaeological lines set the terms for the analysis undertaken by Certeau some three to four hundred years later.

Mystic phrases

Certeau focuses in particular on a text which was deemed necessary to accompany the early Spanish and French editions of the writings of John of the Cross. Written by Diego de Jesus and first published in 1618, it was conceived as an apology for a use of language which was obviously anything but evident for contemporary readers. As translated into English, its title runs: 'Notes and remarks in three discourses, to facilitate the understanding of the mystic phrases and the doctrine of the spiritual works of the blessed John of the Cross'.[24] The text consists of Diego's attempt both to formalize and to rationalize the procedures through which the mystics produced their 'phrases' and 'composed' their words. He also sought to provide what for him was a crucial legitimation for these procedures by constant appeals to canonized authorities. Diego's apology begins by defending the right of mystics to define and use words as they saw fit in order, as thinkers in other emergent disciplines were doing, to constitute a proper 'mystic science'. Paradoxically, however, what was 'proper' to such sciences, and particularly to mystic science as such, turns out for Diego to be a particular sort of *impropriety*. He argued that it was 'sometimes appropriate to use impropriety and barbarisms, and a great wealth of rhetoric, especially when it is a question of very important matters'. One could not 'limit oneself to the literal propriety of terms or elegance'.[25] The conventions of language had for Diego to be subjugated to something else which precisely could never be named as such:

> How will we put order, or bounds, or text, or means in the terms by
> which we must explain so lofty a thing, wanting what is immense
> and unsayable to be subject to the ordinary rules, without exceeding
> the common phrases and guarded terms of the schools of disciples
> and masters, of arts and manners that can be taught and known?[26]

Hence 'mystic phrases' were analysed by Diego as organized manners of treating and mistreating linguistic codes. Yet Certeau notes that this audacity was coupled in the writings of the mystics' apologists (and indeed in those of the mystics themselves) with a fundamental insecurity. On the one hand they strove to defend the advent of certain rhetorical and poetic procedures. They argued that these procedures were necessary if human language was to figure the transcendent force which it could no longer make manifest. On the other hand, they wished to disarm their opponents (and perhaps to reassure themselves) by maintaining that the phrases of the mystics were saying nothing new, and that they were simply repeating what a long spiritual tradition had already formulated many times before. Certeau argues that the symptom of this insecurity was an 'exacerbated erudition' (*MF* 110/153) designed to facilitate a theological and hermeneutical operation which would 'reduce the diverse figures of time to "the Same". This process eliminates the irreducibility of differences through the production of a "tradition", that is, by defining an "essential" which clerical knowledge carves out, claims as its own and regards as the common denominator of an oceanic plurality' (*MF* 111/155). Interpretations which suppose that heterogeneous expressions of religious desire are saying 'the same thing' function for Certeau as screens which occult the exposed contingency of localized historical actions and passions. This is as true for the early modern edification of an apologetic mystic 'tradition' as for modern interpretations of Mysticism in general.

Certeau opts by contrast to approach mystic texts by analysing the kinds of work which they performed on historically specific languages and systems of meaning. It should be emphasized that these languages and systems were in varying states of flux and crisis over the early modern period. They were ceasing to body forth for their speakers the divine presence once believed to support their world. These speakers were now, Certeau suggests, caught between a corpus of opacified or discredited signs and an emergent proliferation of new technical linguistic fabrications. These linguistic combinations produced the (con)text upon which those practices designated as 'mystic' were inscribed:

> Properly speaking, [mystic language] is not a new or artificial language. It is the effect of work carried out upon existent language, a labour applied primarily to the 'vulgar' tongues ... but which extends also to technical languages. The uses which define it reflect operations executed by speakers. Mystic science was not constituted by the creation of a coherent linguistic body (that is, a scientific system), but by defining legitimate operations (that is, by a formalizing of practices). (MF 141–2/196)

It must be stressed that Certeau does not conceive his approach in 'purely' linguistic terms. He seeks rather to retrace how in mystic texts the symbolic order was repeatedly altered, marked, torn or 'wounded' (to use a term which Certeau takes over from the mystics he studies). These wounds betray for Certeau a complex distribution of bodily presence and absence: the absent body of God, the deteriorating substitute bodies of Church and Scripture, the stigmatized or increasingly eroticized body of the mystic, the mystic's relation to the body of the other, etc. Certeau intended to devote the second volume of *The Mystic Fable* to these questions.[27] I shall limit myself here to examining his treatment of such 'wounds' as they are secreted upon a textual surface. The formal principles of the disfigurement inflicted upon ordinary language by mystic phraseology are already discernible in Diego's analysis. I will examine three of these broad principles as they are taken up by Certeau.

(1) The first marks of an 'altered language' analysed by Diego concern the quasi-technical use which the mystics made of certain more or less common terms, such as 'night', 'annihilation' or 'blemish'. Diego argued that the reader had to suspend generally received significations in order to enter a new semantic space. 'Blemish' was to signify less a fault than an impediment to divine

union, 'annihilation' less an absence of being than the abandonment of self, and so forth. If the texts were to be properly 'activated', the mystic transformation of language ideally had to correspond to a transformation of the reader who passed through this language. Certeau emphasizes after Diego the 'operativity' of mystic phraseology. It produces a movement 'characterized both by a *displacement of the subject* within the space of meaning circumscribed by words and by a *technical manipulation* of these words in order to mark the new way in which they are being used' (*MF* 140/195). The mystics cut into the body of language in an attempt to open new textual spaces. Indeed, one is struck here by a distorted reflection of Certeau's own linguistic style, with its strange emphases, its etymological and cross-linguistic derivations and frequent preference for locally appropriate redefinitions (*modes d'emploi*) above the significations facilitated by common usage. Like the authors he studies – although with many important differences – Certeau frequently has recourse to a jarring use of language in order to operate displacements in prescribed configurations of meaning.

(2) Mystic texts manifest another form of lexical re-employment. Both Diego and Certeau analyse how they combine contradictory terms so as to produce what Certeau calls 'split words' (*mots clivés*). Technically, these split words can be called oxymorons. Certeau defines them also as the 'smallest unit' of mystic discourse – a unit which paradoxically consists always of at least two elements. He cites as examples of these figures certain phrases which appear in the writings of John of the Cross, such as 'silent music', 'dark light' or 'blissful wound'. Diego himself focuses on a phrase – or what he also calls the 'composition' of a mystic 'word' – to be found in the writings of the fifth-century theologian Dionysus the Areopagite.[28] This phrase was designed to describe the peculiar rest of 'angels':

> Coming to treat of the quiet they enjoy, [Dionysus] says: '*Immanem quietem*'. That they have a 'cruel repose'. The most dissimilar and contrary thing to quiet that can be. Yet he did it with a divine counsel . . . For whoever hears 'quiet' unqualified seems to be contemplating something lazy, insipid and cold, lax, of low value . . . But whoever adds that it is 'cruel and furious', already removing the imperfection of fury by 'quiet', communicates the power, perfection and intention, and, so to speak, the unbearable and incomprehensible excellence of that 'quiet', and the excess that it has over the imperfect that occurs within ourselves.[29]

Again, such figures are effective less through what they directly signify (this is precisely what they do not do) than through a *movement* which they produce in the reader, a form of passage through and beyond a linguistic space. The reader is taken, so to speak, into and beyond a sense of 'rest', into and beyond a 'cruel and furious' movement. He or she is drawn into a rhetorical process of divergence, dissonance and alteration. The phrases work as particular types of trope. Their constituent parts are removed from their proper sense and twisted so as to point in another direction. Yet the object of this secondary metaphorical reference is not clear. The phrases deliberately present themselves as a kind of non-sense ('silent music', 'cruel rest', etc.). The contradictions which they propose tend to elude even a vestigial semantic ordering in terms of opposition (in contrast say to such hypothetical collocations as 'silent noise' or 'cacophonous harmony'). As tropes, they act to turn semantic expectations askew, mixing as it were 'heterogeneous types of space . . . upon the same site' (*MF* 143/198). The mystics detached individual words from their proper place by introducing them into anomalous combinations. The form of these combinations, however, prevents the reader from supplying or 'filling' them with a new, distinct signification. They were designed to produce a semantic exile.

Certeau conceives these 'split words' as peculiar kinds of deictic. Rather than corresponding to an ideal conceptual content, they worked by pointing beyond the languages which they employed towards an Other which could not be manifested as such by these languages. Indeed one could no doubt see them as formal techniques designed to 'throw' the reader outside the distinctions and divisions of customary language. A series of operations combining a pair of ill-fitting terms in order to point to an absent third term were intended to sap their reader's confidence in the ability of language to comprehend and to name reality. For Certeau, this process 'makes a hole in language. It carves out a space for the unsayable. It is language directed towards non-language. In this sense also, it "disturbs the lexicon". In a world presumed to be entirely written and spoken, and therefore "lexicalizable" . . . it indicates an absence of correspondence between things and words' (*MF* 143/199). Certainly, such formal operations upon language risk degenerating into – or being taken as – mere verbal artifice, a product of duplicitous word-play.[30] One should note, nevertheless, how mystic texts work to throw Certeau himself beyond a conventional interpretative approach. For the interpreter who chooses to 'activate' these texts or read them as they ask to be read runs up against a serious difficulty. How do we set about attributing meaning to them when their internal dynamic rests precisely on the presupposition that none of their sayings present as such the thing which they wanted to say? Their authors maintain that the only way to remain faithful to their object is to break faith with its descriptions. Certeau responds to this challenge by directing his attention towards what these writings effectively do.

(3) Certeau argues that the semantic passages induced by the stylistic micro-unit of the oxymoron are repeated in the form of 'transits' at other levels of mystic discourse. He analyses the use made by Teresa of Avila in *The Interior Castle* of the unstable figure of the 'castle-crystal' in order to represent the 'soul'. The figure is unrepresentable as such. It works for Certeau like a 'fable' which Teresa fabricates by bringing together differently charged connotative elements circulating in diverse religious, poetic and epistemic contexts (*MF* 196–200/267–73). It produces expression precisely through the metaphorical transits which it generates as Teresa plays off the symbolic reverberations of the 'crystal' against the figural spaces opened by the 'castle'. The soul is neither 'that' nor 'this', but finds a voice in the movement which leads from 'this' to 'that'. At another level again, Certeau looks in *L'Absent de l'histoire* at the relation between poetry and prose in the works of John of the Cross and Surin.[31] He discerns in both cases a constant 'tropism' turning each genre to the 'sun' of the other. Thus in John of the Cross,

> the relation between poem and commentary repudiates any immediate and stable reading; it refers incessantly one to the other; it does not allow us to reduce an expression either to the aestheticism which might govern the reception of the poem if it stood alone, or to the moralism to which the commentary would lead if there was not also the poem. A space is created by this movement; meaning is fixed neither here nor there; it is expressed through this very process of referral which localizes it neither in a silence ouside the text, nor in a single type of discursive statement. (*AH* 58–9)

Like the elements of mystic 'split words', neither poetic excess nor discursive control can be interpreted here solely in its own terms or rest in its own truth. Instead, each is always referred beyond itself and altered by its relation to the other.

One should note an analogous relation – or altercation – in Certeau's own writing between the controlled language of analysis and the insinuation of poetic fragments. These fragments can take the form either of his own recourse to deliberate and abrupt figural excess or of citations from other poetic texts (Char, Rimbaud, Bonnefoy, Hölderlin, etc., as well as Surin and John of the Cross themselves). They work as 'fables': unjustified by argument or external authority, they produce transition and discursive possibilities. One might cite as examples the figures of the sea and the shore that we saw above and the concomitant figures of fabrication which inform Certeau's conception of historical interpretation. Likewise I shall discuss in the next chapter how the figures of opacity, chaotic Brownian motion and oceanic indeterminacy give a particular twist to Certeau's attempts to carry out careful formal analyses of contemporary cultural practices. Finally, one should bring into play the metaphorical or iconic figures which saturate the erudite texture of *The Mystic Fable* itself. Certeau's analyses are strangely haunted. He evokes the contours of an edifice traced in the snow (*MF* 79/107), the irruption of a nameless beggarwoman (*MF* 31/48), the garden of delights of Hieronymus Bosch (*MF* 49–72/71–99). The mystics produced their transitory effects by creating 'interference' between different cultural and linguistic registers. It is as if Certeau's writing itself echoed this interference.

Certeau inscribes the transits operated by *mystics* into the linguistic flux and fragmentation of its time. He notes how this symbolic fermentation was intensified by the advent of printing:

> Coming from the East, the North or the South, texts escaped the university institution and professorial interpretation. Languages became passersby, processions of words lived in and practiced differently at each stage of the journey, but continuing to pursue, from region to region, the implanting of foreign thoughts and expressions offered up for new uses. Between lexical capitalization and mobility, novel combinations were produced, preserving, extending or restoring different verbal heritages through the very transits and compromises which they brought about. *Mystics* springs also from this melting pot of languages; it aspired to be the language running across these languages. (*MF* 117/162)

Certeau traces how mystic phrases crossed frontiers, changed names and insinuated their way into different cultures and institutions.

Mystics infiltrated and displaced the proprieties of learned Latin.
It also combined symbolically the elements of other discrete linguistic orders. In Luce Giard's words, it 'turned common language
and standard textual forms into a new poetical instrument'. We
will see below how Certeau treats the detailed processes of such
dissemination.

Yet Certeau presents these transformations as both the products
and the symptoms of a profound ambivalence towards language
as such, which in turn they served to reinforce. The enterprise
of the mystics worked finally to underline the incapacity of their
languages to do what they wanted them to do. Certeau discerns
already in the 'vulgarized' sermons of Meister Eckhart in the thir-
teenth century the scars inflicted by the 'annihilation' of language:

> The German sermons of Meister Eckhart represent to begin with the
> language of the Beguines as it is introduced into the professor's ter-
> ritory, and which he learns from them in order to respond to them,
> while continuing to think in Latin in his treatises. To these two lan-
> guages correspond two different modes of discourse, between which
> there opens up the Eckhartian 'detachment', a silence that flows back
> over them, an absolute transcendence of being, a 'dying of the spirit'.
> The distanciation which the master of Cologne transforms into a
> 'voiding' of language appears everywhere, in more or less theoretical
> or radical ways. A form of mutism rends the configurations of know-
> ledge. An impossibility wounds the expectation that awaits being in
> logos. (*MF* 116/161)[32]

The mystics turned, as it were, silence to speech and speech to
silence. Each stood in want of the other. Where once the presence
of a voice was said to have resounded, there remained only mute
relics or empty space. The mystics in Certeau's reading sought to
inhabit this space and to 'combine' it with the uncertain ferment of
language which they could see and hear around them, and which
welled up equally from 'within'. They moved between aphasia and
glossolalia. They were caught between disruptive verbal artifice
and didacticism. For Certeau, they set out to cultivate

> the art of *hearing* the linguistic flow as it reached their time, the
> rumour of an effectual word, and the art of *producing* combinations
> and artefacts of all kinds. That was the very formula of *mystics*. It set
> up a fabrication of words, expressions and turns of phrase (a language,
> henceforth, was something that had to be produced), but within a

region where a voice that never ceased beginning could be heard.
Such was the paradox of these 'ways of speaking': a production of
language in the field of an attentiveness to what was still speaking.
(*MF* 123–4/171)

Certeau shows how the mystics sought actively to inscribe in their
texts the marks of a fundamental and 'annihilating' passion (passivity). In Surin's terms, they desired, hyperbolically, to 'let God
operate' (*laisser opérer Dieu*).[33] Yet to do this they took recourse to
a series of 'technical' fabrications. They devised, as it were, formal
algorithms for the sacrifice of language. Not only does the space
opened by *mystics* – 'I live, but not I . . .' – oscillate for us between
the Nietzschean and the divine.[34] Their phrases also present us in
Certeau's reading with an ambiguous interstice between the formal alteration of language and the work of something else: 'an
operation is substituted for the Name' (*MF* 150/208).

Contact

The manners of speaking outlined above were designed not just to
disfigure the symbolic order. The mystics did not simply aspire to
turn standardized language into a textual body 'wounded' by a
foreign operation. Certainly, the mystics who figure in Certeau's
account emphatically rejected conventional linguistic and social
contracts. As Surin saw them, they were for the rest of the world
'like savages or strangers whose language it doesn't understand
and whose habits and customs shock it'.[35] Certeau draws attention
to their status as 'wildmen'. In structural terms, their position was
in many ways analogous to that occupied in contemporary epistemic
configurations by the inhabitants of the New World or by cases of
possession. Nevertheless, the mystics were also endeavouring,
precisely through their separation from the symbolic ways of the
'world', to open up spaces for effective contact with an Other
or others. A concern for 'communication', 'correspondence' and
'expression' runs through and indeed generates their texts. The letters of Surin, which Certeau collected and edited in 1966, are saturated with these terms.[36] Certeau also cites as examples the origins
of the writings of Teresa of Avila and John of the Cross, conceived
as responses to requests from others for communication and guidance.[37] Certeau argues that, whatever the outcomes of these multifarious communications, 'the two verbs *speak* and *hear* designate

the uncertain and necessary centre around which circles of language are produced' (*MF* 159/219). He stresses that it was precisely because the possibility of 'speaking' effectively (*orare*, or *conversar*) had become deeply 'uncertain' that it had come to seem both lacking and necessary. He reads the fables produced by the mystics against the background of deteriorating ecclesiastical and scriptural frames of reference. The 'Spirit' (defined by John of the Cross as *el que habla*, that which speaks) seemed to have withdrawn from the world, or to have become indiscernible among the swell of substitutive fabrications. Certeau argues that the enterprise of the mystics was equivalent to an 'anti-Babel' (*MF* 157/216). They sought to set up sites for renewed exchange between speaking subjects.

These sites may perhaps be symbolized fantasmatically by the 'lovers' bubble', a detail from the *Garden of Delights* of Hieronymous Bosch which Certeau included as a frontispiece to *The Mystic Fable*. The image presents what Certeau calls a ' "balloon" of speaking subjects' (*MF* 305/24), two naked figures, encapsulated in a strangely transparent retreat from the 'world', exposed to the gaze and body of each other. Certeau's analyses, however, are founded on the premise that such speaking subjects can, like the possessed at Loudun, speak only with the language of their world. Their *corps à corps* yields no epiphanic *face à face*, no unfolded presence. The truth of the other is not given. 'Contact' must be produced. Certeau shows how the mystics developed treatments for languages – both technical and common – which no longer seemed to yield substance, in such a way as to transform them through speaking into 'a network of allocutions and present alliances' (*MF* 163/224).

Certeau's analysis of these interlocutory networks revolves again around the problematic of utterance. As it did in his study of possessed speech, this theoretical marker provides him with a focusing device for exploring the relations between speaking subjects and languages. It helps him in *The Mystic Fable* to articulate the ephemeral 'scenes' set up by the mystics for their exchanges and transits.

Mystic utterance raises firstly for Certeau an issue which cuts across all forms of knowledge. Putting in question the very possibility of knowledge, the mystics problematize the capacity of the speaking subject initially to enter into the languages of others. Certeau discerns in their texts an aggravated struggle with a 'beginning' upon which ' "all the rest" ' depends. How to speak, how to hear? That beginning that constitutes a threshold for knowledge of the Other must itself have its beginnings (how to start speaking or listening?), its history, its tragedies' (*MF* 161/221). We have already seen how Certeau's own text is set in motion by a distinctive prefatory strategy. He starts by casting a shadow over his own linguistic and cultural 'competence' (*MF* 1/9). He cites later the block which confronts Teresa of Avila at the start of *The Interior Castle* ('I could find neither what to say nor how to begin').[38] Certeau shows how the writings of the mystics both exacerbate and seek to overcome the gap which separates the human subject from the language he or she speaks. This gap was not effaced by their texts. They were always compelled to begin again.

Coupled with this concern for 'beginning', and rejoining again for Certeau the problematic of utterance, is the priority given in mystic texts to the present moment. Certeau sees in these texts a form of historicity stripped, as it were, of historical grounding. The solicitations of present utterance 'relativize the relevance of knowledge guaranteed by an acquisition (a past revelation) and found a historicity of experience (an existential and necessary relation to the passing instant): nothing said yesterday to others can take the place of what I can say or hear, here and now' (*MF* 162/223). He diagnoses in the writings of the mystics a constant anticipation centred on what an Other or others may say. This anticipation frequently takes the form of a frustrated desire. Angelus Silesius, turning away from the now voiceless authority of Scripture, raised such expectation to breaking point:

> The Scripture is scripture, nothing more.
> My consolation is essence,
> And that God in me
> Speaks the word of eternity.[39]

Similarly the 'enlightened illiterate' whose figure Surin painted in his first known dated letter told him that 'should the Gospel pass away, God had taught him enough of it to save him.'[40] Surin himself listened (all too) avidly to the young 'baker's son', captivated by what he experienced as the 'extraordinary efficacy in his words'. These words, projected into the livid sky of Surin's mental world, broke down in a few decisive instants the prison-house of his anxiety. He had been touched within and altered, provisionally unbound by the passing words of a travelling companion, who had voiced for him 'such a great number of good thoughts that I am not equal to writing them down. And I am sure that those three days have been worth many years of my life.'[41]

The exacerbated thirst of the mystics for 'words of life' to be made 'present' works in Certeau's analysis as a symptom of the seeping discredit of an economy of writing founded on the authority of Holy Scripture. The mystics did not, like others, respond to this gradual collapse in credibility by entering into the new economies of writing and production which emerged with modernity. Certeau argues rather that they dwelt precisely in the empty space marked by the ruins of the dilapidated medieval architecture of being:

> The mystic configuration extending from the thirteenth to the seventeenth century . . . was both bound and hostile to a technicalizing of society. It carries to the point of radicalism the confrontation with the vanishing entity of the cosmos. It refuses to mourn it, at a time when this seems acceptable to others who think that they could come to terms with that loss. It accepts the challenge of the unique. Its literature, therefore, has all the traits of what it both opposes and posits: it is the trial, by language, of the ambiguous passage from presence to absence. It bears witness to the slow transformation of the religious setting into an amorous one, or of faith into eroticism. It tells how a body 'touched' by desire and engraved, wounded, written by the other, replaced the revelatory, didactic word. (*MF* 4–5/13)

In the breakdown of the religious cosmos once held to be spoken by God, the mystics sought, in Certeau's account, to devise a series of compensatory tactics for 'utterance'. They aspired to find or to 'invent' spaces where the voices they wished to hear might still nevertheless resound, and where the presences they missed might make themselves felt. Certeau argues that, as the world before them came to seem increasingly silent or duplicitous, the mystics attempted to turn their own bodies into so many vessels of contact. They aspired to convert their own *I* into the site of the Other.

But what was this *I*? Again, a prefatory question threatened perpetually to sabotage the mystic enterprise before it could begin. Certeau cites the opening of *The Interior Castle*:

> It is a great pity and confusion that by our own fault we should not understand [*entendamos*] ourselves nor know who we are. My daughters, would it not be great ignorance if someone were asked who he was and he didn't know, nor who his father and mother were, nor from what region [*tierra*] they came?[42]

Like the subject of possessed speech, the *I* of the mystics could not provide a stable support. They set it up, Certeau suggests, as a sanctuary for the impression of the Word, but were increasingly unable to protect this 'interior' space from the 'corruption' and the unreadability associated with the world outside. Surin's *Science expérimentale*, written some eighty years after *The Interior Castle*, manifests an obsession with the 'great mixture of divine and diabolic operations' which lay siege from within to the self.[43] This vision of the *I* as a site possessed by other forces generates an intensified search in Surin's writing for principles which might permit a 'discernment of spirits' (or what he also theorizes as a discernment of 'operations').[44] Certeau argues, however, that Teresa had already in *The Interior Castle* posed the fundamental question which was to inform and generate *mystics* – the question of a 'foundation':

> This treatise on the soul, prayer and mystic discourse (or itineration) is undoubtedly part of a long Socratic and spiritual tradition of the 'know thyself', but it displaces that tradition from the outset by translating it into two other questions: 'Who else is living inside you?' and 'To whom are you speaking?' A problematic of being and consciousness is at once rerouted towards utterance, that is, towards a dialogical structure of alteration – 'you are the other of yourself.' (*MF* 195/267)

As Emmanuel Lévinas does with a rather different set of references, Certeau turns certain 'dialogical' (or 'heterological') questions which emerge from the debris of a religious tradition against the more 'monological' presuppositions and procedures which have characterized Western philosophy.[45]

For Certeau, *mystics* shows how one's own 'soul' has always already been dispossessed by another. Hence Certeau suggests that this 'soul' may be analysed as an 'echo', and its representations as 'images of an echo':

> If the subject is a response in search of that to which it is responding, this inner speaking is called 'the soul'. It is a speaking that does not know what it echoes. A 'moaning', or a 'murmur', which is missing its own space. . . . In itself, the soul is silent, in that it is formed by being a response to that (God) which it does not know, in that it responds to Unknownness. (*MF* 189/258)

The function of Teresa's 'fable' – the castle-crystal image(s) evoked above – was to create a space in which this echo could reverberate. Being unable to say *what* it was that was speaking to/within her, she endeavoured to find ways to *let* it speak. Her oft-expressed doubts centred around the question of whether this was in fact

taking place, and whether she was through her fabulations saying anything worth hearing: 'I'm, literally, just like the parrots that
are taught to speak; they know no more than what they hear or
are shown, and they often repeat it. If the Lord wants me to say
something new, His Majesty will provide.'[46] As in Beckett's *The
Unnameable*, echoes have reduced speech to a form of repetition
punctuated by hesitation or indifference.

The disowned murmur of mystic utterance draws interpretative
procedure into strange territory. What sense (exorcistic or heuristic) do we make when we attribute to a set of 'fables' the name of
the subject they were designed to 'annihilate'? What do we do
when we assign a place to the speaking (*fari*) that carries her away?
Might this speaking not 'seduce' its prospective interpreter, that is
lead him or her astray into that 'dizzying dissolution of the self'[47]
cultivated by the mystics? Certeau's approach leaves these questions to do their unsettling work. He holds them open by following
the alterations operated in a set of writings conceived as a series of
echoes and responses.

Certeau draws from *mystics* an understanding of the human
subject as always constituted by and dependent on what is Other.
He contrasts this with the subsequent historical development of
the notion of an 'individual' set apart from his social and natural
environment, which he is consequently able to master and strategically to control. I will discuss in the next chapter how Certeau
problematizes certain sociopolitical manifestations of this development. It should also be related to the processes which have produced the figure of the 'author' as we know it today.[48] Certeau
distinguishes in *The Mystic Fable* between the idea of a 'mystic'
subject and that of an 'economic' subject. He argues that the 'economic' subject would come to constitute the dominant figure of
modernity. He suggests that its mythical expression can be found
in Daniel Defoe's *Robinson Crusoe*. Certeau sees a process of inversion by which

> the problematic of alteration through pleasure (or pain) turns into a
> problematic of appropriation through production . . . it is still a ques-
> tion of the subject, but the economic subject displaces the mystic one.
> The island factory replaces the garden of delights. The figure of the *I*,
> which still serves to construct a biographical novel, has become auto-
> nomized from what constituted it as other than itself. (*MF* 200/273)

Mystics and 'economics' (broadly defined) provide Certeau with
two opposing (and to some degree mythical) theoretical models of

human subjectivity. As far as his own work is concerned, it may be more accurate to call them two mutually interfering models. One is characterized by the organizing and compulsive presence of the 'factory'. I have already suggested how this figure structures Certeau's analysis of contemporary historiographical production. The other is associated with the Garden of Earthly Delights (which nevertheless unfolds in Certeau's reading before the inscrutable gaze and vanishing point of melancholia (*MF* 53–4/76–7)). The apparent opposition between the two figures is, needless to say, complicated. Certeau evokes the disturbances, bad dreams and 'fluttering thoughts' which are provoked in Robinson by his encounter with the traces of another.[49] They are footprints in the sand which, like the writing on the wall, bode the demise of his carefully constructed order. The relation of the individual to others continues to provoke echoes.

Mystic utterance emerges from a site voluntarily subject to alterity. Certeau discerns this also in the tactics through which the mystics present their writings to their contemporaries. The citations from Teresa of Avila above adumbrated the uncertainty inherent for mystic writers in such an operation. I would like here to examine further Certeau's analysis of the quasi-military procedure by which Surin set up for his readers' attention the accounts contained in his *Science expérimentale des choses de l'autre vie* [Experimental science of the things of the other life].

I have already outlined the principal moves of this procedure as they are broken down by Certeau. Setting in motion an intricate, shifting play of pronouns (one, they, we, you and I) and 'modal' verbs (know, can, will, should), Surin invoked biblical predecessors for his project of testimony in order to authorize both what he was going to say and the act of saying (and writing) it. He abstracted an evangelical formal sequence to direct the 'production' of his experience for the social body. It may be helpful to quote the last paragraph of Surin's preface:

> It is in the same spirit and with the same intent [as Peter, the biblical author whom Surin has just quoted] that these things that we have known through an adventure we have had during our century, and in which God's providence engaged us, are used in this discourse to strengthen the faith we are engaged to profess by the Catholic religion, and to make us better Christians. All those to whom we speak in this book have an interest in these things. For them I would like to perform a service for eternity.[50]

Through a series of deft rhetorical manoeuvres, Surin constructed
an authorized 'site' from which to speak. He wanted to persuade
his readers that this site was supported not by a solitary human
voice, but by the supposed solidity of what were then more credible authorities. His scriptural 'foundation' rests on a formal repetition. Certeau notes, however, how the final (and first) 'I' of the
preface seems to send retroactive fault-lines running back through
the rest of the text. The conditional 'would like' (*voudrais*) jars
strangely with the confidence of the preceding operation: 'in the
position of strength set up by the text, the *I* is a sort of lapsus' (*MF*
187/256).

Certeau backs up his reading by recalling the circumstances in
which the text was produced. Surin was emerging from twenty
years of isolation, a period of 'madness' characterized by prolonged
bouts of aphasia, an inability even to begin to write anything,
overpowering impressions of damnation and a conviction that he
was excluded from God's kingdom and from the society of the
just. His faith in the possibility of human or religious 'contact' had
been shaken to its foundations. The rhetorical strength of his text
covers for Certeau a more essential fragility. The *I* is not sure of its
place, its purpose, or the validity of its 'vocation':

> Doubtless the public, like the anonymous crowd in which the 'mad-
> men for Christ' lost themselves, represents for the mystic text the real
> figure of the God sought after and presupposed by the solitary *oratio*;
> since for the subject of prayer also, God *must* be there and 'attentive'
> to the discourse addressed to him. . . . Similarly, the preface addressed
> to the readers seems like a prayer. While it makes a show of much
> certainty when speaking in the name of *we*, it becomes hesitant and
> troubled the moment it says *I*. At that point it no longer exorcizes
> doubt. The *I* appears in its dependency on the other. *I* cannot express
> itself except in a desire emanating from elsewhere (rhetorically trans-
> formed into an obligation on the readers' part). *I* speaks only if it is
> awaited (or loved), which is the chanciest thing in the world, even if,
> in principle, it is also the very thing which the religious institution is
> supposed to guarantee. Surin's madness was to begin with the vio-
> lence of that improbability. (*MF* 187/255–6)

With bravura, trepidation or abandonment, the mystic 'I' seeks
itself – its redemption or its effacement – in a proliferation of
others (a proliferation which Certeau supposes to figure in 'real'
terms a transcendent Other). The utterances of the *I* are for Certeau
always a function of an echo and an expectation – dangerous

principles which never cease to alter and to transform the supposedly 'authorial' figure of the writer.

The mystics did not in their writings aspire primarily to produce coherent doctrinal systems – for Surin this would be the task of the 'machines of theology'.[51] Instead they explored the diverse manners in which speaking subjects might be altered, marked, 'annihilated', 'touched' or revived in their relations with an Other or others. They produce in Certeau's interpretative practice two principal displacements. Firstly, 'the interpretable text is transformed into an altered body' (*MF* 149/206). Certeau does not himself extract from mystic texts a stable corpus of verifiable propositions or edifying semantic contents. He sets out instead to trace the ways in which these writings 'respond' to the advent or withdrawal of other presences, and to specify some of the recurrent formal procedures and improprieties through which such responses are marked in the body of the text. Secondly, the mystics' emphasis on the centrality of interlocutory exchange makes it for Certeau unsatisfactory to interpret their practices by a fixation on a limited number of great literary texts and sanctified proper names (Teresa of Avila, John of the Cross, etc.). For the status of these texts as 'literary' is a function precisely of a detachment from the processes and exchanges which produced them. Hence Certeau's work on the ways in which these and other more private texts were disseminated and appropriated.

Appropriations and Alterations

Utterances, whether textual or oral, are always addressed. If they are not received – by a listener or by a reader – then they fall into the folds of oblivion. Yet this act of reception inevitably alters the utterance which it interprets. Certeau's own practice of historical interpretation endeavours, through an erudite attention to an 'underside' of history, to follow the traces of such alterations.

'Correspondence'

One should begin here by referring to the immense work of textual critique and synthesis which Certeau had to undertake to produce for publication in 1966 the *Correspondance* of Surin. From a fragmented corpus of letters, scattered in a multiplicity of archives and collections, censored or 'adapted by pious hands', Certeau had to present something which, with all due reservations, he could call a critical edition. His own labyrinthine circulation among these altered traces seems significantly to have marked his subsequent conceptions of historiographical veracity. As we saw in chapter 1, he considered this to consist in a demanding but properly interminable work of 'falsification'. Certeau's protracted archival explorations seem also, moreover, to have alerted his attention to those other hidden 'circulations' which come together to constitute the massive subterranean reality of history. These circulations, which in this case take the form of the initial exchange and then diffusion of Surin's correspondence, create multiple paths of communication, contact and 'alteration' both within and across different social orders and historical periods.[52]

Certeau takes up again in *The Mystic Fable* the analysis of one such circulation as it was set in motion by the dissemination and series of republications and adaptations of Surin's first known dated letter.[53] I have already quoted above from this letter. It recounts Surin's encounter at a time of spiritual crisis with a young uneducated man on the road from Rouen to Paris. As far as the content of the letter is concerned, it is difficult not to see a significant amount of projection (in the psychoanalytic sense) in Surin's portrayal of his counterpart, without for all that invalidating the hypothesis of an authentic encounter (*MF* 225–34 / 308–20). Certeau also traces how the diverse re-editions of the letter were themselves rewritten (reprojected) in order to suit changing requirements. Nevertheless, Certeau argues that the letter corresponded to an epistemic or spiritual insecurity shared by many contemporaries. Indeed, the very textual corruptions operated by its successive alterations actively point for Certeau to the concerns and obsessions of its readers and rewriters. Surin's story echoed their uncertainties about the new lines being drawn up to divide the empty spaces of ignorance from the emergent configurations of knowledge.

The manifold and obscure itineraries taken by Surin's letter lead Certeau, as he follows them, to devise appropriate interpretative treatments. These treatments yield in their turn a series of intricate and intriguing 'microhistories' of interpretation. The very circulation of such texts leaves traces through which Certeau induces the existence of different 'interpretative communities',[54] bringing together often surprising clusters of readers. Surin's letter for

Certeau works as an 'Ariadne's thread', whose circulation points up – or 'develops' in a quasi-photographic sense – a 'map of spiritual centres [*foyers*]' (*MF* 221/303). Certeau uses a similar technique in *La possession de Loudun* to uncover a series of diabolical 'foci' (or 'abscesses') in seventeenth-century France. The very diffraction of the 'events' at Loudun into a dispersed series of stories and apologetic legends reveals for Certeau as much as it conceals:

> Through their re-emergence in new editions, through their traces or copies, through textual modifications due to changes of milieux, of interests and epochs, these items bring to light, like the voyages of a visible element through the opacity of the body, the socio-religious circuits and, at certain dates, the splits in mentality which diversify the public to which these 'revised and corrected' texts were addressed. (*PL* 268)

This interpretative parallelism discernible over *The Possession of Loudun* and *The Mystic Fable* itself works furthermore to 'develop' the unsettling ambiguity of *mystics*. Certeau finds that both 'mystic' and 'diabolic' currents tended to follow the same sociocultural pathways in early modern France.[55] He uncovers likewise other strange correspondences. The byways taken by Surin's letter are shown to betray secret or anomalous social alliances. Certeau detects, for example, a discreet convergence between the established theologian and censor Jean de Launoy, whose critical severity perhaps led what nevertheless remained of an indubitable faith into the realm of 'devotion', and a more subversive, explicitly 'mystic' spirituality. The passage of differing versions of the letter through heterogeneous sites indicates broadly speaking for Certeau, 'through the fleeting canal of the text, a resurgence of the same waters: an "ignorant" spirituality, sometimes challenging, sometimes hidden. These traces declare or betray a movement of exodus' (*MF* 219/299). Certeau's analyses work at a different level from that of manifest ideological pronouncements. He side-steps, as it were, the history of ideas and the great monuments of literature. He writes 'detective stories' (*MF* 205/278). Investigating here the largely effaced but intermittently sensationalized transits effected by *mystics* and by possession, he suggests how a diffuse but unspoken disquiet insinuated its way into early modern edifices of knowledge.

Certeau endows with significance the very alterations which accompanied the re-employments of Surin's letter. He retraces the different figures which came to take the place of Surin's young interlocutor in succeeding versions of the letter. These conflicting representations combined in diverse ways myths of pastorality, poverty, enlightened ignorance and apologetic hagiography:

> Each of the interpretations along the way of the story's circulation is a manner of understanding it as well as a revealing document about the group that 'met' the young man or shepherd for a moment on its path. Our interpretation, today, is a part of that journey, marking but one more step in a story [*récit*] still moving . . . It is a textual journey, an innumerable series of voyages placed under the fundamental formality of an interweaving between two people. There is no history but that which has been 'revised and corrected'. (*MF* 234/321)

Certeau shows how each interpretation projects – or cites – its 'own' figure of alterity. These figures move between the reassuring edification supplied by an 'other', and the disruptive, irruptive force of an *other*. This genealogy of successive 'interpretations' and their 'others' inevitably implicates its producer. As he suggests, Certeau is caught up in the series of projections which he analyses. Taken together (sym-bolized), the fragmentary itineraries of these texts adumbrate nevertheless a vast and lost Other of the history we can know. They point beyond themselves to an immense Brownian motion of micro-operations, so many spiders' webs tearing and reforming.

The multiple social movements and cross-currents revealed by Certeau's treatment of Surin's letter served in effect to recite the abrupt social transgression recounted in the letter. The narrator (Surin) implicitly rejected the contemporary corpus of scriptural authorities as inefficacious. He testified instead to the 'extraordinary efficacy' of the words of an uneducated servant. The letter enacted a violation of the system of distinction which constituted the social order. The echoes which this move produced are remarkable. *The Mystic Fable* returns repeatedly to the ways in which representatives of scriptural knowledge came to abandon their institutional and epistemic prerogatives. This may have constituted a 'betrayal' of learning (MF 26/43). Influential clerics forsook the conventional keys of their salvation and went in search of that which might, for them, still 'speak'.

Certeau seems to read this move as an archaic variant of his own interpretative strategy as analysed above (see pp. 90–4). He argues that 'their knowledge took leave of its textual "authorities" to become the gloss of "wild" voices' (*MF* 26/43–4). Such glosses, he stresses, were deeply ambivalent. In formal terms, they were equivalent to later fetichizations of the 'popular'. They often revealed more about their interpreters than about the objects of their delight. Nevertheless, Certeau maintains that they represented important symptoms in the context of a general reorganization of contemporary knowledge. They produced an ambiguous interstitial realm which challenged more orthodox instances of social control. Certeau cites a variety of movements which identified

> under various signs (the pauper, the *idiotus*, the illiterate, the woman, or the *affectus*, etc.) . . . a set of spaces that resist the speculation of theologians and professionals. . . . Beneath the multitude of doctrines or experiences, this collective swell of countless muffled voices lends its strength – sometimes seductive, sometimes frightening – to an otherness in the life of the mind. It provides a ballast of disseminated assurance for the construction of a mystic language. It is the elusive referent of a 'place'. (*MF* 105/145)

Certeau uncovers moments of tension, where a *terra incognita* (*MF* 237/325) of the socially undistinguished or excluded seemed to send cracks through edifices of scriptural learning and social authority. Later, the questions which these figures posed would congeal into an alternative system of pastoral or 'popular' myths. I will discuss in chapters 5 and 6 Certeau's critical analyses of the learned concept of 'popular culture', and of its problematic implication in processes both of repression and of aestheticization. These processes, however, cannot readily be dissociated from the more unsettling effects exerted by figures of alterity on configurations of knowledge.

Mystic 'fables' in Certeau's account both enacted and recounted a plurality of social transits and transgressions. They set up problematic connections across heterogeneous social spaces. They shuttled (trans-lated) violent, consolatory or inspiring words from one site to another. They enabled multifarious kinds of transformation at the cost of many kinds of distortion: 'a language of "the other" was generated by the vast labour of these alterations. Mystic speech was fundamentally "translational"' (*MF* 118/164). An 'itinerant operativity' (*MF* 119/165) cut across a multiplicity of interlocutory situations, which were themselves the products of intermeshing social conflicts and 'correspondences'. Certeau's historiographical operation was designed to unravel and to piece together the few remaining threads of this activity.

Hidden histories

It is often assumed that the interpreter is involved in a direct one-to-one encounter with the text or with its author. Certeau's work shows how both texts and interpretations are produced only through multiple forms of social interaction. Emblematic here might be his analysis in L'Absent de l'histoire of Surin's encounter with the writings of John of the Cross. Two points in particular will illustrate my argument.

Firstly, Certeau foregrounds the processes through which an 'authorized' text is established. There was in fact no authorized edition of the writings of John of the Cross for a considerable time after his death, let alone an authorized French translation.[56] Rather there was a circulation of manuscripts and a considerable amount of oral discussion. This was particularly the case in Bordeaux, which worked as something like a seed-bed for the cultivation, transplantation and dissemination of mystic ideas and phrases.[57] Certeau suggests that Surin's encounter with these phrases was less a function of a purely scriptural experience than of his position in a moving network of exchanges and 'translations'. It is therefore for Certeau 'impossible . . . to write a history of Saint John of the Cross at the beginning of the seventeenth century without passing through the alleys and parlours of Bordeaux, places where much of the "received text" attested by Surin was crafted' (AH 50). These exchanges (largely between women) functioned as something like 'living laboratories' (AH 49) in which a spiritual and poetic vocabulary of the sort analysed above was gradually hammered out.

The second point concerns the discreet but decisive intervention of the first French translator of John of the Cross, René Gaultier, whose work appeared in print in 1621. Overshadowed after 1641 by the more famous translation of Cyprien de la Nativité, Gaultier's work was also a function of the kinds of exchanges outlined above. Certeau draws attention in Gaultier's translation precisely to certain apparently miniscule modifications which it produces with regard to the original Spanish text. For Certeau, these modifications were decisive in setting up Surin's encounter with John of the Cross:

Gaultier's sentences create 'regions', are punctuated with 'openings' and come out into 'horizons'. When John of the Cross writes: 'In contemplation', this or that happens, Gaultier translates: 'in the space of contemplation', etc. His prose invents oceans, vast 'expanses', uncharted 'latitudes' and 'immense deserts' . . . A symbolic material, a 'style' of mystic language, something which structures the subject at a more fundamental level than do ideas, organize the experience which emerged at the surface of printed production with the work of Gaultier. Surin belongs to this 'space'. (*AH* 48–9)

A series of creative alterations work here like 'fables', rendering possible new types of experience. Gaultier's translation, literally in this particular case, carries across and insinuates new spaces into a prescribed semantic order. His operation seems to prefigure Certeau's later suggestion that 'the ethical is to social practices what the poetic is to linguistic practices: the opening of a space which is not authorized by the order of facts.'[58] The 'fables' which Gaultier introduced into his authorized translation represent just one form of ethical and poetic activity among many others. Certeau's dedication to his effaced memory anticipates the dedication of his later work to the poetic and ethical ways of 'ordinary' contemporary men and women:[59]

To the worker who has disappeared and become indiscernible in the text of others, this note on the interpretation of John of the Cross by Surin should have been dedicated. The work of erudition, also laborious and hidden, discovers gradually, underneath the mountains which hold captive our gaze, great subterranean expanses, unplumbed circulations and discreet inventions: devout, Carmelite or ecclesiastical translators from Bordeaux effected secretly the transmissions which would emerge in great works. Through these obscure and now faceless figures, displacements were operated, meetings were set up, a common experience was elaborated: the mystic labour of History. (*AH* 70)

Certeau produces for contemporary readers vestiges of historical practice which he supposes to be metonymic (they figure as stray fragments of lost social bodies), and which work as metaphors: they 'carry' modest stories of space and invention into fresh historical worlds.

Certeau seeks constantly in his work to uncover the unspoken forms of constraint and organizing impulses at work in learned interpretation. He sets out to explicate these implicit instances of alterity in so far as they produce paradoxically a repetition of the 'Same' (they form part of the machinery of social reproduction). This is not to say that Certeau aspires to some state of definitive liberation or detachment. He argues in the conclusion to *La possession de Loudun* that

> the possession carries no 'true' historical explanation, since it is never possible to know who is *possessed* and by whom. The problem comes precisely from the fact that there *is* possession [il y a *de* la possession] – we would say 'alienation' – and that the attempt to free oneself from it consists in transferring it, repressing it or displacing it else-where: from a collectivity to an individual, from the devil to state policy, from the demonic to devotion. (*PL* 327)

The implication of interpreters in the 'factories' where they work intermeshes for Certeau with their relation to 'voices', 'visions' or 'fables' which may appear to break in from 'outside'. Indeed, the more one tries to break free from socio-institutional constraints, the more one may by displacement become 'alienated' into these voices and visions. Certeau's analyses present us with a vertiginously com-plex and mobile conception of our 'possession'.

For Certeau, one is, as it were, in the possession of others before one is in possession of oneself. Yet this ineluctable condition of alienation is not connoted purely negatively in his work. It may, for instance, function as the necessary detour through which one can set up an interior space, a properly 'mystic' detachment and unbinding of the will, an aesthetic and ethical 'region to inhabit'.[60] He also analyses it in the form of 'debt'. Surin was indebted to those who interposed themselves between himself and John of the Cross. Likewise Certeau confesses his debt to the fantasmatic and ghostly presence of Surin (*MF* 2/10). He emphasizes that the rela-tion of interpreters to those 'altered and altering others' which they carry within themselves may be one of 'gratitude'. The inescapable indebtedness of the human subject constitutes, as it were, one pole of Certeau's reflection.[61] It may be, however, that its form as such cannot be definitively distinguished from the forms of interpretat-ive 'complicity' to be analysed in the next chapter. For Surin, the operation of the other in the self had the power to damn or to save. Today we might say: to cripple or to heal, to bind or to set free, to engage or to co-opt.

Part III

Strategies and Tactics

5

Strategic Operations

The first two parts of this study have revolved around two fundamental components of Certeau's work. Firstly, he sets out to elucidate forms of otherness which can be described as 'implicit' in
learned or scientific interpretative operations. Secondly, he suggests how such operations may, in their relations to forms of alterity
which they place outside themselves, become caught up in processes of 'alteration'. I shall now take further a set of questions
emerging again from the historical and institutional complexes
which inform interpretative practice. Certeau does not focus exclusively on the kinds of alteration to which this practice may be
exposed. Much of his work aspires instead to uncover how instances of 'implicit' alterity involve interpreters in forms of 'complicity'. He shows how epistemically controlled interpretative
operations may be read as a function of more explicitly political
operations. Rather than being 'altered' by alterity, these operations
work to bring diverse populations into conformity with prescribed
political programmes. In this chapter, I will examine initially how
Certeau detects strategic processes of homogenization in the political and interpretative treatment of 'popular culture' and 'folklore'.
I will then show how he is drawn to the work of Michel Foucault
and Pierre Bourdieu on the 'disciplining' and scientific representation of society, and how his critique of these thinkers opens up a
space for the elucidation of other types of operation which are
generally overlooked by political, administrative and interpretative enterprises.

The Concept of Popular Culture

We have already seen how Certeau traces the emergence of something like the 'popular' in learned discourse over the early modern period. It evolved as the 'other' of productive rationality, epistemic propriety and political power. It constituted a cultural residue or by-product, and its position was clearly subaltern. The effects of its representation were, however, ambivalent. It operated also as a disseminated 'alterity in the life of the mind' (*MF* 105/245). It could take on the disruptive force of the *other*. Certeau's work allows us to follow the questions raised by a popular 'other'/*other* into the nineteenth and twentieth centuries. In the form perhaps of a fragmented Nietzschean genealogy, he examines with suspicion the history of its re-employments and unsettling returns.

In 'The beauty of the dead', an article first published in 1970, and written in conjunction with Dominique Julia and Jacques Revel, Certeau analyses a number of disturbing correlations between specific acts of political repression which took place in the nineteenth century and the establishment of 'popular culture' as an object of study.[1] For Certeau and his co-authors, such correlations were relevant not only to explicitly reactionary nineteenth-century historians, but also to a series of ground-breaking and politically more progressive studies which appeared in the 1960s.[2] Despite important breaks, Certeau, Julia and Revel argued, the latter inherited from the former a persistent structure of perception. Their work was informed by a historical 'archaeology' which was inseparable from an expression of political force.

For Certeau, Julia and Revel, the writings of contemporary historians of popular culture were unconsciously founded upon earlier acts of violence. In 'The beauty of the dead', they trace in particular the links between an erudite concern with the 'popular' and a deliberate police operation. Charles Nisard, whom they consider to be the first historian of popular culture,[3] was also an under-secretary in the Ministry of Police during the Second Empire. He was officially charged with the censorship and with the confiscation of the very books on which he was to base his study. He decreed that three-quarters of the texts distributed among the French people were 'unworthy' of them, and that they should be withdrawn from general circulation. The ensuing selection of an 'exemplary' popular literature was designed to eliminate disturbing elements of popular violence, discontent or depravity which might threaten the stability of the national order.

Certeau, Julia and Revel emphasize that this police operation should be seen in the context of the 1848 uprisings and their brutal subjugation. Moreover, it constituted the condition for a host of subsequent literary operations which fetichized a sanitized notion of the 'popular', converting it somewhat perversely into a reassuring object of learned nostalgia. Nisard's purge laid the bases for what Certeau, Julia and Revel call a 'castrating cult' of the people, which they date in this instance of its manifestation around the period 1850–90. They show how processes of idealization and aestheticization were inseparable from processes of suppression:

> It was at the very moment when chap-books were being pursued with the utmost vigour that fashionable souls turned their attention with glee to popular books and contents. . . . The collector's interest was a correlate of the repression used to exorcize the revolutionary danger which, as the days of June 1848 had demonstrated, was still very close, lying dormant. (*H* 123–4/*CP* 51–2)

Certeau, Julia and Revel show how explicitly political and apparently more innocuous interpretative operations combined to set up a popular culture which could be readily integrated into the national 'heritage' and into a cohesive geographical 'community'. The popular domain was packaged in such a way that it 'ceased to be the disquieting world Nisard had worked so hard to exorcize and confine . . . Folklore ensured the cultural assimilation of a henceforth reassuring museum' (*H* 124/*CP* 53). Nisard's operation was designed to extract from a disturbing 'alterity in the life of the mind' the support of a confirmatory 'other'. Certeau, Julia and Revel foreground the dubious historical origins of superficially anodyne scholarly procedures, and they problematize the literary and aesthetic artefacts which these procedures produce.

For Certeau, Julia and Revel, the effects of the origins outlined above could still be discerned in more recent approaches to popular culture. Modern interpreters, they argued, were unreflectingly taking over a 'preconstituted' literary corpus. Historians such as Robert Mandrou, Geneviève Bollème and Marc Soriano supposed in their turn that this corpus could function as something like a 'support' or 'reflection' of a 'popular mentality'.[4] In fact, by failing to make sufficient inquiry into the historical operations which had provided them with their material, they were reduplicating the separation between this material and the life of the people it was supposed to represent. In choosing 'The beauty of the dead' as the

title of their study, Certeau, Julia and Revel suggest how modern
interpreters inherited as their object a beautified 'corpse' whose
resuscitation could produce only a mirage.

Certeau, Julia and Revel challenge furthermore the operations
which modern historians carried out upon such a 'corpse'. They
stress, perhaps unfairly as it is hard to see how these could be
avoided, the acts of remapping through which sets of documents
designated as 'popular' were organized and classified according to
expressly scientific categories. This resulted in a problematic separation of what was not necessarily separate in effective practice
(for example between the 'properly religious', the 'magical' and
the 'medical'). More importantly, they show how these interpretations inherited certain acts of exclusion. They discuss the suppression – or more accurately the suppression of the suppression
– of more disturbing aspects of the 'popular' (concerning violence,
sexuality and the threatening alterity of the child). They thereby
dismantle a series of interpretative operations which consolidate representations of a popular 'other'. Certeau, Julia and Revel
emphasize that these representations have been abstracted from the
historical conditions in which they were effectively produced. Hence
'"dangerous classes" [and] threatening demands never make an
appearance in this *literature*. . . . Yet the links between these texts
and a political history are fundamental. They alone can explain
how a particular *gaze* was constituted' (*H* 133–4/*CP* 67). The deceptive plenitude of a popular 'spirit' as it emerges from certain
erudite studies is for Certeau and his co-authors founded on an
unavowed absence. They show how the edifying myths of the
'people' which circulate in a variety of administrative, interpretative and ideological discourses imply an excision of less comfort-
able or convenient forms of alterity.

For Certeau, Julia and Revel, such acts of excision nevertheless
produce certain symptoms which remain discernible in the language of learned interpretation. In particular, they argue that one
can detect in erudite studies of popular culture an obsession with
the question of a 'lost origin'.[5] They note how the fantasmatic
presence of a putative origin endows the productions of popular
culture in the eyes of learned observers with a distinctive 'aura'.
The ambiguous charm of this aura tends to overshadow those
elements of popular culture which would otherwise clash with the
purity of the interpreters' preconceptions:

What casts this pall? . . . Henri Marrou said that in the last instance,
'the folksong draws its distinctive character from the popular halo

which covers it in our eyes.' What is then the meaning of this phan-
tom that designates the origin and at the same time conceals it, this
'halo' that manifests while it 'covers'? (*H* 128/*CP* 58–9)

Certeau, Julia and Revel suggest that the ever-receding spectre of
an authentically popular origin performs an essential function in
the works which they analyse. It allows interpreters to set the truth
of the people back, as it were, from the actual texts (or people)
which they have in front of them. Nisard's approach to the mass
of chapbooks which passed through his hands was informed by a
prescribed model of what the 'people' should be. Likewise subsequent interpreters sort through the elements of a 'popular culture' with reference to a predefined model of what constitutes the
'authentically' popular. They present this (fictional) model of authenticity in terms of a seductive 'origin' whose traces and aura are
supposedly discernible in the texts which they interpret. They are
thus able both to mask the nature of their own interpretative intervention and to preserve, despite the inevitably 'corrupted' nature
of their documentary evidence, a reassuringly idealized image of
the people. They can therefore remain deaf to the questions raised
by more unsettling manifestations of popular sensibility.[6]

Of course, there is no such thing as a transparent interpretation,
and this is not the principle of Certeau, Julia and Revel's critique:
'nothing gives itself up, everything has to be seized, and the same
interpretative violence can either create or destroy' (*H* 135/*CP* 69).
This quotation captures something of the 'violence' of the article
itself, which remorselessly and a little one-sidedly sets out to strip
the signifier 'popular' as it figures in learned discourse of any ref-
erential grounding or security.[7] As Certeau does elsewhere, the
authors seek to alert contemporary interpreters to the political and
institutional forces which inform their work, and to the unanalysed
history which inhabits them:

> If the procedures of science are not innocent, if their objectives de-
> pend upon a political set-up, then the discourse of science itself should
> acknowledge the function allotted it by society: to conceal what it
> claims to show. What this means is that a simple improvement in
> methods, or a reversal of conviction, will not change what that scien-
> tific operation does to popular culture. Political action is necessary. (*H*
> 121/*CP* 47–8)

This last remark is crucial, although it is not developed in the text,
save for one or two rather portentous intimations ('The political

act is capable of contesting all of culture and placing all of its divisions in question' (*H* 136/*CP* 71)). For such refinements as the authors propose at the level of specific interpretative procedures are in a sense incidental to the main thrust of the article. The scope of their critique is more general. They wish to challenge the strategic operation which substitutes for the effective practices of the vast majority of the population a stable set of representations. This population is thereby converted into a reassuring 'other'. It is set up as an inert body (or corpus) which can be manipulated and controlled by a ruling elite. This elite, however, becomes for Certeau blind to what it excludes by means of such an operation. More specifically, it occults a panoply of other kinds of operation which run through those regions of society which it supposes to be passive. I will examine Certeau's treatment of these other kinds of operation in chapter 6 of the present study. One could interpret the aggressivity of 'The beauty of the dead', however, as a way of preparing a suitably 'purged' space for these later analyses. Certeau, Julia and Revel suggest that the problem facing studies of popular culture is not that of a progression asymptotic to the veiled truth of the people. Rather, these studies should bring out a neglected capacity of their 'object' to effect important kinds of alteration in political and symbolic distributions of power. I will also consider in chapter 6 whether Certeau's subsequent analyses are able to achieve such an objective without falling into some of the traps so vigorously denounced by this earlier article.

A Politics of Language

Certeau explores further some of the questions raised by 'The beauty of the dead' in *Une politique de la langue. La Révolution française et les patois* [A politics of language: The French Revolution and patois], published in 1975 and again written in collaboration with Julia and Revel.[8] This represents an extremely dense and complex work in its own right, and I do not propose to supply here an exhaustive summary of its contents. Rather, I want to examine again Certeau's analysis of a political operation designed to convert the general population into a passive 'body' upon which further administrative and interpretative operations may then become possible.

The fundamental 'operation' at issue in this study is brutally explicit. It forms the central thrust to the Abbé Grégoire's report to the National Convention in Pririal, Year II, whose title is eloquent enough in itself: 'On the necessity and means of annihilating patois and of universalizing the use of the French language'.[9] The Abbé Grégoire and other members of the Constituent Assembly sought to destroy all patois in so far as they formed the fabric of provincial cultures. These cultures were identified not entirely unreasonably by those in Paris with the injustices of the feudal system. However, they considered that only the universalization of the French language, duly regulated and normalized, could practically enable the capital to 'inform' – to instruct and to give form to – the revolutionary state which they wished to construct.[10] It was with this objective in mind that Grégoire devised a questionnaire concerning the vitality of regional patois throughout France, and the possible means and effects of their elimination. He sent out this questionnaire in August 1790 to a variety of erudite and/or 'patriotic' contacts in the provinces. The analyses of *Une politique de la langue* are based for the most part on the responses which Grégoire received from these provincial correspondents.[11]

Grégoire's aims in disseminating his questionnaire were clearly defined. He sought to eliminate all idioms and dialects which threatened the linguistic unity of the nation. Admittedly, the text of the questionnaire displays his curiosity about the linguistic and cultural artefacts to be found in the provinces. He asked his correspondents to collect interesting examples of patois expressions, stories and inscriptions ('we must look for pearls even in the dunghill of Ennius').[12] For Certeau, however, there was no contradiction between Grégoire's destructive enterprise and this conservationist concern. The first project operated on living cultures in such a way as to turn them into a series of relics. The second project merely confirmed the status of these relics *as* relics. As Nisard was to do sixty years later, Grégoire was preparing a 'beautiful corpse', deftly 'taking hold of *spoken* patois in order to transform it into a collection of *preserved writings*. . . . "Annihilated" as a difference threatening political unity, patois could, and indeed had to, be protected thereafter by the State against "vandalism" – these constituted two interrelated operations' (*UPdL* 15). The spoken dialects circulating in the French provinces were seen in Paris as a principle of anarchy and even of potential treachery.[13] Grégoire set out both to erase them and to integrate them, as museological inscriptions, into a new and cohesive political order (his report was published in the name of 'the one and indivisible Republic'). Certeau suggests that Grégoire's linguistic crusade formed part of a revolutionary 'economy of writing'.

In Certeau's reading, Grégoire aspired to convert the heterogeneous regions of France into a 'blank page' upon which to inscribe, as it were, the institutions and constitutions drawn up in Paris. Certeau notes how, at one level, many of the correspondents also interpreted this political enterprise in 'scriptural' terms. They envisaged in their replies the remodelling of the nation through the propagation of standardized written materials (political catechisms, text-books, etc.). They proposed in addition the creation of a new network of roads and communications – an action which constituted likewise for Certeau 'an operation designed to organize a physical space. It was no longer enough simply to write on paper ... [The correspondents] aspired to "write" upon the ground, as part of an economic and political programme. This geographical planification of "civilization" remained even so a scriptural process' (*UPdL* 157).

Yet Certeau also detects a number of divergences between the conceptions and imaginary configurations which govern Grégoire's writings and those discernible in the texts of his correspondents. Certeau sees in these divergences the localized marks of the correpondents' relation to their own regions. Such differences did not necessarily pose a significant threat to the cooperation which Grégoire required from his provincial agents. Certeau notes nevertheless that, whereas Grégoire tended to conceptualize his programme in an exclusively 'technical' and 'bookish' manner (*UPdL* 165), the correspondents generally evoked a kind of 'agri-culture': they had in Certeau's reading 'an agricultural conception of enlightened culture privileging its rural counterpart. In both registers, their vocabulary spells out the virile activity of traversing, violating and inseminating their mother earth' (*UPdL* 132). The provinces and their patois constituted for the correspondents a 'nature' which needed to be 'cultivated'. They perceived their provinces, and the 'brute' linguistic subjects who inhabited them,[14] as an inert resource which they had to work on and exploit so as to bring them into a productive economic order. Their position, however, remained ambivalent. In so far as they imagined patois to constitute a form of 'nature', it retained an affective charge which threatened perpetually to unsettle their new-found distinction as representatives of 'culture'.

For unlike the ruling elite based in Paris, many of these provincial dignitaries could see before them in the patois of their regions an image of their *own* nature or origin. The voices they could hear were those of a familiar 'infantile' language. Their greater or lesser proximity to these voices called for an active work of separation. In order to satisfy Grégoire's injunctions and to appropriate for themselves the enlightened discourse which would assure their affiliation to Paris, they had to turn their 'nature' into an 'other'. They had to unfold before themselves for ironical scrutiny the provincial idioms which they carried, as it were, within themselves. Certeau traces a constant movement in the writings through which 'these local notables set up representations of their ties to their native land and mother tongue in so far as they were *becoming* either an object of knowledge or else an imaginary recess which could not be articulated before the agents of centralized power' (*UPdL* 18). His reflection on the intermediary status of the correspondents breaks down simple oppositions between identity and alterity. A set of Parisian directives involved these correspondents in an ongoing work of separation which served finally to 'alter' their identities.

However, Certeau shows the results of this alteration to be both ambivalent and unstable. He notes for example in his analysis of a reply from the Abbé Fonvielhe in the Dordogne that

> a cultural asceticism – the bourgeois ethic of *Aufklärung* – characterizes what lies far off and distinguishes it from the place, made up of 'naïvety', 'friendship' and 'songs', from which the response from the Perigord speaks in something like a murmur. It requires an 'effort' to produce in this *we* the transformation which will bring it into conformity with the patriotic and cultural work of Paris, creating also in this way a remainder – *them.* (*UPdL* 58)

The extended process by which Grégoire's provincial correspondents converted themselves into enlightened citizens left in Certeau's reading a particular kind of residue. This residue represented the 'other' of those distinct and controlled operations which issued forth from Paris, and which Grégoire's informants aspired to make their own. It was constituted by these determinate operations as a zone of 'indeterminacy' and 'confusion'. It worked as a vessel for all that which the correspondents had to excise from themselves in order to become active and articulate citizens: passivity, passions and their expression, oral and particularly vocalic flux, nature, animality, etc. In Certeau's conceptual framework, patois were constituted by the correspondents as a variant of the 'fable'. Once more, he presents such 'fables' less as an independent reality than as a by-product of modern economies of writing and rationality. Yet, as with his analysis of Léry's encounter with the Tupinambou,

Certeau seeks to trace how the residues produced by powerful forms of written interpretation or strategic operation do not necessarily remain in the positions of passivity to which they appear to have been confined.

The quotation above itself evokes something of the pull which these patois, destined to become archaic, continued to exert on the correspondents (and no doubt at another level on Certeau himself). Certeau traces in his analyses how that which was set apart as 'passive' returned, as it were, in the guise of 'passion'. The effects of such passions served to unsettle the otherwise clearly defined field of operations laid out by Grégoire. Certeau detects in the texts of the correspondents the symptoms of a peculiar erotic relationship to the body of patois which they sought to leave behind them. Certeau notes for example a heightened sensibility to those sounds and marks of orality which were becoming 'other' for the agents of an order founded on writing:

> The ear is the delicate skin caressed or irritated by sound: an erogeneous zone, exacerbated, so to speak, by the interdictions which banish from language and good manners coarseness, vulgarity and finally passions. A practice of asceticism constructs the code of Parisian and revolutionary culture which is imposed upon local militants. But, rejected by the (written) law, the eroticism exiled from writing seems to make its return in this ear touched by the voices which emerge from the valleys and woods. (*UPdL* 111)

For Certeau, the sounds of patois worked as 'sirens' and 'witches' (*UPdL* 111). They drew the correspondents back over the lines of separation which the correspondents themselves had drawn up. The seductive appeal of patois worked to erode the Parisian 'distinction' to which many of Grégoire's agents aspired.

Certeau also detects in their replies the recurrence of a fantasmatic fear. This concerns again the fragility of the field of operations in which the correspondents sought their new place and identity. For that zone of indeterminacy from which these agents were laboriously separating themselves threatened always to return and to undo the precarious advances of their rational political enterprise:

> The slightest relaxation in the process of instruction, and they could see the re-emergence of what that process was designed to combat. 'Reason' . . . was not inscribed within nature as the movement of its progress, but had to be inscribed therein through a labour which,

pushed to the limit, was a struggle to the death. The elimination of patois was a riposte to the threat of what always 'returns' with them. It is a fight against destiny that is traced (at least in the representations of these notables) by the fatal image of returning spectres impossible to kill. (*UPdL* 105)

Certeau goes on to compare such resilient ghosts to the 'fantastical symptoms' associated with sorcery in earlier struggles against rural opacity (the correspondents also evoke in a stereotypical way an inveterate belief in evil spirits as a characteristic of those who speak patois[15]). In formal terms, the analyses contained in *Une politique de la langue* recall *La possession de Loudun*. In both cases, Certeau examines the repressive strategies designed to convert oral manifestations of difference into prescribed figures of the 'other'. Certeau's own interpretative strategy sets out to follow the mutations and returns of what has been suppressed. He shows how the clear deliberations of expert interpretation and the reasoned deployment of politico-administrative reform are upset by the irruption in fantasmatic form of an *other* which has not been mastered.

One should comment briefly on the way in which Certeau himself presents the sounds and images associated with patois. He seems deliberately to sharpen the imaginary divisions which he detects in the texts of the correspondents. He insinuates into the exposition of his analyses his own poetic figures (voices from woods and valleys, sirens and witches . . .). These figures endow the 'echoes' of historical patois to be found in his historiographical text with a peculiarly seductive resonance. Yet this can also produce a sacrifice of interpretative sobriety. Certeau is led, one feels, to submit his documentary evidence on occasion to a form of poeticization. Certainly, this poeticization is extremely effective. Once again, it suggests something of the historical interpreter's involvement (or com-plicity) in his material. One should none the less remain alert to the intermittent turbulence which it introduces into the analytic unfolding of Certeau's historiographical operation.

Despite his underscoring of such fantasmatic forms, Certeau argues finally that their effectivity in this particular instance was severely circumscribed. The engineers of the Jacobine 'steam-roller' in Paris were not exposed to the vicissitudes resulting from the intermediary positions of Grégoire's provincial correspondents. Grégoire and his successors could start simply to 'collect' that which did not fit immediately into their programmes and to place this in the reassuring but remote category of folklore. This process, which

Certeau calls the 'folklorization of difference', did not contest but
rather complemented a policy of national unity, in so far as 'the
place of a centralized power and that of the Archives where it files
away patois belong to the same set-up. Certainly, the assimilation
of citizens leaves a *remainder*: disseminated words and monuments. But this too is managed by the Administration' (*UPdL* 167).
One cannot automatically assume that the residue produced by
powerful forms of rationality will return always and everywhere
as a disruptive force. Certeau nevertheless turns his own
historiographical practice against the strategic models which govern a centralized administrative machinery, and focuses on what is
lost or marginalized through the workings of this machinery. He
reconfigures the abandoned verbal matter and the 'frozen words'
which are cited by his sources in such a way as to put in question
the very operation which consigned them as relics to the archives.

It may be that Certeau demonizes to some degree the work of
centralization as such. He underplays what often emerges in the
replies to Grégoire as an urgent need for specific forms of standardization. Those letters included in the appendix to *Une politique
de la langue* evoke for example the sheer logistical problems inherent in situations where 'people often have trouble understanding
each other from one parish to the next,'[16] as well as the difficulties
of instructing people about new improved agricultural techniques
or legal rights.[17] Only by giving more weight to such problems
could Certeau forestall the danger of a facile or romanticized appropriation of his analyses. Yet his rather exclusive focus on the
deleterious effects of centralization produces even so an interesting
instance of regressive diagnosis. He argues in the conclusion to
Une politique de la langue that the administrative machinery under-
pinning Grégoire's enterprise was soon to become detached from
those moral imperatives which initially provided its ideological
rationale. Shorn of the evangelical and philanthropic spirit which
motivated Grégoire's zeal, 'this ideology would collapse, but not
the apparatus created in its name. The Administration was soon
serving Napoleonic policy' (*UPdL* 167). Certeau suggests that the
operations of this refined 'apparatus' would in the nineteenth century begin to eliminate forms of social alterity in more insidious a
manner than that which distinguished the Jacobine elite of the
revolution. They would work also to iron out the more nuanced
positions proper to the likes of Grégoire's correspondents. The
strategies which they served to implement would become less ideological but if anything more implacable. They require for Certeau
particular forms of critical analysis.

The Disciplining of Society (Foucault)

Une politique de la langue was published in the same year as Michel Foucault's *Discipline and Punish*.[18] For Certeau, this constituted Foucault's most powerful work, and I shall suggest below some of the main reasons for Certeau's sustained interest in the book. It develops in an incisive manner many of the issues which run through Certeau's own work, and it takes further in particular the questions raised so far in this chapter. However, Certeau considers the general thrust of Foucault's arguments in *Discipline and Punish* to be deeply problematic. Luce Giard has suggested that Certeau's resistance originates to some degree in a pretheoretical 'elective anti-affinity . . . which does not preclude an interest or fascination for opposing theories'.[19] I will also examine therefore those aspects of Foucault's thought which Certeau is loath to accept, and which form the bases for their divergences.

The basic plot of Foucault's historical account is now well known. Its protagonists are impersonal disciplinary procedures which organize social space through operations of gridding, timetabling and surveillance. For Foucault these procedures came to prominence first in certain monastic, pedagogical and military institutions of the ancien régime before going on to colonize ever larger domains of social existence. He describes them as 'always meticulous, often minute, techniques', which nevertheless 'had their importance: because they defined a certain mode of detailed political investment of the body, a "new micro-physics" of power' (*DP* 139). Foucault seeks to demonstrate how such techniques came to infest and finally to conquer the social body. He argues that their success could not be attributed to any consciously devised strategy or grand design. Rather, it was a function precisely of their anonymity and mute, mechanistic punctiliousness. They represent 'acts of cunning, not so much of the greater reason that works even in its sleep and gives meaning to the insignificant, as of the attentive "malevolence" that turns everything to account. Discipline is a political anatomy of detail' (*DP* 139). Moreover Foucault suggests that this impersonal panoply of disciplinary apparatuses constituted the seedbed for the ostensibly nobler interpretative operations of the human sciences. He traces for example how the dissemination of recorded 'examinations' drew biological individuals into a variety of 'disciplinary' structures. He argues that the

> small techniques of notation, of registration, of constituting files, of
> arranging facts in columns and tables that are so familiar to us now,

were of decisive importance in the epistemological 'thaw' of the sciences of the individual. . . . The birth of the sciences of man . . . is probably to be found in these 'ignoble' archives, where the modern play of coercion over bodies, gestures and behaviour has its beginnings. (*DP* 190–1)

These 'archives' recall those dossiers which Grégoire was in the process of constructing, and which were in Certeau's account due to be taken over in a more systematic fashion by the Napoleonic administration. However, Foucault's analyses tend to erase the notion that the information in question may be collected and ordered as a result of any deliberate central plan or ideologically inspired enterprise. He seeks to reconfigure common conceptions which strictly divide centres of decision-making and institutional islands of scientificity from a periphery which they control. For Foucault, the quasi-autonomous logic of 'discipline' cuts across such oppositions between an 'inside' and an 'outside'. Instead, science and knowledge are constituted in his account by mechanisms which permeate the social body. One should note the permanent ambiguity in his book of words like 'operation', 'analysis' (literally a separation into parts), 'control' and 'distribution'. These terms can signify both the deliberate steps in scientific and interpretative procedure, but also the impersonal, microbe-like mechanisms which he sees as moving across and organizing social space. Foucault describes, for example, an apparently disparate set of scientific methods, political and economic strategies, military disciplinary procedures and hospital arrangements at the end of the eighteenth century as so many 'twin operations in which the two elements – distribution and analysis, control and intelligibility – are inextricably bound up' (*DP* 148). In uncovering such disciplinary complexes, Foucault points to accentuated forms of the interpretative 'complicity' which represents for Certeau a recurrent object of analysis.

Foucault seeks to expose the interpretative activity of the human sciences as a function of a disciplinary machinery which constitutes particular kinds of object. This machinery was designed to fabricate 'docile bodies' which would 'operate' in rigorously prescribed manners (*DP* 137–8). Interpretation worked, so to speak, as a cog in this process of production. The history of 'delinquency' shows for example in Foucault's account how interpretative operations have served to reinforce more fundamental disciplinary structures.[20] Foucault distinguishes between the concept of a lawbreaker (a legal subject who infringes an article of a juridical code) and the category of a delinquent (an individual who cannot lead a responsible social life outside the confines of a disciplinary institution). He argues that the insertion of law-breakers into intensive disciplinary networks served finally to *produce* delinquents. In the interpretative discourse of criminal psychology, however, the category of 'delinquency' referred to a supposedly essential or genetic attribute of particular kinds of criminal. It was used precisely as a reason to enmesh legal offenders ever more tightly in the machinery of disciplinary institutions. Interpretation thereby served merely to perpetuate and to reinforce the very symptom which it purported to diagnose. Foucault's argument is less than convincing as a total explanation for delinquency. However, it does demonstrate very suggestively how certified/certifying practices of interpretation operate upon objects (or subjects) which have been 'preconstituted' by other kinds of operation. In the case of delinquency, Foucault shows how the official language of legal discourse, which proclaimed its concern with the apt punishment and/or with the rehabilitation of the offender, could in fact be hijacked or 'diverted' (*détourné*) by an unspectacular set of mute coercive procedures.

Certeau argues that Foucault's analyses have set up a major new field of inquiry. We can see how they correspond to a number of his own concerns. They are designed to cut beneath the 'chatter' of 'ideology' (*PE* 46/77) and to focus on the complicities and distortions which are sealed at the level of effective practice ('operations'). Certeau takes a particular interest therefore in

the transformations that Foucault has introduced into the analysis of procedures and the perspectives that have opened up since his study. By showing, in one case, the heterogeneity and equivocal relations between apparatuses [*dispositifs*] and ideologies, he has constituted as a treatable historical object that zone where technological procedures have specific *effects of power*, function according to their own *logics*, and can produce a fundamental *diversion* within the institutions of order and knowledge. (*PE* 49/81)

We have seen that Certeau was already addressing in his work the disjunctions between manifest discursive contents and effective procedures. Yet Certeau also takes further the forms of 'heterogeneity' and 'diversion' diagnosed by Foucault. He examines most notably the ways in which the sorts of procedure discerned by Foucault may themselves be 'diverted' by other forms of operation. I will explore this development in chapter 6. I want here just to suggest how it arises from a conception of the social order which is radically different from that contained in Foucault's book.

Foucault extrapolates from his analysis of a 'microphysics' of power to present in *Discipline and Punish* a dystopian vision of the social body as a whole. In the same movement by which he inserts interpretations of social reality into a disconcerting 'genealogy', he himself also produces what could appear to Certeau only as an extremely problematic representation of that social reality. For in Foucault's account, disciplinary mechanisms have not simply constituted the human sciences, or restricted themselves to localized institutional appearances. Rather, in their alarming proliferation, he considers that they have insidiously invaded and colonized all of social space, which thereby becomes gridded, measured and surveyed in an implacable, impersonal light. He talks for example of 'the infinitely minute web of panoptic techniques' (*DP* 224), or of 'the carceral texture of society' (*DP* 304). One can no longer even talk here of repression, for in such a perspective there is nothing left to repress. It seems that for Foucault in *Discipline and Punish*, there is no 'outside'. Any conceivable form of social alterity has always already, so to speak, been entrapped and processed by the workings of a disciplinary apparatus:

> It is not that the beautiful totality of the individual is amputated, repressed, altered by our social order, it is rather that the individual is carefully fabricated in it, according to a whole tactical range [*toute une tactique*] of forces and bodies. We are much less Greek than we believe. We are neither in the amphitheatre, nor on the stage, but inside the panoptic machine, invested by its effects of power, which we ourselves reactivate since we are part of its mechanism. (*DP* 217)

For Foucault, a series of 'meticulous' tactics are integrated into anonymous strategies in such a way as to homogenize the entire social order. I will outline below how Certeau proposes an alternative theoretical model of 'strategies' and 'tactics' in *The Practice of Everyday Life*. One should note here simply that Foucault's bleak hyperbole is profoundly antipathetic to the general style and orientation of Certeau's thought. Certeau is perpetually alert to the ways in which forms of alterity may break into and 'alter' forms of identity, and it is this alertness – or faith – which sets his thought in motion. Hence he seeks to expose forms of interpretative 'complicity' in order to suggest how they serve to occult the objects which interpreters aspire ostensibly to bring to light. Foucault wants to demonstrate in *Discipline and Punish* that interpretative operations are functions of disciplinary 'complexes' in order to suggest instead that little else exists. This represents a conclusion which, were he to accept it, could only stifle Certeau's thought.

Certeau argues instead that Foucault's work indirectly perpetuates the same interpretative and disciplinary violence which it uncovers at the heart of the human sciences and in carceral institutions. Foucault's work in Certeau's eyes inverts but also 'preserves' certain deep-rooted conceptions concerning forms of social control and organization. Certeau considers that Foucault shares with political and technocratic strategists the assumption that disciplinary procedures have the capacity to mould fully a docile social body. It may even be that this tendency is more marked in the work of Foucault than in the thought of more pragmatically minded administrators. Foucault's wider analyses evince the mark of a long preoccupation with the workings of monolithic and 'total' institutions. He talks of a generalization of 'the carceral' (*DP* 303), and asks, intensifying his point with a movement of rhetorical closure, whether it is 'surprising that prisons resemble factories, schools, barracks, hospitals, which all resemble prisons' (*DP* 228).

Certeau does not subscribe to these evocations of a seamless disciplinary web which emerge at recurrent intervals throughout *Discipline and Punish*.[21] In order to sustain the characteristic movement of his thought, Certeau needs to find openings in the social fabric which undermine what appears sometimes to be the totalizing ambition of Foucault's account. Certeau looks for limits both to those strategic politico-administrative and interpretative operations which he analyses in his own work, and to the proliferating mechanisms of 'discipline' diagnosed by Foucault. These limits work for him as signs of practices which are not reducible to such forms of social control. The problems posed by Certeau's own intellectual 'need' for resistant forms of alterity will themselves be addressed in chapter 6. I want next, however, to show how Certeau's recourse to the thought of Pierre Bourdieu may be analysed in the context of this general orientation.

Theory and Practice (Bourdieu)

Bourdieu, like Foucault, constitutes a pervasive presence in *The Practice of Everyday Life*. While Certeau incorporates important aspects of Bourdieu's reflection into his work, his reading of Bourdieu is informed again by a kind of intellectual allergy or 'irritation' (*PE* 59/94).[22] I shall examine below how Bourdieu's writings are appropriated by Certeau in his work on the limits of interpretative operations. I will point out the principal divergences between the two thinkers, and I will assess the implications of the critique which Certeau addresses to Bourdieu's key concept of the 'habitus'.

Foucault argues that the disciplining of modern society has been based on a 'panoptic' surveillance and control of all social practices. For him, the human sciences have performed an essential function in this process. We looked above at his provocative reassessment of their 'small techniques of notation, of registration, of constituting files, of arranging facts in columns and tables' (*DP* 190). No doubt most analysts would not subscribe to Foucault's uniformly bleak portrayal of the role of the human sciences in modern society. It is generally assumed, however, that a major rationale of these sciences is to provide a coherent overview of diverse social processes. Bourdieu devotes a considerable amount of epistemological reflection to the limits of the different 'overviews' which scientifically controlled interpretative procedures are able to produce. Like Certeau, he begins by challenging naive conceptions of interpretative mastery.

Bourdieu problematizes what he calls the 'synoptic' representations constructed by social scientists in order to survey fields of social practices. These representations can take the form of maps on which to chart the itineraries of individuals or groups, of calendars or chronologies on which to draw up their organization of time, of tables, graphs, diagrams and so forth. Such artefacts permit the rapid synthesis of controlled samples of data. They are invaluable tools which enable the investigator to bring a disparate array of information under simultaneous scrutiny. Bourdieu argues nevertheless that the very process by which these artefacts are assembled must itself be submitted to critical scrutiny. He refers to this process as one of 'objectification' which is itself in need of objectification.[23] Certeau, in his reading of Bourdieu, seems less confident about the practicability of this supplementary objectification. He speaks rather of an unavowed 'operation of withdrawal and power' (*PE* 53/86) which itself needs to be made explicit. Like Bourdieu, however, Certeau emphasizes that the operations which produce these interpretative artefacts falsify in important ways the 'nodes of heterogeneous operations' (that is, social practices) whose forms they are designed to display.

Bourdieu argues that social scientists pay insufficient attention to the intrinsic effects of their own technical operations. He shows, for example, how the very process through which these interpreters represent ordinary spatial practices itself tends to occult the nature of these practices.[24] They become abstract components in a 'theoretical' space which bears little resemblance to the sort of 'practical' space defined by Poincaré as the 'system of axes invariably attached to our body, and which we transport with us everywhere we go' (*ETP* 159). Bourdieu questions the capacity of synoptic representations to capture the moving reality of the practices which they examine. He argues that they convert 'a practical succession into a represented succession, an action oriented in relation to a space objectively constituted as a structure of demands, calls, prohibitions or threats (things "to do" or "not to do") into a reversible operation executed within a continuous and homogeneous space' (*ETP* 212). For Bourdieu, the very power which socially authorized interpreters and planners have to 'map' or to 'grid' social space leads them to forget the existence of other kinds of relation to the same social space. Bourdieu attributes this amnesia less to specific class differences than to a different 'relation to necessity' implied by scientific and interpretative practice as such. Institutionally based interpreters tend to be more or less set off from the world which they profess to interpret. Bourdieu foregrounds an important divergence between an 'interpretative' disposition and a necessarily 'practical' disposition, which an adequate theory of theory and practice would have to take into account (although one should stress that one could use Bourdieu's own work to reconfigure substantially this opposition). These contrasting dispositions produce different approaches to social reality:

> Knowledge depends not only, as an elementary relativism teaches us, on the particular point of view which a 'situated and dated' observer takes upon an object, but also on the very fact that as a spectator who takes a *point of view* upon action, who withdraws from it in order to observe it, to examine it from afar and from on high, he constitutes practical activity as an *object of observation and analysis*. Architects took a long time to notice that the cavalier perspective of their plans and models led them to construct cities for some kind of divine spectator and not for the people whose lot it would be to move about in them. (*ETP* 160)

For Bourdieu, it becomes progressively easier to adopt such a 'point of view' on social reality as one ascends the social hierarchy, and as one is provided with the technical means to carry out the requisite operations. Bourdieu does not wish to deny the uses of the overviews which scientific observation can produce.[25] He does, however, show the sort of 'panoptic' power often attributed to these overviews to be based on an interpretative quid pro quo. A theoretical artefact is mistaken for reality itself. I will discuss in the next chapter how Certeau takes up these ideas, and how he develops the critique adumbrated above of the 'divine spectator' in conceptions of urban space.

For Bourdieu, scientific interpretation of 'unscientific' (or ordinary) social practices tends to be led further astray by the very nature of its theoretical rigour. He argues that interpreters endeavour to abstract stable logical models from their material, without reflecting adequately on the status of the logic which they employ. A controlled scientific logic aspires, for example, to define elements through laws of identity, equivalence and non-contradiction, and to arrange these elements in a coherent system. Bourdieu contrasts this with what he calls a specifically 'practical' (or 'polythetic') logic. People resort to this logic precisely because they do not have the 'leisure' (*skholê*), means or inclination to arrange their practices in a more strictly systematic manner. The scientific interpreter's systematization therefore runs the risk of falsifying what is most characteristic about these practices. In his work on ritual practices in Kabylia, Bourdieu uncovers a series of inconsistencies in the diverse correlations made by members of indigenous communities among a set of homologies which facilitate the symbolic, if not effective, control of the world (these correlations draw on analogies and 'family resemblances' between autumn, winter, spring, summer, evening, night, morning, noon, insemination, gestation, birth, maturity, west, north, east, south, etc.). Bourdieu argues that such agents do not operate in terms of ready-made structures, but seek rather to exploit any apparently auspicious combination which may come to hand:

What distinguishes the complete *series* of temporal oppositions produced by the work of the interpreter is that it is not actually mobilized or indeed mobilizable as such, in its entirety and in all its details. For the needs of existence never demand such a synoptic grasp, even when they do not actively discourage it by their urgency. In short, what we shall call *polythetism* constitutes, along with polysemy, the condition for the functioning of a practical logic. This logic can only organize all thoughts, perceptions and actions by means of a limited number of principles ... because its entire *economy* presupposes the sacrifice of clarity and distinctions in the interests of simplicity and generality. (*ETP* 219–20)

In this polythetic or 'economical' logic, items are assigned meaning not in terms of a prescribed essence, identity or consistent function. This meaning is defined rather by the different and sometimes opposing ways in which a given element may be used. As Certeau puts it in his reading of Bourdieu, 'the same thing has employments and properties that vary according to the arrangements into which it enters' (*PE* 54/88). For Certeau, Bourdieu's 'polythetic' logic appears as a variant of his own conception of 're-employments'. It serves first and foremost to delineate the manners in which scientifically incompetent practitioners elude the types of identity thrust upon them by controlled forms of interpretative operation.

One should therefore note a divergence discernible in Bourdieu's own attitude towards a 'practical' logic. In a manner which becomes more marked in *The Logic of Practice*, published in the same year as *The Practice of Everyday Life*, Bourdieu is careful to emphasize the weaknesses of this logic. It constitutes a response to misfortune or to insecurity in the context of powerlessness and of a paucity of information. Individuals are thereby *reduced* to seeking the maximization of a purely 'magical' profit (*ETP* 56–8; *LP* 264, 282). He even goes so far in *The Logic of Practice* as to talk of a 'demon of analogy' at work in practical logic, a demon which can effectively 'possess' those who possess it.[26] Certeau tends to pass over such weaknesses in his concern to uncover a kind of polymorphous flexibility where most interpreters had assumed too readily only an inert passivity. By occulting such problems, Certeau's analyses run the risk of lapsing intermittently into an unqualified apologetics for ordinary practices.

The construction of synoptic representations and the recourse to a technical logic constitute key components of standard interpretative strategies. Such strategies are designed to uncover 'rules' through which scientific communities can bring predetermined fields under intellectual or social control. The question of 'rules', whether these are understood in an explanatory, descriptive, regulative or normative sense, is subjected to incisive critical scrutiny in *Esquisse d'une théorie de la pratique*.[27] Bourdieu exposes the limits of the rules which may be held at a given level of interpretation to account adequately for the conduct of particular groups and individuals. He shows how these rules may in fact be appropriated by the latter as a function of more complicated strategies. Bourdieu draws evidence for this argument from an analysis of matrimonial strategies in Kabylia, where both official and tacit rules governing dowry, social status, inheritance and genealogy are not so much obeyed as manipulated, orchestrated and reshuffled.[28] Instead of a set of strict regulations, he uncovers a process of negotiation combined with a subtle and often devious interplay of substitutions, elisions and compensations. For Certeau, Bourdieu hereby introduces a heightened complexity into his object of analysis. Scientific interpretative strategies are, so to speak, set against other strategies, interpretative or otherwise, which 'do not "apply" principles or rules; they choose among them to make up the repertory of their operations' (*PE* 54/88). Bourdieu seems to introduce the scientific interpreter into an unsettling and intriguing vortex. Given the proliferation of supplementary manipulations outlined above, the interpreter could never be absolutely sure of possessing a set of valid rules which were not being turned this way or that by strategies more wily than his own.

In Certeau's reading, however, Bourdieu does his utmost to escape the consequences of this disarming insight. He does this by appealing to a second-order principle of regulation which he calls the 'habitus'. This signifies, to use the concise definition provided by the English translator of *Homo Academicus*, 'a system of shared social dispositions and cognitive structures which generates perceptions, appreciations and actions'.[29] In Bourdieu's account, this system is acquired primarily in the course of an individual's upbringing. It is a direct function of an objective social structure which indelibly marks the individual, and it determines and regulates the forms of his or her subsequent practice. For Bourdieu, the habitus contains within it a set of unanalysed implicit rules which determine the way in which the subject takes up and *appears* to manipulate the explicit rules prevailing in a social environment. Hence Bourdieu can, with the help of the habitus, show how improvisations on rules are themselves 'regulated', but by rules unknown to the agents themselves. Thus Bourdieu maintains that

> the subtlest trap lies no doubt in the fact that the agents' discourse resorts willingly to the highly ambiguous vocabulary of *rules*, those of grammar, morality and law, in order to express a social practice which

actually obeys very different principles . . . The explication of their practice which can be supplied by the agents themselves, at the cost of a quasi-theoretical review of their practice, conceals from their own eyes the truth of their practical mastery as *docta ignorantia*, that is as a mode of practical knowledge which does not contain within itself the knowledge of its own principles. (*ETP* 202)

For Certeau, such a passage would in effect constitute Bourdieu's own subtlest trap. For in the move which takes away from agents the understanding of their practical understanding, Bourdieu creates the gap – the 'learned ignorance' – in which the scientific interpreter can come and install himself, armed with the interpretative master-key of the habitus. This alone for Bourdieu can render properly explicit that which for the agents themselves must remain forever implicit or unconscious. It is not the notion of the unconscious structuration of experience as such which troubles Certeau. Rather, Certeau declares himself to be 'irritated' by a dogmatic aggressivity in Bourdieu's work which belies the labyrinthine intricacy of his actual analyses. Certeau sees the habitus as a theoretical or heuristic artefact which tends to conceal its status as such and to congeal into the fundamental or 'mystical' reality of practices. Indeed, the term shows a striking tendency in Bourdieu's writing to take over as the subject of these practices:

If agents are possessed by their habitus more than they possess it, that is primarily because they only possess it in so far as it acts within them as the organizing principle of their actions, that is to say in such a mode that they are at the same time dispossessed of it in the symbolic mode. (*ETP* 202)

For Bourdieu, it is ultimately the socio-logician who symbolically possesses the habitus of others. At one level, Certeau certainly remains intrigued by Bourdieu's analyses in so far as they converge with his own attempts to expose the limits of authoritative strategies of interpretation. He emphatically resists, however, the claims of Bourdieu to have reached a definitive scientific understanding of other peoples' practices. He suggests that this interpretative mastery, which Bourdieu denies both to other interpreters and to the practitioners themselves, is itself best seen as part of a strategy of intellectual bluff and counter-bluff.[30]

Certeau's own intellectual wager, by contrast, consists in an attempt to remain open to the unsettling proliferation of manipulations, combinations and orchestrations evoked above. He sets up as a focus of analysis the points where organized politico-administrative and interpretative complexes give way to something else. He argues that the strategic operations designed to inform or to control the social order are liable to become overrun by a multiplicity of other kinds of operation which he calls 'tactics':

> Such tactics, through their criteria and procedures, would use the institutional and symbolic organization in such an autonomous manner that if it were to take them seriously the scientific representation of society would get lost in them, in every sense of the word. Its postulates and ambitions could not resist them. Norms, generalizations, and segmentations would yield to the transverse and 'metaphorizing' pullulation of these *different* micro-activities. (*PE* 59/95)

I will outline in the next chapter the precise nature of the distinction which Certeau draws between 'strategies' and 'tactics'. One could say that Certeau, in contrast to Bourdieu, endeavours to introduce his analyses *into* the swarm of tactical operations which he discerns around him. These analyses constitute, as it were, a metonymic and reflexive instance of the procedures which they examine. This move produces in Certeau's case new and exciting results, but it is not without its problems. One might for example question in Certeau's work the figural presence of the 'crowd' – that ambivalent figure of the 'real' – into which he can disappear.[31] More seriously, perhaps, an ethical surrender of interpretative 'mastery' may conflict with an equally ethical responsibility to exert a degree of critical control.

Imaginary Displacements

One may experience a temptation to lay down all tools of analysis before this proliferation of 'tactics', and to relapse into a series of modified imaginary figures. Certeau's writings offer the reader a number of tropes which seem to encourage such an appropriation:

> As one examines carefully this fleeting and permanent reality, one has the impression of exploring the night-side of societies, a night longer than their days, an obscure sea from which successive institutions emerge, a maritime immensity on which socioeconomic and political structures appear as ephemeral islands. (*PE* 41/67)

Certainly, the recurrent figures of indeterminacy and of a bewildering multiplicity are an important feature both of *La culture au pluriel* and of *The Practice of Everyday Life*. The passage above illustrates Certeau's recourse to images of the night and of the sea. Both metaphors seem to dissolve and to carry away with them the clear demarcations of analytic thought. He uses to analogous effect terms like 'rumour' and 'murmur' to characterize his perception of the teeming plurality of different practices at work around him. He speaks of 'the oceanic rumour of the ordinary' (*PE* 5/19) and of 'the poetic or tragic murmurings of the everyday' (*PE* 70/109). The interpreter apprehends a commotion of confused 'sounds' rather than the functionally ordered phonemes of effective and economical signification. An excess of apparently disjointed, peculiarly combined or now incomprehensible fragments resists the articulatory thrust of analysis. The invocation of these 'innumerable lexicons and strange vocabularies' (*CP* 213) sets up an ironic perspective both on the kinds of strategic operation discussed above and on Certeau's own research. The cumulative effect of such stylistic devices, inserted moreover into the very grain of Certeau's writing, is considerable. In this respect, it is not quite accurate to talk as Françoise Choay does of a 'permanent counterpoint' between the rigour of Certeau's writing and the richness of the metaphors which animate it.[32] The persistent resurgence of the figures outlined above threatens to overturn the very balance connoted by Choay's evocation of a quasi-musical harmony.

These figures are, however, also dangerous in another way, in so far as they risk simply converting incomprehension into aesthetic pleasure. Taken by themselves, they may serve to cover over a disconcerting proliferation of practices with a series of poetically satisfying images. The 'beautiful corpse' of a popular culture is never far away. The intellectual fantasm which Certeau had previously dissected mutates, as it were, and returns to haunt the imaginary dimension of his work. One must emphasize nevertheless that it is not a case of simple repetition. Certeau himself hints at the existence of such a latent continuity:

> The imaginary landscape of an inquiry is not without value, even if it does lack rigour. It restores what was once indicated under the term 'popular culture', but it does so in order to transform what was represented as a matrix-force of history into a mobile infinity of tactics. It thus keeps before our eyes the structure of a social imagination from which our questions never cease to take different forms and to set out again. (*PE* 41/67)

For Certeau, the 'imaginary landscape' of his work has more than a reductively aesthetic or ornamental value. By framing his material in particular ways, and by foregrounding especially that which exceeds conventional political and interpretative frameworks, it helps to open up new kinds of investigation. It focuses the mind on phenomena which tend to remain below the threshold of attention. I shall examine in the next chapter the formal analyses which Certeau is able to produce as a result of this reorientation. These analyses may remain 'contaminated' by that aestheticization which to some degree renders them possible. They also serve, however, to uncover a vast range of operations which exceed the kinds of strategic operation discussed above. This range of operations appears to constitute for learned interpretation a diffuse and massive form of alterity.

6

Turns and Diversions

Strategies and Tactics

Certeau's historical analyses show that one cannot identify the truth of the 'popular' with the representations which have traditionally circulated in its name. His approach to contemporary culture is designed precisely to drive a wedge between such representations and the multiple practices through which they are appropriated. He sets up as the object of his inquiries the ways in which texts and images are 'manipulated' by 'practitioners who are not their makers'. He argues that such a move is essential if we are to 'gauge the gap or similarity between the production of an image [or of any cultural artefact] and the secondary production hidden in the processes of its utilization' (PE xiii/xxxviii). This gap is that introduced by the forms of 're-employment' to which agents subject the objects with which they are presented. The diversity of such practices inevitably splinters the apparent stability of the images on which they work – including that of the 'popular' itself. Nevertheless, one should note how Certeau himself re-employs this resilient epithet. In his work, the term 'popular' is applied no longer to standardized sets of constructed representations, but rather to the heterogeneous and largely invisible operations of construction and destruction governing the reception of these representations.

We have already seen in chapter 1 how Certeau advocates in historiography a transition from a preoccupation with representations to a focus on practices and beliefs, and how he places this shift under the conceptual rubric of the 'formality' of practices. It is a shift which informs nearly all of Certeau's writing. It generated in 1968 the analyses of *La prise de parole*. For Certeau, it corresponded to a series of fault-lines which the events of May '68 had both drawn out and aggravated in contemporary French society:

> Our speech, which has become a 'symbolic site', designates the space created by the distance separating those represented from their representations, the members of a society from the modes of their association. It is essential, and at the same time it is nothing, since it announces a dislocation in the very element of social exchanges and an emptiness, a withdrawal of assent, in the very place where social apparatuses should be joined to what they claim to express. Our speech is moving outside social structures, but to indicate what they *lack*, that is, the adhesion and the participation of their subjects. (*PP* 38)

Certeau traced how this very much 'symbolic' (which does not mean ineffective) revolution was set in motion through a series of operations which 'created a network of symbols by taking a society's signs and inverting their sense' (*PP* 35). These two fundamental problematics – the gap between representations and those they are supposed to represent; the gap between orthodox symbolic languages and their utilization – again inform and generate the analyses of *La culture au pluriel* (1974) and *The Practice of Everyday Life* (1980). The latter, however, are no longer primarily concerned with the directly 'revolutionary' potential of these gaps. They operate in another cultural climate.

Roger Chartier has drawn attention to the lucidity which distinguished *La prise de parole*.[1] The book's subtitle – *Pour une nouvelle culture* [Towards a new culture] – nevertheless underlines the hopes which Certeau placed in the emergent forces which were rocking the symbolic equilibrium of the country. It has become a commonplace of cultural history to say that such hopes were to a large extent condemned to frustration.[2] Certeau's subsequent work on contemporary cultural practices retains, however, a modified but equally distinctive form of lucidity. He did not, like many contemporaries, lapse simply into a facile demonization of 'capitalist society' imagined as a monolithic bloc, nor did he indulge in compensatory utopian fantasy. His texts betray rather a fascination with the effective 'plurality', the disseminated multiplicity of contemporary societies. In this respect, the shifts symbolized by May

'68 have left their mark. 'Culture', for Certeau, like Christianity, had become 'shattered' (*éclaté*) into myriad pieces.[3] It could no longer be approached in terms of a universal literary or exclusively 'scriptural' model. His texts evince as a consequence an acute sense of the limits inherent in his own place and practice of writing:

> Analyses concerning culture border upon a silent immensity. As they walk along these shores of the inaccessible, they discover their irreducible limitation and, through this, their relation to a death. Obsessed by this rumour of a different country, I have to recognize that no text or institution could ever control the place where the rumble of machines, of tools, of kitchens, and the thousand sounds of creative activity all rise into the air. Innumerable lexicons, strange vocabularies. (*CP* 212–13)

Neither *La culture au pluriel* nor *The Practice of Everyday Life* address themselves in general to questions of comprehensive social reform. They cannot and do not claim to provide us in themselves with a self-sufficient framework for political action. They set out instead to contribute in a necessarily partial way to the opening of new symbolic and conceptual spaces. They suggest how other practices, with their 'foreign' or semi-effaced vocabularies, may insinuate their ways into the kinds of strategic programmes outlined in chapter 5 above. Certeau hopes thereby himself to 'alter' such programmes.

Certeau tends to conceive these 'other' practices as so many 'turns' which people carry out with regard to those mechanisms of control and standardized forms which set the terms of their existence. He organizes his analyses around the elements of a distinctive theoretical lexis: 'turn' (*tour*), 'detour', 'diversion' (*détournement*), 'inversion', 'conversion', 'subversion', 'torsion', 'trope', etc.[4] Such turns have in a sense a parasitical relation to the imposed order upon which they operate. Yet *The Practice of Everyday Life* in particular suggests how they also constitute the irreducible mark of the human subject within this order (the parasite here is essential to what life the host may possess). They correspond for Certeau to a series of tears in the superficial homogeneity of the social fabric. His work can in this respect be considered as an essential 'supplement' to analyses like that of Foucault in *Discipline and Punish*:

> If it is true that the grid of 'surveillance' is becoming everywhere more minute and extensive, it then becomes all the more urgent to uncover

the ways in which it does not absorb an entire society, what popular
procedures . . . play upon the mechanisms of discipline and conform
to them only in order to turn them around. (*PE* xiv/xxxix–xl)

Certeau carries out a series of displacements on standard interpretative approaches to non-institutionalized cultural fields. He
analyses the 'opacity' of popular cultures not as a function of archaic mystery or sheer incoherence but rather as the product of
specific 'techniques' of secretion or masking. He experimentally
defines a popular 'art' (*technè*) in terms of 'the tactical and joyful
dexterity involved in the mastery of a technique', and of 'a pleasure in getting around [*tourner*] the rules of a constraining space'
(*PE* 18/35–6). He argues that the stories circulating in popular
milieux should not be converted into repositories of some authentically popular 'spirit'. They can be considered instead as narrative
resources, repertories containing 'models of the good or bad tricks
[*tours*] that can be used each day' (*PE* 23/42). He envisages a
'popular art of speaking' not as a symbol of enchanting or disparaged naivety, but as so many 'turns of phrase (or "tropes") [which]
inscribe in ordinary language the ruses, displacements, ellipses,
etc., that scientific reason has eliminated from operational discourses
in order to constitute "proper" meanings' (*PE* 24/43). Likewise
Certeau explores ways of tracing the 'discreet inversions' (*PE* 31/
53) which take place when an official ideology is disseminated
among the people whom it is supposed to inform. He cites in this
respect the supposed Christianization of certain South American
Indian tribes. He also proposes as a quasi-paradigmatic figure for
these manifold 'turns' the practice of the *perruque*, whereby factory
workers 'divert' impersonal corporate time and residual industrial
material in order to create in makeshift fashion items which will
find their place in a network of family or friends.
    The Practice of Everyday Life is studded with such paradig-
matic figures (the poaching reader, graffiti on the underground . . .),
whose metonymic force of suggestion to some degree becomes
detached from their grounding in effective reality. Thus the example of the *perruque* is employed by Certeau as a mnemonic emblem.
He uses it both to demonstrate and to incite – in other places – 'the
resurgence of "popular" practices within industrial and scientific
modernity' (*PE* 25/45). These practices are in Certeau's view constrained but not defined by an order imposed from 'above', since
'the actual order of things is precisely what "popular" tactics turn
to their own ends, without any illusion that it is about to change'

(*PE* 26/46). There is nothing retarded or quaintly outdated about such practices. They constitute instead for Certeau constantly mutating responses to constantly mutating distributions of power in successive socioeconomic and symbolic formations.

The adjective 'popular', with or without scare-quotes, re-emerges in Certeau's writing in order to designate these practices. This does not mean that Certeau is simply repeating the interpretative move discussed above which forcefully defines and fixes its hypothetical object (see pp. 132–6). Certeau does not suppose either that the practices in question possess (are possessed by) an underlying 'essence', or even that they belong only to a particular place in society. Firstly, Certeau stresses how the sorts of 'turn' outlined above can take place within institutions of power and knowledge, and are thus not the distinguishing, quasi-exotic characteristic of a single socioeconomic class.[5] Secondly, the 'popular' is understood here neither as a transhistorical constant nor as an aesthetic category. It works rather as an unstable term for the analysis of hierarchical social organizations which divide a culturally 'productive' minority from a vast majority of apparently passive consumers. Indeed, the very term 'popular' comes to constitute a somewhat unwieldy and tautological tool through which to characterize the cultural practices of this majority. It tends to presuppose the homogeneity of these practices, which is precisely one of the problems of representation which must be addressed. Likewise it prohibits a meaningful approach to distributions of power which cut across the division between popular and elite, involving for example questions of gender, race, generation or language. Certeau experiments, therefore, with an alternative and more obviously conflictual analytic distinction – that between 'strategies' and 'tactics'.

Certeau's distinction between 'strategies' and 'tactics' presents a relative degree of conceptual clarity. It also constitutes an interpretative model which, while transportable, fosters by its very nature a close attention to the differences between the various divisions of power in heterogeneous social fields. Certeau defines the components of his theoretical artefact as follows:

I call a *strategy* the calculation (or manipulation) of power relationships that becomes possible as soon as a subject with will and power (a business, an army, a city, a scientific institution) can be isolated. It postulates a *place* that can be delimited as its *own* and serve as the base from which relations with an *exteriority* composed of targets or threats can be managed. (*PE* 35–6/59)

One can cite as examples of 'strategies' the political and epistemic operations discussed in the previous chapter. Such operations require an accumulated financial, symbolic and/or scientific 'capital', together with a corresponding measure of security and stability. 'Tactics', on the other hand, correspond to what I am presenting in this chapter as operations (or counter-operations) of 'diversion'. They are characterized for Certeau by insecurity, ephemerality and a high degree of mobility:

> I call a *tactic* a calculated action determined by the absence of a proper locus. . . . A tactic has no place but that of the other. Thus it must play on and with a terrain imposed on it and organized by the law of a foreign power. . . . It is a manoeuvre 'within the enemy's field of vision', as von Bülow put it, and within enemy territory. (*PE* 36–7/60–1)

'Tactical' practices are exposed upon a field controlled by a stronger force. They lack the fortifications and the assurances provided by multifarious kinds of capital. They must in Certeau's account make up for this by operating in a different way. Tactical agents must cater to their needs and desires by 'manipulating' and 'diverting' those spaces which strategies alone are able to 'produce, tabulate and impose' (*PE* 30/51). To tactics, as it were, the nocturnal stealth of the poacher; to strategies the infernal glare of surveillance.

It is worth pausing to consider a problematic aspect of this theoretical artefact as it is presented in *The Practice of Everyday Life*. If anything, the lines which it draws are too clear-cut. They occult some of the confusions which characterize the operations of power in contemporary society. The appeal which Certeau himself makes to the 'strategic' authority of Clausewitz masks a weak link in his argument:

> Tactics are an art of the weak. Clausewitz noted this fact in discussing trickery in his treatise *On War*. The more a power grows, the less it can allow itself to mobilize part of its means in the service of deception: it is dangerous to deploy large forces for the sake of appearances; this sort of 'demonstration' is generally useless and 'the gravity of bitter necessity makes direct action so urgent that it leaves no room for this sort of game.' One deploys one's forces, one does not take chances with feints. Power is bound by its very visibility. (*PE* 37/61)

This seems mistaken. The more strategic resources which an agency of power has at its disposal, the *more* it can afford to 'waste' on tactics designed to confuse, mislead or seduce its targets. One does not have to look far in contemporary society for the fragmentary evidence of simulative tactics in the service of more systematized forms of strategic 'intelligence'.[6] 'Strategies' and 'tactics' cannot necessarily be set against each other as opposing forces in a clearly defined zone of combat. Rather, as Certeau presents them, they enable us as concepts to discern a number of heterogeneous movements across different distributions of power.

Tactical 'turns' as Certeau conceives them alter the configuration of the sites and artefacts upon which they work. He analyses them as operations which set up and grasp so many 'occasions', drawing sustenance for this approach from the work of Marcel Détienne and Jean-Pierre Vernant on practical intelligence in classical Greece.[7] I shall to begin with abstract simply the broad lines of his analytic scheme. This scheme may be considered as an appendix to the model of systems and re-employments outlined in chapter 1.

At an initial level, Certeau posits 'turns' as operations upon an imposed spatial field. They exercise 'an aptitude for always being in the territory of the other without possessing it' (*PE* 87/131). They work on this synchronically conceived order by, as Certeau puts it, 'insinuating' into it other things. Fragments (citations, schemes, metaphors) are, for example, selected from memory and inserted into the present situation so as to turn it around. The memory of the individual (accumulated 'experience') operates here for Certeau in an analogous manner to the manifold historical archives of humankind. It constitutes a reserve of alterity, supplying 'heterological' resources and expedients which can be applied in different contexts. It 'mediates spatial transformations. Intervening at the "opportune moment" . . . it produces a founding rupture or break. Its foreignness makes possible a transgression of the law prevailing in a particular place. Emerging from its unplumbable and mobile secrets, a deft move [*coup*] modifies the local order' (*PE* 85/129). Memory has the capacity to alter contemporary space. The transformative 'insinuation' of an anomalous supplementary element into a prescribed order – an 'inscription of a private act upon a public register', to use the old French legal definition of the term[8] – represents for Certeau a basic formal model for the turn.

However, this operation cannot be reduced to one of mechanical insertion. If memory as such can necessarily only be acquired over a long duration, it can only be effective for the purposes of the 'turn' if the requisite fragment can be extracted, altered and applied in an instant. 'Tactical' practitioners do not have time at their disposal. They must respond to situations as they are affected, and retaliate as they are 'touched'. Certeau underlines the crucial importance of 'tact' (from the Latin, *tangere*, to touch) in the skill of successful 'insinuation', defining its art as 'the very transformation of touch into response, a "re-turning" of the surprise expected without being foreseen' (*PE* 88/132). The events which break in constantly to alter, say, a professional interlocutory exchange (oral interjections and interdictions, veiled threats, contractual slippages) must themselves be constantly negotiated, altered and 'returned' to their utterer. Indeed, this process of ongoing alteration takes us beyond the heuristic scheme opposing the strategic domination of a spatial field and the tactical insinuation of temporal alterity. The clear contours of this scheme fall away to show how the 'turn' must operate in an essentially mobile element. Opportunities and ripostes are not offered up as such but must be seized as they pass, set up as moving targets in transit. They come into existence only through the act itself which forcefully combines disparate elements to constitute unpredictable, ephemeral conjunctions. Whether broadly 'poetic' or retaliatory, tactical 'chances' for Certeau are grasped through a series of '*torsions* generated in a situation by the bringing together of qualitatively heterogeneous dimensions which are not merely contraries or contradictories' (*PE* 84/127).

I will show below how such fleeting and unstable syntheses organize Certeau's theorization of reading and spatial practices. More generally, they seem to work in his thought as a keystone of 'heterological' practice. We have already seen in chapter 4 how the poetic tropes of the mystics combine for him 'heterogeneous types of space . . . in the same setting' (*MF* 143/198). Such combinations turn conventional arrangements askew and take standard expectations by surprise. Certeau returns repeatedly to the manners in which diverse sets of circumstances may be altered or turned around by the tactical insinuation of foreign elements – 'everything seems the same within the structure into which a detail is introduced which nevertheless changes both its functioning and equilibrium' (*PE* 89/134). His analyses of cultural practices are characterized by a sustained focus on the virtual presences secreted by such insinuations into the deceptively homogeneous order of cultural representations.

Readings

Reading in an economy of writing

Certeau's concept of a 'scriptural economy' represents a guiding scheme in his thought. I have traced how he analyses European and colonial history by focusing on projects designed to 'produce a society through a "scriptural" system' (*PE* 167/241). I want now to explore the place which Certeau attributes to reading within such economies. As he does with regard to 'fables', Certeau problematizes the ways in which reading is suppressed or standardized, and he seeks to uncover the forms of its unsolicited returns.[9] This approach also serves to reconfigure a number of the questions raised in his work concerning the relation of interpretation to its 'other'. It suggests how these questions can be reconceived in terms of the complex tensions and interplay between certain types of 'writing' and certain types of 'reading'.

It may be helpful to begin by recapitulating the rudiments of Certeau's theory of a scriptural economy. Writing, then, assumes with modernity a 'mythical' status due to its operational capacity to articulate (to bring together and to repartition) in a strategic and quasi-encyclopedic manner a vast multiplicity of practices. It institutes the idea of a 'blank page' on which to order the elements of the social and natural world. Certeau talks of a 'capitalist and conquering scriptural enterprise' which combines 'the power of accumulating the past and that of bringing the alterity of the universe into conformity with its models' (*PE* 135/201). We have already explored in previous chapters certain political, linguistic and scientific facets of such strategic enterprises. One can speak of an 'economy' in so far as 'writing' (operations of recording, stocking, accumulation, standardization and so forth) constitutes the basis for an informational system governing the ways in which societies manage their resources and organize their practices. One can speak of 'myth' in so far as this activity ambivalently 'takes the place' of the authoritative 'origins' invoked by religiously ordered societies: 'the origin is no longer a story that is told, but is constituted rather by the multiform and murmuring activity of producing text and producing society as text' (*PE* 134/198).

Certeau sees a correlative of this myth in what he refers to as the ideology of '"information" by the book' (*PE* 166/240). By this he means the presupposition of cultural elites that what is written in places of authority has the power directly to mould or to in-form the social body into which it is disseminated. Of course such an assumption has a complicated archaeology. One could invoke the history of the Bible (the Book) and of its certified interpreters; of the 'enlightenment project' to rewrite and rationalize the social order; of the assumptions governing the circulation of information and cultural artefacts in a modern consumer society. Yet running through these discontinuous moments, Certeau discerns an enduring 'conviction that with greater or lesser degrees of resistance, the public is modelled by writing, whether verbal or iconic, that it becomes similar to what it receives, and finally that it is *imprinted* by and like the text which is imposed upon it' (*PE* 167/ 241). Successive economies of writing have for Certeau consistently occulted the act of reading as a specific operation. The ordinary reader has become nothing but the passive wax upon which competent interpreters, social engineers or machines write.

An overlooked activity

Reading as such constitutes a disconcerting object for theoretical reflection or historical analysis. As Certeau notes, 'the story of humankind's travels through its own texts remains in large measure unknown' (*PE* 170/246). The very nature of the activity, which leaves no lasting trace and which seldom speaks publicly of itself outside the restricted circles of more or less 'professional' readers, discourages – if it does not seduce – prospective scientific inquiry.

Certainly, a number of theories of 'reception' and 'reader-response' have developed and grown in sophistication over recent decades.[10] In a French context, a key reference here would be the pioneering work of Roland Barthes,[11] despite his quasi-programmatic disclaimers concerning his theoretical competence in this domain:

> I don't know if we have to have a *doctrine* on reading; I don't know if reading is not, constitutively, a plural field of dispersed practices, irreducible effects, and if, as a consequence, the reading of reading, a Meta-reading, is itself anything other than a scintillation of ideas, fears, desires, delights and oppressions.[12]

Subsequent thinkers have provisionally bracketed Barthes's deliberately assumed doctrinal 'disarray' in order to develop experimental approaches to the reality of reading. Michel Charles has mapped out notably what he calls a 'rhetorics of reading', a textual approach designed to uncover the ways in which writings carry within themselves the readings which they allow, and hence the ways in which they 'impose' themselves and 'demand' to be read.[13] Evidently, as intriguing as it is, such an approach can give only a rather one-sided account of the act of reading. Roger Chartier, by contrast, working after Certeau, has sought to set up as a historical object of study 'reading as a distinctive space of appropriation which is never reducible simply to what is read'.[14] He explores the ways in which the material and social conditions of the act of reading alter the meaning which this act produces. Chartier remains, however, acutely aware of the precariousness of such analyses. He speaks of the 'paradox underlying any history of reading, which is that it must postulate the liberty of a practice that it can only grasp, massively, in its determinations'.[15] Like the textual approach of Charles, Chartier's historiography ultimately runs up against the self-confessed limit of trying to think through a relationship while missing one of its terms.[16]

The blind spot and focus of a history or poetics of reading is thus the question of appropriation. What do specific readers 'make of' specific texts? The hermeneutics of Paul Ricoeur provides a helpful preliminary outline of the problem – although with his hermeneutical reverence for the letter of the text, Ricoeur tends to concentrate on what texts in general might make of a reader in general. Firstly, then, appropriation is a function of the 'distanciation' inherent in and constitutive of writing: 'An essential characteristic of a literary work' – and 'literary' should be understood here in a very wide sense – 'is that it transcends its own psycho-sociological conditions of production and thereby opens itself to an unlimited series of readings, themselves situated in different socio-cultural conditions.'[17] Yet there are limits to each reading in this potentially unlimited series. Most obviously, perhaps, there are textual limits: one cannot read *anything* in(to) a given text. In Ricoeur's account it is rather the reverse. The text appears as the dominant term in its relation to the reader and seems to dictate not only how it is to be read, but what the reader himself must become:

> Henceforth, to understand is *to understand oneself in front of the text*. It is not a question of imposing upon the text our finite capacity of understanding, but of exposing ourselves to the text and receiving from it an enlarged self, which would be the proposed existence corresponding in the most suitable way to the world proposed.... In this respect, it would be more correct to say that the *self* is constituted by the 'matter' of the text.[18]

Ricoeur's account of reading/appropriation can be used as a useful foil to that provided by Certeau. By way of transition, one should note three points of divergence with regard to the passages quoted above. Firstly, Certeau concentrates – at least in *The Practice of Everyday Life* – less on the self's exposure to the text than on the text's 'exposure' to the reading subject. Secondly, Certeau problematizes the question of 'corresponding in the most suitable way to the world proposed' by the text. For Certeau, the myriad demands and injunctions constitutive of such a 'proposal' should be situated in the force-field of socioeconomic constraints and institutional instances – a 'world' which Ricoeur's account seems consistently unwilling to take into consideration. Thirdly, if Certeau could accept in general that the reading subject is constituted by 'textual matter', he would none the less argue that, in each specific instance, a text is constituted only by a subject who is the carrier of a host of other by no means compatible 'texts'. In all but the most exceptional cases, it is an exaggeration to say that the self is constituted by the act of reading a single text. Rather, one could say that for Certeau the operation of reading enmeshes a text into an *agon* (or hypertext) of other texts, resulting in a series of collisions, elisions, displacements and acts of subjugation.[19] At one level, Certeau makes acts of reading more banal than Ricoeur. He emphasizes that interpretations must force their way through and defend themselves in a socioeconomic order. However, he also makes them more elusive (and seductive?). He shows how the 'matter' of the text forms the basis for a series of uncontrolled and errant 'metaphorizations'. I shall explore now these two opposing facets to Certeau's analyses of reading practices.

The institution of the 'literal sense'

The ideology of 'information by the book' evoked above rests on an essential presupposition, namely that the texts through which one wishes to 'inform' a given readership can be tied down to a limited number of 'literal' meanings. It is only when such a univocal sense can be established that the book becomes an efficacious means for social control. Certeau emphasizes, however, that literal significations are in fact the products of particular readings (or *lectiones*[20]) among others which tend to mask their status as such:

> The use made of the book by privileged readers sets it up as a secret of which they are the 'true' interpreters. It interposes a frontier between the text and its readers that can be crossed only if one has a passport delivered by these official interpreters, who transform their own reading (which is *also* a legitimate one) into an orthodox 'literality' which makes other (equally legitimate) readings either heretical (not 'in conformity' with the meaning of the text) or insignificant (abandoned to oblivion). (*PE* 171/248)

Writings, one could conclude, are never presented as such, but have always already been configured by particular manners of reading. Certainly, the text-in-itself does not exist. Yet this does not in Certeau's account lead simply to an indeterminate proliferation of readings. For the 'literal' meanings evoked above necessarily impose themselves. They are always constituted and disseminated according to specific socioeconomic constraints, institutional instances of certification and the fluctuating trends of what Pierre Bourdieu would call symbolic capital. Hence one can simply not *afford* to ignore the panoply of literal, socially endorsed meanings – meanings which can moreover be more or less conflictual according to the locus of their social legitimation. There is no such thing as an unproblematically free or wild reading. The shifting set of literal meanings may simply be possible readings among others, yet their social, epistemic and institutional leverage is such that they set the terms for more vagabondish or insecure practices of reading. They represent for Certeau 'the index and the result of a social power, that of an elite. In itself offered up for a plural reading, the text becomes a cultural weapon, a private hunting reserve, the pretext for a law that legitimizes as "literal" the interpretation given by *socially* authorized professionals and intellectuals' (*PE* 171/248).

Literal readings are thus overdetermined operations which must be analysed according to their function in a social and institutional network. We saw in chapter 1 how Certeau adopts a similar perspective in his work on contemporary historiography. Indeed, this work also points to the necessity of diverse forms of discursive control. Certain types of discourse aspiring to make certain kinds of truth-claim must be exposed to the 'falsifying' scrutiny of scientific or interpretative communities. This is a question which Certeau rather underplays in *The Practice of Everyday Life*. The book nevertheless demonstrates that other ('metaphorical') kinds of reading should not be treated in isolation. They should themselves be read in the shadow of multifarious instances of cultural disqualification or excommunication.

Poaching

The all too imposing reality of 'literal' readings should not, in Certeau's view, mislead us into believing that nothing else exists. There seem in Certeau's account to be at least two broad modes of living with these readings ('making do') without necessarily being taken in by or identifying with them. One could define the first mode as an 'impertinent absence'.[21] The second consists in various operations of 'diversion'.

At the heart of the 'impertinent absence' of the reader lies the vanishing point of unpredictable irony. If readers are not 'with the text', where are they? There is a distanciation constitutive of the act of reading (the same in the end as that constitutive of writing) which can, in a dubitative or hyperbolic moment, turn this activity against the economy of writing in which it takes place. Such instances of disenchantment or resistance figure in Certeau's writing as a series of marks or smudges between the lines of a quasi-autonomous scriptural production. One should invoke here Certeau's analysis of the 'celibate machines' which figure in the reflexive texts of early twentieth-century writers such as Franz Kafka. These figures problematize the process of writing as such. They present in the fantasmatic form of a nightmare a self-enclosed system of written production cut off from the altering effects of what lies outside it. They function in Certeau's thought as 'myths of an incarceration within the operations of a writing whose machinations extend indefinitely, and which never encounters anything but itself' (*PE* 150/220). He suggests how readers may keep their reservations with regard to this proliferation of concoctions. These reservations are by definition invisible to the producers of writing, too preoccupied with what they are putting together and with the enforcement of its correct interpretation to detect 'behind the theatrical décor of this . . . orthodoxy . . . the silent, transgressive, ironic or poetic activity of readers (or television viewers) who maintain their own views in private and without the knowledge of the "masters"' (*PE* 172/249). It is the guiding premise of Certeau's analyses that this silent activity exists in differing forms. Naturally, one cannot dogmatically affirm that this is always and everywhere the case. Against the spectacular colonizing successes of scriptural economies, however, Certeau postulates a multiplicity of effaced blind spots. These represent in his writing the virtual alterity of obliquely reading subjects.[22]

Indeed, Certeau suggests how ordinary reading practices may serve precisely to produce a 'reserve'. They may constitute spaces set off from the compound pressures exerted by instances of socio-economic control and constraint. The distanciation inherent in the act of reading would here work to set up unlikely sites of pleasure or solace. It both fosters an ironic detachment from the world imposed on the reader, and secretes, as it were, a strangely protective opacity. To read is to be transported 'elsewhere, where *they* are not, in another world; it is to set up a secret scene, a place one can enter and leave as one wishes; to create recesses of shadow and night in an existence subjected to technocratic transparency' (*PE* 173/250). Reading provides here in Certeau's account a retreat from 'them' – from a form of *autrui* ('other people') understood perhaps in the infernal Sartrean sense, as much as from the inscrutable scribes and the jealous guardians of a senseless law which haunt the writings of Franz Kafka.

Naturally, this space of relative autonomy must find its place in a socioeconomic force-field. It risks degenerating into a mere alibi, a rather weak insistence that 'life is elsewhere' (Kundera) and a pretext for manifold forms of escapist fantasy. Equally, it becomes easier (potentially more 'facile') to establish such retreats as one ascends the sociocultural hierarchy. Nevertheless, Certeau seeks to foreground at least in a metaphorical manner the disseminated indices of an immense 'virtual' space. He points to an uncertified and invisible movement across the organized textual surfaces of written production. This movement – gleaning, poaching, making do – ought to make any cultural history based (inevitably) on writings and representations appear merely as the tip of an iceberg, a drop in the ocean:

> Far from being writers – founders of their own place, heirs of the peasants of earlier ages now working on the soil of language, diggers of wells and builders of houses – readers are travellers; they pass through lands belonging to someone else, like nomads poaching their way across fields they did not write, despoiling the wealth of Egypt to enjoy it themselves. (*PE* 174/251)

Yet it is also too easy to invoke an impertinent absence or opacity as the paradoxical guarantee of a relative autonomy. Precisely because the 'impertinent reader' is not there, he or she can be insinuated *in absentia* into any argumentative or poetic edifice. Hence Certeau explores also more nuanced approaches to the study of common and aberrant textual itineraries.

Certeau's own 'manner of reading' these readings operates by abstracting some of their recurrent forms. He focuses again on the 'formality' of practices in order to suggest how these formalities themselves work on the standardized forms which they appropriate. It is worth pausing briefly to ask what relation these formal

analyses bear to more conventional kinds of interpretative practice. On the one hand, much of Certeau's enterprise seems to be
directed against the desire to interpret, in so far as this aspires
to catch ordinary practices with their serpentine mobility in the
unwieldy nets of scientific explanation. On the other hand, interpretation of one sort or another is surely inevitable. It seems most
helpful to see Certeau as forging a series of interpretative tools for
what Jacques Revel has called a 'hermeneutics of the present'.[23]
Certainly, such a hermeneutics would be a paradoxical enterprise
(Certeau himself shows something of an allergy towards the term).
It belongs perhaps to the second stage of a larger interpretative
project. It points the way beyond an exclusive preoccupation with
representations and texts, together with their manifest or 'deep'
meanings, towards questions of practice and usage. Its interpretative
ambition is apparent in its attempt to expose the limits of strategically simplified conceptions of the social order. Its supplementary
paradox is that it takes as its object precisely those practices which
destabilize interpretative categories and fixations. In the light of
this displacement, the interpretative tools refined by Certeau can
be considered as limited formal models. They cannot be automatically applied to any situation, but can enable us to discern
more clearly the overlooked implications of practices disseminated
throughout the social body. I shall isolate here three models for
reading which Certeau offers in the course of his analyses.

(1) I have already discussed the logic of 're-employments' as it
operates in Certeau's work. It is relatively straightforward to transfer this as a model to the practice of reading – indeed it could have
been introduced as a generalized model of reading in the first place.
Certeau analyses reading as an operation which takes elements
from the writings it traverses and 're-employs' them in different
ways, taking them up in a series of unpredictable conjunctions and
elisions. The reader 'invents in texts something different from what
they "intended". He detaches them from their origin, now lost or
merely incidental. He combines their fragments and creates something un-known in the space organized by their capacity for allow-
ing an indefinite plurality of meanings' (*PE* 169/245). Texts are
thus 'diverted' or rerouted as one can divert a river, capital or
traffic. They are consciously or unconsciously fragmented and their
constituent parts turned this way and that to enter into makeshift
transitory conglomerates. 'Following' an act of reading (as an interpreter 'follows' a musical score) thus becomes an impossible and

intriguing operation in its own right. Certeau evokes analyses which pursue 'the activity of reading in its detours, drifts across the page, metamorphoses and anamorphoses of the text produced by the travelling eye, imaginary or meditative flights taking off from a few words, overlappings of spaces on the militarily organized surfaces of writing, and ephemeral dances' (*PE* 170/246).

Certeau compares this activity of selection and recombination, creation and concomitant destruction, to the practice of intellectual 'bricolage' as defined by Lévi-Strauss. The latter opposes 'bricolage' to the strategic operations of the modern scientist or social engineer, who conceive and implement their plans through recourse to specifically designed technical apparatuses. Lévi-Strauss contrasts these with the 'diverted means' (*moyens détournés*) employed by the 'bricoleur', who sets his or her ideas in motion 'with the help of a repertoire whose composition is heterogeneous and . . . limited'. He speaks of the compromises by which one 'makes do with "whatever is at hand"' and of a makeshift 'poetry of bricolage', through which the different fragments of a repertoire are put together.[24] Certeau emphasizes the agonistic as well as the poetic possibilities of these circumstantial combinations. They may work as 'tactical' operations of re-employment in situations where resources are scant and where there is limited room for manoeuvre.

(2) 'Metaphorization', a recurrent term in Certeau's writing, provides him with a further model for reading practices. The term signifies here quite simply the transfer of a sign from one thing to another.[25] He uses it to designate the proliferation of quid pro quo's which take place in the process of reading, as one thing is repeatedly 'taken for' another. A word, a passage, an image come to stand for something quite different to the sense intended by their producer. They stir in the reader strange new resonances, they are incorporated in unpredictable ways. There is an 'errance du sémantique' (Derrida), a transport of signs and sense. The oblique appropriations of readers carry out a metaphorical twist upon the letter of a text.

In this respect the text assumes in Certeau's analysis a peculiar in-between status. It only exists for the reader in the act of appropriation, and yet this act alters it. The reader reflects 'upon' the text, and yet the text operates 'upon' (within) the reader. We have already seen how a chiastic structure of two-way transformation (an 'abyss of alteration') informs Certeau's reading of history (see pp. 38–43 and 90–4 above). The realm of the quid pro quo (who and what is where?) dissolves analytic demarcations between reading subject and written text:

> A television viewer says of the programme she watched the previous evening: 'It was stupid, but I sat there all the same.' What place captivated her, which was and yet was not that of the image she saw? It is the same with the reader: his place is not *here* or *there*, one or the other, but neither one nor the other, simultaneously inside and outside, dissolving both by mixing them together, associating dormant texts which he brings to life and to which he plays host, but which he never owns. (*PE* 174/251)

Certeau's phrasing recalls here the vertiginous, mobile stratifications which he conceives elsewhere as so many historical 'archaeologies'. His analyses suggest how the social and institutional instance of the 'literal' sense is transported and finally diffracted – 'shattered through the universe into a thousand bodies'[26] – in the labyrinthine detours of the reader's secret historicity.

(3) We saw at the beginning of this chapter how the concept of 'insinuation' informs Certeau's analysis of the 'turn'. He understands by this the introduction of a supplementary element, bearing the mark of the individual subject, into a structured composition of other elements in such a way as to alter the configuration and hence the signification of these elements. Certeau evokes the theory and practice of medieval poets, who subtly inserted innovatory devices into the terms of a literary tradition. He suggests that this can supply a model for the analysis of modern reading practices. He thereby places them in what could be seen as an alternative, strictly speaking paradoxical tradition of 'insinuation': 'these poetic ruses, which are not bound to the creation of a proper (written) place of their own, have endured through the centuries and into contemporary reading, which is just as agile in practicing diversions and metaphorizations that sometimes are hardly even indicated by a shrug of the shoulders' (*PE* 175/252). Certeau's work explores the ways in which agents may bring something of their own to the received texts and representations through which they move (or which move through them). One ought nevertheless to note the questionable exemplarity of the example cited above. The minimal nature of this insinuation – a disparaging shrug of the shoulders – evokes the more problematic side of the forms of distanciation which Certeau is seeking to analyse. I will examine

such problems at greater length in the concluding section of this chapter.

Certeau works on models designed to exhume ordinary practices of reading from the night of their supposed passivity. He shows how they can be understood as a series of operations generated according to distinctive 'poetic' principles (he recalls the etymological force of the Greek, *poiein*: to create, invent, generate). In this respect,

> reading is situated at the intersection of a *social* stratification (class relationships) and *poetic* operations (the textual constructions of practitioners): a social hierarchization works to bring readers into conformity with the 'information' distributed by an elite (or semi-elite); readers use their wits ... to insinuate through their operations their inventiveness into the cracks of cultural orthodoxy. (*PE* 172/249)

In the first instance this leads to an opposition between 'writers' and 'readers', as between proprietors and poachers. There are, however, plenty of elements in Certeau's own writing which complicate this opposition. The emphasis on the 'poetic', creative nature of reading practices, for example, brings these to figure as types of active 'writing' – albeit writings which are always more or less under erasure. Generally such writings are covered over by the imposition of a 'literal' sense, but Certeau notes how 'as the institution weakens, there appears the reciprocity between the text and its readers, previously hidden by the institution. It is as though it brought to the surface through its withdrawal the indefinite plurality of the "writings" produced by readings' (*PE* 172/249).

We saw in chapter 2 how Certeau invoked the possibility of this 'reciprocity' (or altercation) between reader and prescribed forms in order to challenge modern interpretations of early modern popular religious practices. On the one hand, Certeau argues that both early modern and modern societies can usefully be analysed in terms of differing 'economies of writing'. On the other hand, his own analyses problematize in acute fashion the workings of these economies. His work suggests how they may be overrun by a swarm of other readings, writings and voices. At one level, Certeau's 'economical' conceptual models serve perhaps as a necessary textual platform on which to stage these excessive movements and crosscurrents. They set out the conditions in which such movements must operate, but also place them in dramatic relief. Certeau thereby confronts authoritative interpretations with a set of practices which they cannot assimilate, and which work directly to expose the limits of such interpretations.

The reconception of reading practices as forms of rewriting produces a significant displacement in the movement of Certeau's thought. I shall now explore his treatment of spatial practices in terms of a tension between effaced tactical 'writings' and the failure of strategic attempts to read these writings.

Itineraries

Unreadable writings

Certeau opens his discussion of spatial practices in *The Practice of Everyday Life* with a striking figure. He presents the view over New York from the top of the World Trade Center, a powerful experience for the elevated spectator whereby the 'agitation' of the metropolis is converted into a strange 'texturology' (*PE* 91/139). Certeau evokes an absorption/detachment in a peculiar optical intoxication, a kind of rush or fantasy of power, as if the city were handed over for an absolute (unbound) reading: the 'elevation transfigures one into a voyeur. It puts one at a distance. It transforms the bewitching world by which one was "possessed" into a text that lies before one's eyes. It allows one to read it, to be a solar Eye, a divine gaze' (*PE* 92/140). Yet this ecstatic reading is predicated for Certeau upon a form of amnesia. In order to survey the city, the onlooker loses sight of the myriad of tangled practices which form the obscure fabric of urban experience: 'like Icarus flying above these waters, he can ignore the devices of Daedalus in mobile and endless labyrinths far below' (*PE* 92/140). The function of his initiatory ascent is to manufacture a simulacrum of interpretative control. Certeau elevates the World Trade Center into a paradigmatic operator of strategic readings: 'the 1370 foot high tower that serves as a prow for Manhattan continues to construct the fiction that creates readers, that transforms the complexity of the city into readability and freezes its opaque mobility in a transparent text' (*PE* 92/141).

The 'complexity' of the city, rather like the fantasmatic stratification of Freud's Rome (see above p. 43), cannot for Certeau be reproduced on a flat surface. Neither can it be made directly visible to the naked eye. We have already seen how Pierre Bourdieu problematizes the interpretative operations which produce 'synoptic' readings. Like Bourdieu, Certeau emphasizes that the representation which the onlooker has before his eyes is a seductive but finally deceptive artefact. It substitutes for the effective practices of passers-by a more or less stable configuration of retinal traces. A similar quid pro quo takes place for Certeau when itineraries are charted upon a map – cartographic 'traces of journeys miss what was: the act itself of passing by. The operation of walking, wandering . . . is transposed into points that draw upon the map a totalizing and reversible line' (*PE* 97/147). Certeau does not dispute the heuristic validity of such procedures, but challenges rather any implicit assumption that they master reality. As he does with regard to the documentation of the historian, he foregrounds the absences which professional surveyors are all too willing to mask.

Beneath or between the facsimiles produced by panoramic readings, Certeau projects an imbricated multiplicity of transitory 'writings'. These correspond to criss-crossing movements traversing the social order, whose traces, so to speak, have 'always already' been erased or altered, taken up or absorbed into the alterations they themselves produce in this social order or in other 'writings'. Certeau attempts to introduce into his analyses – or perhaps just metaphorically to stage – a proliferation of fleeting, unreadable inscriptions upon the deceptive stability of urban space:

> The ordinary practitioners of the city live 'down below', below the thresholds at which visibility begins. They walk – an elementary form of this experience of the city; they are walkers, *Wandersmänner*, whose bodies follow the ups and downs of an urban 'text' they write without being able to read it. . . . The paths which respond to each other in this intertwinement, unrecognized poems of which each body is an element signed by many others, elude legibility. It is as though the practices organizing a bustling city were characterized by a form of blindness. The networks of these moving, intersecting writings compose a manifold history that has neither author nor spectator. (*PE* 93/141)

The 'blindness' which Certeau evokes is ambivalent. On the one hand it signifies the demise of the panoptic desire to read the peripatetic 'writings' of the city. On the other hand it characterizes these writings themselves, caught up in the labyrinthine twists and turns which they seek to negotiate and of which they form a part.

They are both 'knowing' (artful, street-wise, in touch) and unknowing (parts of a mutating whole). Certeau adopts implicitly himself the fiction of a bird's eye view in order to present the blindness of these 'networks of moving, intersecting writings' while at the same time demonstrating this fiction itself to be 'blind'. There is no way out. One should nevertheless comment briefly on the work which the figure of blindness performs in Certeau's own reading of urban spatial practices. It is significant that he evokes in a footnote Descartes's invocation of the blind man as the guarantor of the true (tactile) knowledge of things against the illusions of sight (*PE* 218/ 321). There is a rhetorical opposition at work in these pages of *The Practice of Everyday Life* between a 'visual' knowledge fissured by the very distanciation which constitutes it and a 'tactile' knowledge all the more authentic or 'immediate' for its lack of vision. This opposition is clearly problematic. It holds out a metaphorical opportunity for a facile rehabilitation of 'common sense' as it is conventionally opposed to the alienating abstraction of critique. This danger should be borne in mind even as the figure operates an important conceptual transition in Certeau's writing: those who see are shown in an important sense to be blind, those deemed blind are shown to operate or to 'write' according to complex forms of logic and knowledge.

It may be helpful to develop further the idea of these itinerant 'writings' in so far as they cannot immediately be identified with the practice of arranging signs upon a standard textual support. They may be conceived as an activity of 'insinuation'. In an earlier piece, and in a rather different context, Certeau gives a useful definition of what we can understand for our present purposes as 'writing':

> In a very broad sense, I call 'writing' the tracing of a desire in the system of a language (this language can be professional, political, scientific, etc., and not simply literary) – and hence also, as one says in law, the 'insinuation' into a body (a corpus of laws, a social body, the body of a language) of a movement which alters it.[27]

The 'writing' in question inscribes itself upon a corpus of the already written. It is therefore inseparable from a 'body', which Certeau goes on in the same passage to describe as 'the historical and social being-there of an organized site'. Writings in this broad sense would thus be signifying practices which operate upon, alter and displace the variously significant material which they meet through their movement. Their ephemeral trace would be precisely this alteration – an alteration which affects them as much as the urban or linguistic 'body' which they move across. Moreover, any such mark which they leave would be rapidly effaced and/or incorporated by other 'writings'. They correspond to errant operations at work below the threshold of readability.

Certeau proposes another paradigmatic, excessive figure for this teeming swarm of insinuatory activity (indeed, the deliberate sublegal connotations of this and other rhetorical figures in *The Practice of Everyday Life* raise problems which we will consider below):

> If despite everything an illustration were required, then it would be the images in transit, yellow-green and metallic blue calligraphies that howl without raising their voices and streak the subterranean passages of the city, traceries of letters and numbers, perfect gestures of violence painted with a pistol, Shivas in writing, dancing graphics whose fleeting apparitions are accompanied by the rumble of subway trains: the graffiti of New York. (*PE* 102/154)

The sort of aberrant (bio)graphical itineraries which Certeau retraces in *The Mystic Fable* are dispersed also in metaphorical fragments in his analyses of contemporary culture. Certainly, what Samuel Kinser calls the 'superbly idealistic' partiality of this part of Certeau's oeuvre is nowhere more apparent than here.[28] Many readers would not want to describe in such choreographic terms the inscriptions and defacements which they may have encountered in the course of their own banal transits through different metropolitan subways. Nevertheless, one should note how the figure of these invisible underground transports (*metaphorai*) combines symbolically in Certeau's text with the panoptic figure of the World Trade Center. The two images serve in conjunction to project a peculiar asymmetry between redefined practices of 'writing' and 'reading'. This figural asymmetry dislocates in its turn the conception of an orthodox 'economy of writing'. This concept is thrown strangely off balance. It is as though Certeau wanted to show both how a modern economy of writing works – and also how it does not work, how it breaks down, overrun by a proliferation of other kinds of 'writing' which it cannot control.

Prescribed path and rhetorical trope

Certeau employs a basic analogy to take his analysis of spatial practices beyond a mere critique of representations. This analogy follows on from the interpretative move which turns ambulatory itineraries into so many 'writings' (and vice versa). Certeau suggests that one can usefully transfer to manners of inhabiting and moving across a spatial order those interpretative categories generally applied to manners of inhabiting and traversing a linguistic order: 'the courses taken by passers-by present a series of turns and detours that can be compared to "turns of phrase" or "stylistic figures". There is a rhetoric of walking. The art of "turning" phrases finds an equivalent in an art of "diverting" itineraries' (*PE* 100/151).[29] He situates such spatial 'turns' in a field of signifying practices analogous to that constituted by the institutions of literal meaning and the proliferation of errant readings discussed above. He supposes that 'practices of space are, like the tropes of rhetoric, deviations relative to a sort of "literal meaning" defined by the urbanistic system' (*PE* 100/151). Of course, as with the interpretation of texts, such a literal sense is not grounded in a single underlying reality. Rather, it is the necessarily artificial production of powerful readings and writings. Moreover, in the context of an urban order, it works to a greater degree as a virtual, heuristic object than is the case with authoritative textual readings, which can more readily be identified as such. The symbolic environment of the city, beyond the misleading clarity of the street-plan, is set up by a shifting network of prescribed routes, standard itineraries, rumour, social divisions and prohibitions against which individual detours take their meaning and direction.

Certeau, after Augoyard, sees two fundamental rhetorical tropes at work in ordinary spatial practices: synecdoche and asyndeton.[30] Synecdoche first: one can usefully approach urban experience by following the way in which parts come to stand for wholes. A street becomes represented for a pedestrian by a favourite café, the forbidding or reassuring presence of a police patrol, a familiar window, the evocative power of a name. A train station becomes detached from its surroundings, a factory or sports ground absorbs into itself the meaning of a district. The city becomes cut up into a multiplicity of fragments which operate as invisible, quasi-subliminal poles of attraction and repulsion. The affective charge of these fragments interferes with the strictly functional negotiation of a spatial order. Asyndeton is in effect an inevitable corollary to this process of selection and recombination. The standard liaisons and connections which constitute the objective or 'literal' cohesion of the city fall away. Differing instrumentations of these fundamental tropes produce for Certeau characteristic itinerant 'styles', breaking open a multiplicity of singular paths upon a prescribed spatial order: 'through these swellings, shrinkings, and fragmentations – that is, through a work of rhetoric – a spatial phrasing of a particular type is created, both anthological (composed of juxtaposed citations) and elliptical (made up of gaps, lapses, and allusions)' (*PE* 101–2/153). The tropes of synecdoche and asyndeton supply again basic 'models'. They help us to describe the ways in which inhabitants appropriate their environment. Firstly, the subject detaches and cathects isolated fragments of larger wholes (this activity could be analysed also as an insinuation of metaphor). Secondly, these fragments are concatenated to create what Certeau calls 'spatial stories'.[31]

The function of place names in individual itineraries provides a suggestive illustration of metaphorical insinuation into an objective order. It also constitutes a significant bridge between a strictly linguistic and a spatial 'rhetoric' (the analogy between a 'linguistic' and a 'spatial' order may be problematic for some, but a strict demarcation between the two is surely impossible). With time and practice, the proper names of places become overdetermined. They become incorporated by passers-by in ways irreducible to their strictly designatory function in an urban layout. Certeau cites names like *Place de l'Étoile, Concorde, Poissonnière*, which for him become transformed into metaphors, abstracted and reincarnated in a multiplicity of experiential cityscapes:

> Bringing together movements and footsteps, opening up meanings and directions, these words operate through an emptying-out and wearing-away of their primary role. They thereby become liberated spaces that can be occupied. A rich indetermination gives them, through a semantic rarefaction, the function of articulating a second, poetic geography on top of the geography of literal, forbidden or permitted meaning. They insinuate other routes into the functionalist and historical order of urban movement. (*PE* 105/157–8)

These metaphorical by-ways represent, as it were, other forms of those lapses of history which Certeau discerns in the history of *mystics*. They can be analysed as 'turns'. They insinuate a 'folded' time into the dimensions of public space. The com-plications of an individual social existence (associations, desires, fears), buried in the unreadability of an opaque past, form the basis for his or her appropriation of an objective order. In this respect, the manifest existence of the city's landmarks and streets ceases to figure as a self-evident given. As with the documents/monuments of history, the meaning they hold for others is withdrawn from the onlooker's gaze. Places become for Certeau 'fragmentary histories, folded away as pasts that others are not allowed to read, accumulated layers of time that can be unfolded but tend rather to remain there as stories waiting to be told, as rebuses or mute symbolizations encysted in the pain or pleasure of the body' (*PE* 108/163).

This second, poetic geography is not a reductively aestheticized or ethereal construct. It represents rather a 'practical' geography in so far as it is a product of the ways in which inhabitants actually put their environments 'into practice'. Nor is it opposed to a 'literal' geography as private to public, individual to social. Certeau works with a notion of *poeisis* which is inseparable from the realm of everyday social exchanges, ties and constraints, and which displaces the more narrowly literary affiliations of the term. This is not to say that a distinction between private and public is irrelevant for the analysis of the metaphorizations outlined above. Indeed at one stage Certeau proposes – a little disturbingly – the 'wandering lines' (*lignes d'erre*) produced by autistic children as an emblem of the itineraries which he is analysing (*PE* 34/57). Nevertheless, the poetic geographies which emerge from Certeau's analyses are informed through and through by social pressures and configurations (which may themselves work to produce forms of social autism[32]). We can see this very clearly in the suggestive analyses contained in the second volume of *L'Invention du quotidien*, where Pierre Mayol and Luce Giard take up respectively the ways in which a group of working-class residents appropriate the Croix-Rousse quarter of Lyons, and the 'implications' of ordinary cooking practices.[33]

Stories

The 'poetic' fragments evoked above do not remain in isolation. They are recombined and strung together to form distinctive sequential itineraries. Certeau refers to these as 'spatial stories' (*récits d'espace*). By extension, these stories are also metaphors. They take figures out of a pre-established context and they appropriate them as 'transports'. They incessantly reconfigure the urban and rural environment. They twist received senses and directions, 'carrying' people from one symbolic place to another. Certeau notes how 'in Athens today, the vehicles of public transport are called *metaphorai....* Stories could also carry this fine name: every day, they traverse and organize places; they select and bind them together; they make sentences and itineraries out of them. They are spatial journeys' (*PE* 115/170). These stories work as the cultural life-blood of any social environment. They form through their exchange a general and predominantly oral narrative flux. The banalized, sensational or totalizing 'rumours' produced by diverse 'media' (*PE* 107–8/161–2) combine with the stratified and proliferating murmur of singular, aberrant or effaced itineraries (every story is in one sense a travel story).

We saw in chapter 1 how, for Certeau, the 'historiographical operation' may constitute a particular form of critical intervention in this narrative flux. The professional historian cuts into the scripturally uncontrolled myths carried by hearsay. At another level, of course, he or she supplies new myths, new stories. Certeau evokes powerfully the disorientation which confronts individual subjects when they are deprived of stories which 'speak' to them, or which promise convincingly to lead them somewhere:

> Where stories disappear (or are reduced to museographical objects), there is a loss of space: deprived of narrations (as we see now in the city, now in the country), the group or the individual regresses towards the disturbing, fatalistic experience of a formless, indistinct and nocturnal totality. (*PE* 123/182)

Stories open paths. They introduce otherness into familiar space (they are 'citations and recitations of the other'). They implicate speakers and hearers in a disseminated multiplicity of 'heterologies'. They constitute for Certeau perhaps the fundamental fable upon which we inscribe our truths. They refigure and prefigure the forms taken by an itinerant *poeisis*.

The products of the metaphorizations analysed by Certeau are stories or 'writings' whose ins and outs combine beneath the threshold of any single readable surface. They are what make a city inhabitable, they are commonplace, and yet by their very nature they elude the schemes and representations produced in institutions of interpretative and scientific control. Against varying odds, urban inhabitants thread their complex and makeshift ways through the places which others have constructed. They create 'within the planned city a "metaphorical" or mobile city, as dreamed of by Kandinsky: "a great city built according to all the rules of architecture and then suddenly shaken by a force that defies all calculation"' (*PE* 110/164). The plurality of such 'metaphorical' towns and itineraries constitute both the object of Certeau's analyses in *The Practice of Everyday Life* and the book's vertiginous backdrop.

Problems

Certeau's work problematizes the mastery which forms of scientific or learned interpretative practice aspire to achieve with regard to their uninformed 'others'. He translates the 'turns' produced by ordinary readers and walkers into forms of active 'writing'. He seeks thereby to contest the representations of a largely passive and controllable exterior space which tend to prevail in 'strategic' milieux. He uncovers a range of procedures which convert urban environments into migrational patchworks and a 'common poetics' whose indices emerge – 'like bubbles rising up from watery depths' (*PE* 172/249) – to challenge more exclusively cultivated displays of reading. He shows how the textual and architectural spaces instituted by diverse forms of strategic operation may be seen, as it were, to 'secrete' a host of other operations. He aspires less to interpret other representations and texts (to explicate their meaning) than to specify some of the practices through which representations and texts may be appropriated and subverted. This is not to say that he can avoid the partiality implied by a set of interpretative presuppositions ('it is always good to remind ourselves that we musn't take people for fools' (*PE* 176/255)). Nevertheless, Certeau thereby obliges the reader to rethink what is generally too easily thought as the 'social order', the constitution of the *polis*. This intellectual task is in Certeau's work both marked and induced by a corresponding imaginary displacement in representations of urban life (see pp. 154–6 above). He foregrounds the operative nature of practices effaced by the clamourous productions of a society organized around a 'scriptural economy'. He postulates – or extrapolates from – a hidden reserve of creativity and inventiveness which he places under the rubric of the common *poeisis* evoked above – a designation which, as we saw, draws on the etymological force of the Greek term signifying creation, invention, generation. This *poeisis* does not take place in an exclusively 'cultural' sphere, but corresponds rather to modes of operation which are always relative to changing socioeconomic circumstances.

For Certeau, a full conception of political life is inseparable from the reality of this diffuse 'poetics'.

The central thrust of *The Practice of Everyday Life* is thus to affirm the resilience and inventiveness of 'ordinary men and women' against the analyses which present them as entirely informed or crushed by the economic and cultural apparatuses which set the terms of social life. Certainly, it is extremely reductive to schematize the book as belonging on one pole of a 'populist–miserabilist' debate.[34] I discussed in chapter 5 the seminal critique which Certeau addressed in *La culture au pluriel* to idealizing constructions of 'popular culture'. Nevertheless, Certeau clearly intended *The Practice of Everyday Life* to work as a corrective intervention in an intellectual field dominated by bleak constatations of the 'miserabilist' variety. As a consequence, his writing is not entirely immune from the dangers inherent in advocating on principle the worth of the 'popular' (despite the displacement effected by the critical dissection of this term). It seems therefore useful, in order to preserve the tension which characterizes the book, to return to some of the fundamental theses laid out in 1957 by Richard Hoggart in his classic work *The Uses of Literacy*. These concern in particular the question of 'resilience' and the figure of the 'ordinary man'.

Much of Hoggart's book is devoted to exhuming forms of resilience in a way which prefigures to some degree Certeau's later analyses. Hoggart sounds, however, a note of caution:

> The resilience to be found in individuals and local groups is healthy and important. But it can clearly be another form of democratic self-indulgence to overstress this resilience, to brush aside any suggestion of increasingly dangerous pressures by a reference to the innate right-headedness of man; to point out that people still do persist in living lives by no means as rootless and shallow as the new influences seem to invite, and from that to assume that this will always be so, that 'human nature will always save itself.'[35]

Of course, Certeau does not invoke human nature as such as a guarantee of the resilience and reserve which he sets up as objects of analysis. Yet he tends to assume that there will always be a given quota of inventiveness to ensure that people can 'get round' whatever mechanisms seek to organize and inform them. One misses in Certeau's account a note of threat, the sense that what he is analysing can never be guaranteed but can undeniably be stamped out in specific cases (an extreme example would be the behaviour of the popular majorities in Nazi or totalitarian states[36]).

Likewise Certeau tends to valorize resistance as such, whereas this may constitute in some cases a damaging problem which has to be addressed. To cite Hoggart again:

> Eventually, nothing in this big world can move the 'common man' as a 'common man'. He is infinitely cagey; he puts up so powerful a silent resistance that it can threaten to become a spiritual death, a creeping paralysis of the moral will. We hear much of the gullibility of working-class people, and have seen that there is plenty of evidence for its existence. But this disillusionment presents as great a danger now, and one which . . . they share with other classes. Outside the personal life they will believe almost nothing consciously; the springs of assent have nearly dried up.[37]

Hoggart saw such generalized disillusionment leading to a 'contracting-out', a 'loss of moral tension'.[38] Certainly, Certeau is acutely aware of the problems associated with a generalized loss of credibility as regards the political and institutional fabric of a society.[39] But one needs to supplement this with an account of the vicious circle by which a loss of credibility breeds 'resistance', the valorization of which in turn further saps the credibility (the necessary symbolic 'credit') without which a democracy ceases to function as such, while its subjects greet with self-confirming cynicism all forms of state intervention.

Moreover, the forms of metaphorically charged sublegal 'resistance' which emerge at intervals in Certeau's writing may well provoke in their turn a resistance or malaise in the mind of a contemporary reader – the symptom, perhaps, of a shift which has taken place over recent years in the symbolization of our social environment. There is a darker side to conflictual tactics, graphic violence, poaching, misappropriations (*détournements*) and sublegal groupings which is not addressed in *The Practice of Everyday Life*. As Samuel Kinser asks:

> Are the tactical shortcuts and tricks that we sometimes develop and sometimes forget the same as the ones used on occasion by the poor huddled masses yearning to be free, who, tired of waiting, kick open the golden door with the ruses of racketeering? . . . Violence today . . . appears as multiform as the ordinary person's ruses. It shocks us not merely in a newspaper's sensational accents but in more intimate ways – unemployed friends, acquaintances mugged on the subway, children's bicycles stolen repeatedly, hands and hats outstretched along the streets. This kind of daily life cannot be countered with more

trickery, just as appeals to total, violent replacement of ill-working social arrangements seem . . . derisively unrealistic.[40]

The Practice of Everyday Life proposes what Kinser calls an 'inspiring vision' of how social life might be conducted. This should not blind its contemporary readers to the inevitable limitations of the book.

A final reservation I should express here concerns the question of the 'ordinary man' to whom, albeit with a distinctive form of irony and qualification, Certeau dedicates *The Practice of Everyday Life*.[41] For it is easy to forget that he does not exist. In Hoggart's words, we must 'remember, every day and more and more, that in the last resort there is no such person as "the common man". If we do not, we may in the end have allowed individual decision to slip away in our dutiful democratic identification of ourselves with a hypothetical figure whose main value is to those who will mislead us.'[42] It is not that Certeau urges any such identification. But his invocation 'at the threshold of his stories' (*PE* v/11) of this fantasmatic, impossible figure (his *other*), needs to be read with half an eye on other rhetorical invocations of the term (by the Moral Majority, by the tabloid press, by every kind of politician). Only then could Certeau's arresting re-employment of the term be read less as ballast to his writing than as a powerful perspectival displacement upon the operations of learned analysis.[43]

Certeau envisages the analyses contained in *The Practice of Everyday Life* as belonging to a properly political enterprise. He argues for example that 'a politics of reading must . . . be joined to an analysis which, describing practices that have long been in effect, makes them politicizable' (*PE* 173/250). Yet this process of 'politicization' is less evident than it might seem. Not only are the political repercussions of such analyses hard to specify and easy to exaggerate. Their principal burden is also to show how their objects are defined precisely by a resistance or recalcitrance to standard forms of political intervention. Indeed, the relative autonomy which these forms of *poeisis* put into play need not always correspond directly to forms of 'resistance', which are always thoroughly implicated in and conflictually bound by the strategic operations against which they work. Certeau shows how they may serve to set up spaces removed from the reach of what is usually understood as the political. They produce so many 'lapses of history' (*MF* 174/239) or ' "balloon[s]" of speaking subjects' (*MF* 305/24).

Yet even these lapses and pockets are not created in utopian space, and I would like to conclude this chapter by suggesting two potential effects of politicization operated by *The Practice of Everyday Life*.

Firstly, Certeau's work helps to provide a space of cultural legitimacy for readings and writings which are generally disqualified as illegitimate or uninformed. He himself would no doubt have remained highly ironical with regard to any such effects of rehabilitation, arguing that ordinary reading (and other) practices have no need of a sanction from on high – Certeau's ordinary man 'comes before texts. He doesn't even expect them. He couldn't care less about them' (*PE* v/11). Yet I wonder if there is not a trace of hyperbole or fantasmatic dialogue here. One could turn to Pierre Bourdieu for a rather different account of a typical encounter with learned culture:

> I think that one of the effects of an average contact with intellectual writings is to crush popular experience, leaving people tremendously exposed, that is to say caught between two cultures, between an originary culture now abolished and a learned culture that they've frequented enough to feel that they can't just carry on chatting about the weather, to know all the things that you're not meant to say, without having anything else to say.[44]

Bourdieu's proposition points up a properly political effect of Certeau's analyses, in so far as they work to undo the debilitating opposition between originary and learned culture. The analyses contained in *The Practice of Everyday Life*, in a more direct manner than Certeau's historical studies, offer a set of new perspectives on 'ordinary' kinds of operation and intelligence. They show how the latter can be (re)appropriated without simply occupying an empty position in their relation to Knowledge. Certainly, such a redistribution of cultural practices is largely 'symbolic'. Yet it is easy to forget that it is precisely such symbolically effective divisions between what is legitimate and what is illegitimate or void which constitute the operative fabric of modern democratic societies. A given analysis – a drop in the ocean – constitutes a more or less effective intervention in such mobile processes of 'symbolic' distribution, as they are more or often less obliquely appropriated or incorporated by political subjects.

Secondly, Certeau sets up what could be defined as a distinctively Certalian working space situated in the gap between, say, political, pedagogical and urban programmes and what different people 'make of' these programmes. Of course, it is unsatisfactory simply to keep repeating that such a gap exists. To treat it, however, as a working space in the full sense of the term, to focus in different cases on the specific modalities of such problematic articulations or disjunctions, would constitute again a properly political enterprise (if, as Jacques Revel suggests, we can describe as 'political' a project designed to uncover the processes through which new social forms are 'invented').[45] The cumulative effect of such work would be to shift the centre of gravity as it operates in administrative, political and pedagogical 'centres' of decision-making. Such work is easier to invoke than to carry out, but it is the work which Certeau's analyses exemplify and demand.[46]

Conclusion: Thought in Motion

I would like to conclude this introduction to Certeau's work by drawing together the elements of a distinctive pattern discernible in the movement of his writing. This pattern is not set out as such by Certeau, but corresponds to something like a model – at once ethical and aesthetic – which runs through and to some extent generates the extraordinary range of his work. It informs his practice of both pushing forms of thought towards their limits and opening them up to others.

The model in question can be presented as a threefold sequence. Firstly, Certeau delimits a figure of homogeneity which encloses the subject, either protecting him or isolating him from the world, enveloping or suffocating him. Secondly, he shows how this structure of enclosure is (always already) fissured by the irruption or insinuation of manifold instances of alterity. These may be either desired or feared. Finally, this irruption results in an alteration or even a shattering (*éclatement*) of identity, which itself may be experienced either in the mode of panic (possession) or release (dilation).[1] This final stage does not efface identity, limitation and enclosure, which always return, in altered forms, as marks of the speaking subject's irreducible difference and separation.

The structures of 'enclosure' outlined above are often associated with 'certified' forms of writing. They correspond to strategies of interpretative and sociopolitical control. As Certeau presents them, they work to bring others into conformity with the canons of orthodox signification and with the criteria of epistemic propriety.

They map out or grid (*quadriller*) the spaces which others must inhabit. Yet Certeau suggests how, in the very exercise of this power, they also cut themselves off from the others they are supposed to control. He raises the fantasmatic spectre of 'an incarceration within the operations of a writing whose machinations extend indefinitely, and which never encounters anything but itself' (*PE* 150/220). I have already discussed how Certeau's own writing may intermittently lapse (or be raised) into myth. The problems which it articulates – whether conceptually or metaphorically – nevertheless seem real enough. What are our options before the quasi-anonymous and no doubt relatively chaotic tangle of capitalizing, conquering and self-reproducing strategies which prescribe the terms of our social existence? Or, at a more intimate level, how can we ourselves move beyond a compulsive complicity in 'the disease of identity' (*E* 179) towards a form of ethical/aesthetic 'dilation'?

Certeau looks for interruptions and fissures which put in question strategies of control and reproduction. They figure as so many breaches in edifices of confinement. He cultivates these breaches in his own writing. His work shows, for example, how epistemic strategies have always already sacrificed their propriety to 'implicit' forms of social and historical alterity. He cites moreover in his texts 'particularities that block the demonstrations of meaning', and which produce 'a suspension of meaning in the continuum of interpretation' (*MF* 9–10/19). These fragments are designed to 'give' us nothing but a sense of withdrawal, the overwhelming impression that 'there is otherness' (*il y a de l'autre*). Certeau manipulates them so as to 'falsify' the schemes and models which make sense from our world. Likewise he analyses how diverse figures of a reassuring or exotic 'other' projected by interpretative strategies mutate and return in the form of a disruptive *other* (to use the differentiation I have adopted above). Finally, he draws out the 'virtual' or 'secreted' presence of other kinds of operation, both conflictual and poetic, which strategic operations tend to occult. He works to take away a naive confidence in interpretative, epistemic and political 'controls', and to expose us to something else.

It may be that the disruptive impulse which runs through much of Certeau's writing provokes a sense of malaise in today's cultural climate. At a time when so many forces in our social, symbolic and biological surroundings seem to be breaking away from any kind of responsible control, an ethics generated by fissure and dehiscence might seem something of an inadequate response. How are we collectively to 'control' (in an inevitably flawed way) transnational fluxes of information, misinformation and capital, the dramatic mutation of symbolic and other environments, internecine nationalist passions, the consequences of social dislocation (to cite just some of our mental commonplaces)? The sort of global/holistic strategical planning eschewed by Certeau may now appear less as an instrument of mastery than as an indispensable framework through which to evaluate necessarily more localized initiatives.

Yet one should not lapse into static oppositional thinking. The effect of Certeau's ethics/aesthetics is precisely to open the individual subject to what lies beyond him or her, and to uncover his or her implication in larger complexes. Certeau himself never ceases to hope both for an 'alteration' and a 'dilation'. The individual, for Certeau, does not hold his or her own truth, but may develop a differential truth by responding to a series of solicitations and disruptions which come from 'outside'. We have seen how this ethic/aesthetic informs Certeau's interpretative techniques. He attempts to stage, to follow or to facilitate the altering effects of such solicitations and disruptions. He does this through the insinuation of anomalous historical and cultural fragments; by exposing writing to other 'voices' and fables; through an attention to the forms of other peoples' practices; by setting up encounters with the itinerant stories which circulate through 'metaphorical' towns or which lie dormant in archival recesses. Certeau directs us to the unending heterological work of introducing otherness into familiar space, and of uncovering the otherness which already inhabits that space.

Certainly, this 'otherness' constitutes an ambivalent force in Certeau's thought: it may 'possess' individual subjects, and deprive them of the space which they aspire to inhabit. It may, however, provide them with what Certeau saw already in the correspondence of Surin as a way out of confinement and into a 'common life'.[2] The breakdown of possessive identity and of certified interpretative control may open the way for a form of 'hospitality' – a 'means of becoming host to an other who disquiets us and brings us to life' (*FC* 313), and a patient endeavour to 'take upon oneself what the other lacks' (*MF* 46/68). A more developed 'sense of others' (as we talk of a good or bad 'sense of direction') would reorient multiple kinds of contemporary operation.[3] It is not a sense we are born with, but Certeau's work can provide us with an invaluable guide through the inveiglements and diversions which lie on the way to its interminable acquisition.

Notes

Introduction

1 See R. Chartier, 'L'histoire ou le savoir de l'autre'; M. Augé, 'Présence, absence'; E. Jabès, 'La voix où elle s'est tue', in L. Giard (ed.), *Michel de Certeau* (Paris: Éditions du Centre Pompidou, 1987), pp. 155–67 (p. 156), pp. 81–4 (p. 84), pp. 237–41 (p. 237), and J. Kristeva, 'Éclairer la tradition mystique', in *Libération*, 11–12 January 1986. My epigraph is taken from J. Kristeva, *Étrangers à nous-mêmes* (Paris: Fayard, 1988), in English as *Strangers to Ourselves*, tr. L. Roudiez (London: Harvester, 1991), see p. 40.

2 For translations after *The Practice of Everyday Life*, see *Heterologies* (1986), *The Writing of History* (1988) and *The Mystic Fable* (1992). Translations of *La possession de Loudun*, *La culture au pluriel* and *La prise de parole* are currently under way. Full details of all of Certeau's books can be found in the bibliography at the end of this study. For a representative sample of his reception in the English-speaking world, see the special edition of *Diacritics*, 22/2 (1992).

3 See Luce Giard, 'Histoire d'une recherche', her introduction to the second edition of *L'Invention du quotidien*, vol. 1: *Arts de faire* (1990), pp. i–xxx. For more detailed biographical accounts, see also Giard's studies 'La passion de l'altérité' and 'Biobibliographie' in *Michel de Certeau*, pp. 17–38, 245–53, and 'Mystique et politique, ou l'institution comme objet second', in L. Giard, H. Martin and J. Revel, *Histoire, mystique et politique. Michel de Certeau* (Grenoble: Jérôme Millon, 1991), pp. 9–45.

4 *Libération*, 11–12 January 1986.
5 See *FC* 183–226, and the comments of Luce Giard in 'Mystique et politique', pp. 15–17.
6 The term 'éclatement' appears for example in *L'Étranger ou l'union dans la différence* (*E* 85), as does 'la vie commune' ('common life', *E* 91–6), a term which Certeau takes from Jan van Ruysbroeck (*E* 11). For formal anticipations of Certeau's later itinerary which are still substantially bound to a circumscribed tradition, see e.g. chapters 3 and 4 of *L'Étranger*, first published in *Christus* in 1964 and 1963 under the titles 'Donner la parole' and 'La conversion du missionnaire'. These analyse how teachers and missionaries may be 'altered' and questioned as to their 'foundation' through their encounters with others.
7 See L. Giard, 'La passion de l'altérité', p. 27. Certeau had published Surin's *Guide spirituel pour la perfection* (Paris: Desclée de Brouwer, 1963) and a monumental edition of his *Correspondance* (Paris: Desclée de Brouwer, 1966).

Chapter 1 The Historiographical Operation

1 On Certeau's choice of professional position on election in 1984 to the École des Hautes Études en Sciences Sociales in Paris, see Roger Chartier, 'L'histoire, ou le savoir de l'autre', in L. Giard (ed.), *Michel de Certeau* (Paris: Éditions du Centre Pompidou, 1987), pp. 155–67 (pp. 155–6). Certeau had also taught under the aegis of theology (Catholic Institute of Paris, 1964–78); of psychoanalysis (University of Paris VIII (Vincennes), 1968–71); of cultural anthropology (University of Paris VII (Jussieu), 1971–8); and of comparative literature (University of California at San Diego, 1978–84). See Luce Giard, 'Biobibliographie', in *Michel de Certeau*, pp. 245–253 (pp. 248–50).
2 Cf. for example *MF* 79/107, *PE* 21/39, *WH* 339–40/349–50, etc. On the function of the 'trace' in the production of historical time, see also Paul Ricoeur, *Time and Narrative*, vol. 3: *Narrated Time*, tr. K. Blamey and D. Palmer (1985; Chicago: University of Chicago, 1988), pp. 119–26, 155–6.
3 For a discussion of the epistemological status of sight in classical historiography, and the setting aside after Herodotus of the question of 'hearsay', see François Hartog, 'Herodotus and the historiographical operation', *Diacritics*, 22/2 (1992), pp. 83–93.
4 This frontispiece reproduces an allegorical etching by Jan Van de Straet, first published in 1619. See Certeau's commentary (re-allegorization?) at *WH* 1/3.

5 Cf. Hervé Martin, 'Michel de Certeau et l'institution historique' in
  L. Giard, H. Martin and J. Revel, *Histoire, mystique et politique. Michel
  de Certeau* (Grenoble: Jérôme Millon, 1991), pp. 57–97. Martin, tracing
  the reception by French historians of a work 'considered initially as
  impenetrable, if not incomprehensible' (p. 58), and whose repercussions
  he analyses in terms of a 'Certalian theoretical earthquake' (p. 83),
  observes that 'paradoxically, Certeau's influence seems to have taken
  the form of a return to the concreteness of ordinary practices' (p. 91).
6 Cf. the title of the first chapter of *WH*: '*Making* history' – '*Faire* de
  l'histoire' – my emphasis. This chapter, which first appeared as an
  article in *Recherches de Science Religieuse*, 58 (1970), pp. 481–520, subsequently gave its title to the important collection in three volumes
  edited by Jacques Le Goff and Pierre Nora, *Faire de l'histoire* (1974; Paris:
  Gallimard, 1986). Certeau also wrote the first chapter for this collection, entitled 'L'opération historique' (ibid., pp. 19–68). A substantially
  extended version of this piece, entitled 'The historiographical operation', constitutes chapter 2 of *WH*.
7 For Mikhail Bakhtin's account of François Rabelais's rather different
  exercises of 'debasement', see *Rabelais and His World*, tr. H. Iswolsky
  (1965; Cambridge, Mass: MIT Press, 1968).
8 See R. Aron, *Introduction to the Philosophy of History: An Essay on the
  Limits of Historical Objectivity*, tr. G. Irwin (1938; Boston: Beacon, 1961).
9 Cf. e.g. the emblematic title given by Luce Giard to the posthumous
  collection of essays by Certeau, *Histoire et psychanalyse entre science et
  fiction* (1987).
10 Certeau closes the introduction to *WH* by recalling some of Marx's
  classic propositions on the nature of economic 'production', and by
  suggesting how these can usefully be transferred to the field of
  historiography (see *WH* 11–14/19–23).
11 See for example *PE* 24–8/43–9, and chapters 4 and 6 below. One
  should also note here Certeau's own practice (which cannot be proposed
  as a universal model) of moving between a plurality of institutional
  positions.
12 See for example the recourse to Certeau's work in Philippe Carrard,
  *Poetics of the New History: French Historical Discourse from Braudel
  to Chartier* (Baltimore: Johns Hopkins University Press, 1992), pp. 90,
  93–4, and in Joan Scott, 'Women's history', in P. Burke (ed.), *New
  Perspectives on Historical Writing* (Cambridge: Polity, 1991), pp. 42–66
  (pp. 51–2).
13 Françoise Choay describes Certeau as an 'artist, no doubt one of the
  greatest of our time, through the grace of a permanent counterpoint
  between the rigour of his writing and the richness of the metaphors
  which invigorate it without ever congealing into a fixed system';
  see 'Tours et traverses du quotidien', in Giard (ed.), *Michel de Certeau*,
  pp. 85–90 (p. 87).

14 One might compare also Paul Ricoeur's reflection on the relation between formal analysis and the claims of intuitive comprehension, that is between what he calls after Wilhelm Dilthey 'explanation' and 'understanding'; see for example 'What is a text? Explanation and understanding', in Paul Ricoeur, *Hermeneutics and the Human Sciences*, ed. and tr. John B. Thompson (Cambridge: Cambridge University Press, 1981), pp. 145–64.

15 One can find analogous instances of this strategy in the work of Michel Foucault and Pierre Bourdieu, both of whom also set out to show in different ways how social reality is 'constructed' rather than 'given'. I discuss the relation of their work to that of Certeau in chapter 5.

16 T. Hawkes, *Structuralism and Semiotics* (London: Methuen, 1983), p. 133.

17 For developments in modern historiography (quantification, the influence of ethnology, etc.) which have displaced the status of writing as such, see WH 69–77/79–89, and François Furet, 'Le quantitatif en histoire', in Le Goff and Nora (eds), *Faire de l'histoire*, vol. 1: *Nouveaux problèmes*, pp. 69–93, esp. pp. 75–83. Cf. also more recently Peter Burke, *The French Historical Revolution: The Annales School 1929–1989* (Cambridge: Polity, 1990), and in P. Burke (ed.), *New Perspectives on Historical Writing* (Cambridge: Polity, 1991), articles by Jim Sharpe on 'History from below' (pp. 24–41), by Gwyn Prins on 'Oral history' (pp. 114–39), and by Robert Darnton on the 'History of reading' (pp. 140–67).

18 See WH 115–205/121–212.

19 For an account of quantitative approaches to religious history, see J. Delumeau, *Catholicism between Luther and Voltaire* (1971; London: Burnes and Oates, 1977), pp. 129–53. For a more recent use of quantitative methods for the analysis of the spread of literacy, see F. Furet and J. Ozouf, *Reading and Writing: Literacy in France from Calvin to Jules Ferry* (1977; Cambridge: Cambridge University Press, 1982).

20 Cf. the comments of Carlo Ginzburg in *The Cheese and the Worms: The Cosmos of a Sixteenth-Century Miller*, tr. J. and A. Tedeschi (1976; London: Routledge and Kegan Paul, 1980), pp. xiii–xxiii, 125–6, etc.

21 L. Goldmann, *The Hidden God: A Study of Tragic Vision in the Pensées of Pascal and the Tragedies of Racine*, tr. P. Thody (1959; London: Routledge and Kegan Paul, 1964).

22 One should note here that Stephen Greenblatt cites Michel de Certeau, along with Michel Foucault, Raymond Williams, Mikhail Bakhtin and Kenneth Burke, as a powerful influence in his movement towards what can schematically be called the New Historicism; S. Greenblatt, *Learning to Curse: Essays in Early Modern Culture* (London: Routledge, 1990), p. 3. For a comparison between Certeau's historiographical practice and the 'history from below' produced in the wake of E. P. Thompson by a number of anglophone historians, see Mark Poster, 'The question

of agency: Michel de Certeau and the history of consumerism', *Diacritics*, 22/2 (1992), pp. 94–107 (pp. 101–3).

23 I have taken the phrase 'permanent anticipation' from Hervé Martin, who describes Certeau as an 'indefatigable pioneer, who indicated to historians other domains that had to be reached, doing so all the more forcefully since he knew perfectly the rules of the "corporation". He had put them to work precociously and brilliantly, thereby uncovering more effectively their limits'; H. Martin, 'Michel de Certeau et l'institution historique', p. 59.

24 Tom Conley, 'Translator's introduction: for a *literary* historiography', at *WH* vii–xxviii (p. xvii).

25 Cf. R. Barthes, 'The discourse of history' (1967) and 'The reality effect' (1968), both available in *The Rustle of Language*, tr. R. Howard (Oxford: Blackwell, 1986), pp. 127–48. See also Certeau's discussion at *WH* 41–3/53–6.

26 Conley, 'Translator's introduction', pp. xvi–xviii.

27 For Certeau's distinction between 'general' historiography and the controlled form of 'specialized' historiography as practised by professional historians, see 'History: science and fiction', *H* 199–221/*HP* 66–96, esp. pp. 205–7/73–6.

28 For Pierre Bourdieu's assessment of the contemporary status of 'structural' or 'relational' thought as a disseminated, quasi-anonymous, but by no means self-evident resource, see P. Bourdieu, *The Logic of Practice*, tr. R. Nice (1980; Cambridge: Polity, 1990), p. 4.

29 P. Boutry, 'De l'histoire des mentalités à l'histoire des croyances. La possession de Loudun', *Le Débat*, 49 (1988), pp. 85–96 (p. 88).

30 Timothy Armstrong notes that there is no straightforward way of translating *dispositif* into English, and proposes the terms 'social apparatus' or 'apparatus' as the closest equivalents; see his translation of Gilles Deleuze, 'What is a *dispositif*?', in *Michel Foucault Philosopher* (1989; London: Harvester Wheatsheaf, 1992), pp. 159–68.

31 Jacques Revel, 'Michel de Certeau historien: l'institution et son contraire', in Giard, Martin and Revel, *Histoire, mystique et politique*, pp. 109–27 (p. 126).

32 Ibid.

33 Boutry, 'De l'histoire des mentalités à l'histoire des croyances', p. 88.

34 Cf. *WH* 120–2/127–9.

35 Cf. Paul Ricoeur, *Interpretation Theory: Discourse and the Surplus of Meaning* (Fort Worth: Texas Christian University Press, 1976), p. 9.

36 See M. Foucault, *The Order of Things: An Archaeology of the Human Sciences*, tr. A. Sheridan-Smith (1966; New York: Random House, 1970), and Certeau's 1967 review, 'The black sun of language: Foucault', *H* 171–84/*HP* 15–36.

37 Cf., in a rather different perspective again, the first chapter of *CP*,

entitled 'Les révolutions du "croyable"' (*CP* 15–32), and the last section of *PE*, entitled 'Ways of believing' (*PE* 177–98/257–87). Certeau notes that the status of 'belief' is complicated in modernity by the fact that one begins to label as 'beliefs' only those beliefs in which one does not believe; see 'Croire: une pratique de la différence', in *Documents de travail et prépublications*, Centro Internazionale di Semiotica e Linguistica, University of Urbino, no. 106 (1981), series A, pp. 1–19 (p. 6). Towards the end of his life, Certeau was working on what he called an 'anthropology of belief'; see Louis Panier, 'Pour une anthropologie du croire. Aspects de la problématique chez Michel de Certeau', in *Michel de Certeau ou la différence chrétienne*, ed. C. Geffré (Paris: Cerf, 1991), pp. 37–59.

38 M. de Certeau, 'La rupture instauratrice ou le christianisme dans la culture contemporaine' (first published in *Esprit*, June 1971, pp. 1177–214), *FC* 183–226 (pp. 191–3).

39 Jacques Le Brun, 'Le secret d'un travail', in L. Giard (ed.), *Le voyage mystique. Michel de Certeau* (Paris: Cerf/RSR, 1988), pp. 77–91 (p. 87).

40 The notion of a 'structure of perception' ('structure perceptive') derives from the work of Michel Foucault. See for example *The Birth of the Clinic: An Archaeology of Medical Perception*, tr. A. Sheridan-Smith (1963; New York: Vintage Books, 1973). One could also compare Pierre Bourdieu's somewhat differently directed critique of 'economic' interpretations of traditional societies which fail to pay adequate attention to the workings of other kinds of 'economies' (notably 'symbolic' economies) (recently formulated in P. Bourdieu, *The Logic of Practice*, pp. 112–21), as well as Certeau's own late piece, 'Economies ethniques', included at *PP* 225–71.

41 See chapter 4 of *WH*, entitled 'The formality of practices: from religious systems to the ethics of the Enlightenment (the seventeenth and eighteenth centuries)', first published as a study in *Ricerche di Storia Sociale e Religiosa* (Rome), 1/2 (1972), pp. 31–94.

42 See *WH* 150–60/157–71. Cf. also the remarks of Alphonse Dupront, 'Réflexions sur l'hérésie moderne', in J. Le Goff (ed.), *Hérésies et sociétés* (Paris: Mouton, 1968), pp. 291–300.

43 See *PL* 97–114.

44 Cf. Leszek Kolakowski, *Chrétiens sans Église. La conscience religieuse et le lien confessionel au XVIIe siècle*, tr. from Polish by A. Posner (1965; Paris: Gallimard, 1969), and Certeau's review, 'La mort de l'histoire globale?', *Politique Aujourd'hui*, Feb. 1970, pp. 56–8 (republished at *AH* 109–14).

45 See R. Mandrou, *Magistrats et sorciers en France au XVIIe siècle. Une analyse de psychologie historique* (Paris: Plon, 1968), and Certeau's appreciation and critique, 'La magistrature devant la sorcellerie au XVIIe siècle', *AH* 13–39 (first published in *Revue d'Histoire de l'Eglise de France*,

55 (1969), pp. 300–19). Certeau's provocative reinterpretation also needs to be qualified. Robin Briggs, for example, argues on the basis of archival work in Lorraine that the apparatus of witchcraft did not constitute an instance of resistance to the representatives of orthodoxy, but represented rather a traditional means of playing out village conflicts and tensions. Briggs finds evidence that peasant communities would turn to ecclesiastical authorities in order to have confirmed the ostracizations which they themselves had already carried out; R. Briggs, *Communities of Belief: Cultural and Social Tension in Early Modern France* (Oxford: Oxford University Press, 1989), pp. 7–65.

46 See e.g. below pp. 46–52, 121–7, 157–64. It would also be worth tracing how Roger Chartier has turned this project into one of the central axes of his research. See e.g. the English collections *The Cultural Uses of Print in Early Modern France*, tr. L. Cochrane (Princeton: Princeton University Press, 1987), or the aptly titled *Cultural History: Between Practices and Representations*, tr. L. Cochrane (Cambridge: Polity, 1988).

47 See P. Veyne, *Writing History: Essay on Epistemology* (1971; Middletown, Conn.: Wesleyan University Press, 1984), and Certeau's review, 'Une épistémologie de transition: Paul Veyne', *Annales ESC*, 27 (1972), pp. 1317–27.

48 K. Popper, *The Logic of Scientific Discovery* (1934; London: Hutchinson, 1959).

49 Cf. e.g. *MF* 9–10/19–20, 71–2/99, 179/246, etc.

50 See for example the short preamble presenting *UPdL* as a piece of 'experimental' historiography (*UPdL* 7).

Chapter 2 Interpretation and its Archaeology

1 See for example Hervé Martin, 'Michel de Certeau et l'institution historique', in L. Giard, H. Martin and J. Revel, *Histoire, mystique et politique. Michel de Certeau* (Grenoble: Jérôme Millon, 1991), pp. 57–97, or Roger Chartier, 'L'histoire ou le savoir de l'autre', in L. Giard (ed.), *Michel de Certeau* (Paris: Éditions du Centre Pompidou, 1987), pp. 155–67.

2 Hence, although Certeau's description of an economy of historiographical production can usefully be compared to certain 'field studies' of Pierre Bourdieu, one must emphasize that Certeau does not invest this sociological conceptual apparatus with an unrivalled explanatory power. Hence also Paul Ricoeur's charge that Certeau presents too 'linear' and 'mechanical' a relation between historiographical production and social organization (in *Time and Narrative*, vol. 3: *Narrated Time*

(1985; Chicago: University of Chicago, 1988), p. 309 n27) is based on a rather one-sided appropriation of Certeau's work. Ricoeur himself suggests as much in the note on Certeau's conception of the historian's 'debt' to the past with which he closes this chapter of his study (ibid., p. 312 n42).

3 See e.g. M. Foucault, *The Order of Things: An Archaeology of the Human Sciences*, tr. A. Sheridan-Smith (1966; New York: Random House, 1970), and *The Archaeology of Knowledge*, tr. A. Sheridan-Smith (1969; London: Routledge, 1992).

4 For a reading endorsed by Foucault himself, see H. Dreyfus and P. Rabinow, *Michel Foucault: Beyond Structuralism and Hermeneutics* (Brighton: Harvester Press, 1982), in particular ch. 4, 'The methodological failure of archaeology', pp. 79–100.

5 Foucault, *The Archaeology of Knowledge*, p. 7.

6 See ibid. Cf. also Dominique Julia, 'Une histoire en actes', in L. Giard (ed.), *Le voyage mystique. Michel de Certeau* (Paris: RSR/Cerf, 1988), pp. 103–23 (p. 106).

7 See the first section of chapter 1 above. One should note that at the time Foucault was using his 'archaeological' descriptive methods for the analysis of formal epistemic configurations. No doubt these were for Foucault more amenable to a programme of depersonalization and petrification than were for Certeau the forms of religious and spiritual history which constituted his main object of study in the sixties.

8 This review, available at *H* 171–84/*HP* 15–36, was first published under the title 'Les sciences humaines et la mort de l'homme' in the Jesuit journal *Études*, 326 (1967), pp. 344–60. It would constitute in itself a valuable document for a history of the reception of Foucault's thought; see Ian Maclean, 'The heterologies of Michel de Certeau', *Paragraph*, 9 (1987), pp. 83–7 (p. 83).

9 This attitude undergoes a significant change in Foucault's later, explicitly 'genealogical' work. *Discipline and Punish* (1975; Harmondsworth: Penguin, 1991) closes dramatically with an evocation of the 'roar of battle' (p. 308). I discuss Certeau's appropriation of this book in chapter 5.

10 On the fantasmatic significance of archaeology for Freud, see also Malcolm Bowie, 'Freud's dreams of knowledge', *Paragraph*, 2 (1983), pp. 53–87 (esp. pp. 57–70).

11 See the chapter 'History: science and fiction', at *H* 199–221/*HP* 66–96. For the rather complicated textual history of this piece, whose original version dates from 1977, see Luce Giard's introduction to *HP*, pp. 11–12.

12 Cf. e.g. E. Le Roy Ladurie, 'The historian and the computer' (1968) and 'The quantitative revolution and French historians: record of a generation (1932–1968)' (1969), republished in *The Territory of the Historian* (1973; Hassocks: Harvester, 1979), pp. 3–15 (one should note, however,

that Le Roy Ladurie's excessive propositions are placed in a more nuanced context than is sometimes admitted).

13 See Chartier, 'L'histoire ou le savoir de l'autre', pp. 157–64. I have also drawn here on his contribution to the radio programme on Certeau produced by Antoine Spire and broadcast in two parts on France-Culture on 10 and 17 September 1992.

14 See also François Furet, 'Le quantitatif en histoire', in J. Le Goff and P. Nora (ed.), *Faire de l'histoire*, vol. 1: *Nouveaux problèmes* (1974; Paris: Gallimard, 1986), pp. 69–93.

15 Cf. also Philippe Carrard, 'The rites of quantification', in his *Poetics of the New History* (Baltimore: Johns Hopkins University Press, 1992), pp. 166–81.

16 We will see in chapter 6 how Certeau proposes a similar move for the analysis of contemporary cultural practices.

17 Certeau refers especially to the pioneering work of Gabriel Le Bras (1891–1970). See for example Le Bras's *Introduction à la pratique religieuse en France*, vol. 1 (Paris: PUF, 1942), and the bibliographical presentation of Henri Desroches, 'Domaines et méthodes de la Sociologie religieuse dans l'oeuvre de G. Le Bras', *Revue d'Histoire et de Philosophie Religieuse*, 2 (1954), pp. 128–58.

18 See for example Jean Delumeau, *Catholicism between Luther and Voltaire* (1971; London: Burns and Oates, 1977), pp. 175–231, and more recently Robin Briggs on 'agencies of control' in *Communities of Belief: Cultural and Social Tension in Early Modern France* (Oxford: Oxford University Press, 1989), pp. 179–380.

19 See for example Jean Orcibal, *Louis XIV et les Protestants* (Paris: Vrin, 1951), and above, p. 30.

20 For the development of 'registers' from the end of the Middle Ages and especially in association with the programmes of the Counter-Reformation, see Le Bras, *Introduction à la pratique religieuse*, pp. 62–70.

21 J.-J. Surin, *Guide spirituel pour la perfection*, ed. and introd. M. de Certeau (Paris: Desclée de Brouwer, 1963), pp. 24–5. Certeau takes the quotation in this passage from Surin himself.

22 On the unprecedented use of educational institutions around this time by an emergent bureaucratic elite in order to secure also their own place of distinction in a mutating social hierarchy, see for example Pierre Bourdieu's recent study, *La noblesse d'État. Grandes écoles et esprit de corps* (Paris: Minuit, 1989), pp. 533–48; in English as *The State Nobility: Grandes Écoles and Esprit de Corps*, tr. Lauretta Clough (Cambridge: Polity, 1995). Elisabeth Rapley nevertheless makes some interesting comments on the complex designs, effects and side-effects of educational strategy in early modern France. She notes that the enormous rise over the seventeenth century in female teaching orders was often experienced as a threat to the status quo; see the chapter 'Development of a feminine pedagogy', in *The Dévotes: Women and Church*

in Seventeenth-Century France (Montreal: McGill-Queen's, 1990), pp. 142–66 (p. 163).

23 See also Jacques Revel, 'Forms of expertise: intellectuals and "popular" culture in France (1650–1800)', in S. L. Kaplan (ed.), *Understanding Popular Culture: Europe from the Middle Ages to the Nineteenth Century* (New York: Mouton, 1984), pp. 255–73.

24 These 'economies of writing' may usefully be compared to the forms of cybernetic 'ecology' mapped out by Pierre Lévy in *Les technologies de l'intelligence. L'avenir de la pensée à l'ère informatique* (Paris: La Découverte, 1990).

25 For an analysis of the complex relations between the historian (the writer of history) and those in positions of administrative or governmental power and authority (i.e. those who effectively 'write history'), see *WH* 6–11/13–19.

26 See especially the analyses developed over the course of *PL, WH, MF* and *UPdL,* treated in chapters 3, 4 and 5 below.

27 On the sometimes problematic status of the rupture which Certeau posits between a quasi-mythical 'Middle Ages' and an age in which belief no longer has an institutional foundation, see the comments of Pierre Vallin and Jean-Claude Eslin in Giard, Martin and Revel, *Histoire, mystique et politique,* pp. 54 and 142–3. One should note that, while this rupture undoubtedly provides Certeau with a characteristic interpretative structure, its clear-cut contours are freqently complicated in the detail of his analyses (cf. e.g. *WH* 7 n14/14 n14, *MF* 85–90/114–21). On the more intimate processes of severance which the telling of this historical 'story' may serve intermittently to stage, see the first section of chapter 4 below.

28 See the section 'Christian formalities of philosophical practices?' at *WH* 175–9/190–6.

29 See Jacques Le Brun, 'Le secret d'un travail', in L. Giard (ed.), *Le voyage mystique. Michel de Certeau* (Paris: Cerf/RSR, 1988), pp. 77–91 (p. 87).

30 See in particular *WH* 168–79/182–96.

31 Cf. Pierre Bourdieu's sociological 'objectifications' of the processes of interpretative objectification (e.g. in *Esquisse d'une théorie de la pratique* (Geneva: Droz, 1972), pp. 157–62, and more recently in *The Logic of Practice* (1980; Cambridge: Polity, 1990), pp. 30–41). I discuss Certeau's reading of Bourdieu in chapter 5.

Chapter 3 Voices in the Text

1 On the differences and interferences between orally and scripturally based thought-processes, and on the corresponding mutations in the

controls which govern the production of truth, cf. J. Goody, *The Domestication of the Savage Mind* (Cambridge: Cambridge University Press, 1977), and W. Ong, *Orality and Literacy: The Technologizing of the Word* (London: Routledge, 1982). I will discuss below the relation between Certeau's conception of 'voice' and that articulated in the work of Jacques Derrida.

2 This section is based on Certeau's analysis of Léry's text, 'Ethno-graphy. Speech, or the space of the other: Jean de Léry' (*WH* 209–43/215–48). Certeau uses Paul Gafferel's 1880 re-edition of the text (2 vols, Paris: A. Lemerre), based on the 1580 edition. There is now available a facsimile reproduction of this edition, edited by J.-C. Morisot (Geneva: Droz, 1975), and an English translation by Janet Whatley, *History of a Voyage to the Land of Brazil* (Berkeley: University of California Press, 1990).

3 In Claude Lévi-Strauss, *Tristes Tropiques*, tr. J. Russell (1955; New York: Atheneum, 1970), p. 85.

4 See her introduction to her abridged and modernized edition, J. de Léry, *Indiens de la renaissance. Histoire d'un voyage fait en la terre du Brésil*, ed. A.-M. Chartier (Paris: Epi, 1972), esp. pp. 12–27.

5 Ibid., p. 18.

6 Cited at *WH* 213/221.

7 The most appropriate term here would be the French word *frayage*, which translates the Freudian concept of *Bahnung* (see Freud's 'Project for a scientific psychology' (1895), in Freud, *The Standard Edition of the Complete Psychological Works* (London: Hogarth Press and The Institute of Psychoanalysis, 1953–74), vol. 1). Unfortunately, the term 'facilitation', which is the standard English translation, does not carry all the connotations which I have in mind.

8 See for example the section 'Amériques: le réveil politique' at *PP* 131–61 (part of which can be found in translation at *H* 225–33), and also *FC* 129–56. Certeau was involved from the late 1960s onwards in diverse kinds of academic and political work in Latin America.

9 See note 7 above.

10 J. Derrida, *Of Grammatology*, tr. G. Spivak (1967; Baltimore: Johns Hopkins University Press, 1976), p. 11. Cf. also Monique Schneider, 'La voix et le texte', in L. Giard (ed.), *Michel de Certeau* (Paris: Éditions du Centre Pompidou, 1987), pp. 133–46. For an exposition of Derrida's work on Rousseau, see e.g. Christopher Norris, *Derrida* (London: Fontana, 1987), pp. 97–141.

11 See *WH* 236/248; Certeau takes this phrase from Lacan.

12 The heading above is taken from *WH* 212/218.

13 See J. Derrida, 'The violence of the letter: from Lévi-Strauss to Rousseau' in Derrida, *Of Grammatology*, pp. 101–140, esp. p. 139: 'The ethic of speech is the *delusion* (*leurre*) of presence mastered. Like the *bricole*, the

delusion or lure designates first a hunter's stratagem. It is a term of falconry: "a piece of red leather", says Littré, "in the form of a bird, which serves to recall the bird of prey when it does not return straight to the fist." '

14 L. Giard, 'Epilogue: Michel de Certeau's heterology and the New World', *Representations*, 33 (1991), pp. 212–21 (p. 216).

15 Cf. Emmanuel Le Roy Ladurie: 'Father de Certeau, in this collection of texts which he has brought magnificently together, has succeeded in playing upon everybody's words and in taking up every kind of language. He becomes by turn a medical and social historian, a theologian-psychoanalyst, a quantifier, a disciple of Freud or Foucault . . .': Le Roy Ladurie seems both intrigued and a little unsettled by the transverse movement of Certeau's thought; see 'Le diable archiviste', in *Le territoire de l'historien* (Paris: Gallimard, 1973), pp. 404–7 (p. 406). Philippe Boutry suggests that *PL* may contain the first use of psychoanalysis in a non-theoretical piece of French historiography; see his article 'De l'histoire des mentalités à l'histoire des croyances. La possession de Loudun', *Le Débat* 49 (1988), pp. 85–96, pp. 88–9. For a semiotic approach, see *WH* 244–68/249–73.

16 For a suggestive treatment of these nevertheless important considerations, see Aldous Huxley, *The Devils of Loudun* (1952; London: Grafton, 1977), pp. 96f.

17 See for example the image entitled 'The Devil leaving La Rochelle', on the tenth page of illustrations in *PL*.

18 The first sense which the modern *Trésor de la langue française* gives of 'produire' is: 'Faire exister, naturellement ou non, ce qui n'existe pas encore; créer.' The 1690 edition of Furetière's dictionary elides what for us now generally seem two distinct senses of the verb: 'Donner la naissance à quelque chose, la faire paroistre au jour', giving as an example: 'La mer *produit* souvent et fait voir des monstres.'

19 See the third page of illustrations in *PL*.

20 It may be worth noting that an earlier title for *The Writing of History* was 'La production de l'histoire' ('The production of history' – see the proleptic references at *AH* 173).

21 For the details of other possessions and witchcraft trials in early modern France, see J. Michelet, *La sorcière* (1862; Paris: Garnier-Flammarion, 1966), and more recently R. Mandrou, *Magistrats et sorciers en France au XVIIe siècle. Une analyse de psychologie historique* (Paris: Plon, 1968), together with Certeau's analysis of the latter at *AH* 13–39.

22 In M. Foucault, *The History of Sexuality*, vol. 1: *An Introduction* (1976; Harmondsworth: Penguin, 1990), pp. 45–6. For an interpretation based on the idea of 'induction', see Huxley, *The Devils of Loudun*, pp. 184–90.

23 Quoted by Certeau in his edition of Jean-Joseph Surin's *Correspondance* (Paris: Desclée de Brouwer, 1966), p. 245.
24 See the discussion in L. Giard, H. Martin and J. Revel, *Histoire, mystique et politique. Michel de Certeau* (Grenoble: Jérôme Millon, 1991), p. 158.
25 'Thus there continues . . . this fine duel of doctor against Devil, of science and light against dark deception'; J. Michelet, *La sorcière*, p. 203.
26 Certeau's use of the concept of a common epistemological framework is indebted to the work of Michel Foucault.
27 See T. Todorov, *Introduction à la littérature fantastique* (Paris: Seuil, 1970). This comparison also needs to be qualified. Todorov's analysis is based on the specific nineteenth-century genre of 'fantastic' literature, where the hesitation occurs between nineteenth-century conceptions of 'scientific' and 'supernatural' explanations. The hesitation which Certeau produces is both more complex and historically 'staggered'. To begin with, it is produced by his presentation of the divergent and mutually destabilizing positions of a seventeenth-century interpretative field. This uncertainty is then redoubled by his refusal to supplement this presentation with a decisive modern interpretative master-key. Instead, the reader seems to be confronted with a series of uncertain reflections of his or her own desire to interpret.
28 Quoted by Derrida in *Of Grammatology*, p. 109, in the section entitled 'The battle of proper names' (pp. 107–18).
29 There is also the case of the *a posteriori* written self-analyses of erstwhile 'demoniacs'. Cf. e.g. the *Autobiographie* of Jeanne des Anges (1644; ed. Legué and de la Tourette, 1886; re-ed. Grenoble: Jérôme Millon, 1990), or, for the case of a 'possessed exorcist', J.-J. Surin, *Triomphe de l'amour divin sur les puissances de l'Enfer et Science expérimentale des choses de l'autre vie* (1653–1660; re-ed. Grenoble: Jérôme Millon, 1990). Certeau stresses that in order to constitute themselves as discourses 'on' a possession (as opposed to possessed speech), these writings had to base themselves on contemporary interpretative systems. They too are 'altered documents' (see *WH* 254/259–60).
30 Michelet, *La sorcière*, p. 204.
31 See the section 'Man and language' in Émile Benveniste, *Problems in General Linguistics*, tr. M. Meek (1966; Miami: University of Miami Press, 1971), pp. 193–246, and the chapter 'L'appareil formel de l'énonciation' in *Problèmes de linguistique générale*, vol. 2 (Paris: Gallimard, 1974), pp. 79–88. There is also a range of helpful articles on the concept of 'énonciation' in the special edition of *Langages*, 17 (1970), ed. T. Todorov. On its fundamental role in Certeau's thought, see Louis Marin, 'L'aventure sémiotique, le tombeau mystique', in Giard (ed.), *Michel de Certeau*, pp. 207–23, esp. pp. 207–14.

32 See Benveniste, 'L'appareil formel de l'énonciation'.
33 *PE* xiii/XXXVIII, quoted by Marin, 'L'aventure sémiotique', p. 208. I take up this 'marker' again in chapters 4 and 6.
34 Exorcism of May 10 1634; quoted at *PL* 68.
35 Cf. Louis Marin: 'These uttered utterances, marks and traces of the utterance through which it can become an object of knowledge, reveal . . . a remarkable affinity with a logic and an economy of the secret in so far as they insinuate the unknowable "virtual", in so far as they "secrete" its withdrawal in the mesh of their network, and designate obliquely and indirectly its "hidden" presence'; 'L'aventure sémiotique', p. 210.
36 Schneider, 'La voix et le texte', p. 136.
37 For the Rabelaisian fable of the 'frozen words', see *The Fourth Book*, ch. 55, in François Rabelais, *The Histories of Gargantua and Pantagruel*, tr. J. M. Cohen (Harmondsworth: Penguin, 1955), pp. 566–8.
38 For Jacques Derrida's analysis of the 'undecidable' character of the supplement, see *Of Grammatology*, pp. 141–64.

Chapter 4 *Mystics*

1 J. Revel, 'Michel de Certeau historien: l'institution et son contraire', in L. Giard, H. Martin and J. Revel, *Histoire, mystique et politique. Michel de Certeau* (Grenoble: Jérôme Millon, 1991), pp. 109–27 (p. 125).
2 Luce Giard is currently preparing an edition of this work based on the notes and drafts already written by Certeau.
3 For a reading of *MF* based on a more general (though erudite) conception of mysticism, see for example Alain de Libéra and Frédéric Nef, 'Le discours mystique. Histoire et méthode', *Littoral*, 9 (1983), pp. 79–102, and Certeau's reply, pp. 115–16. For an analysis of diverse sociohistorical figures of 'mysticism', see Certeau's article 'Mystique' in the *Encyclopedia Universalis* (1971; reprinted in the 1990 edition), and also translated by Marsanne Brammer in *Diacritics*, 22/2 (1992), pp. 11–25.
4 M. Smith, 'Translator's note', at *MF* ix–x.
5 See Luce Giard's comments in *Histoire, mystique et politique*, at p. 161, and Marsanne Brammer, 'Thinking Practice', *Diacritics*, 22/2 (1992), pp. 26–48.
6 Certeau, 'Histoire et mystique', in *AH* 153–67 (first published in *Revue d'Histoire de la Spiritualité*, 48 (1972), pp. 69–82). See in particular his editions of Pierre Favre, *Mémorial* (Paris: Desclée de Brouwer, 1960); Jean-Joseph Surin, *Guide spirituel pour la perfection* (Paris: Desclée de

Brouwer, 1963); Jean-Joseph Surin, *Correspondance* (Paris: Desclée de Brouwer, 1966); and *La possession de Loudun* (Paris: Julliard, 1970).

7 See *Libération*, 11–12 January 1986.

8 L. Giard, 'La passion de l'altérité', in Giard (ed.), *Michel de Certeau* (Paris: Éditions du Centre Pompidou, 1987), pp. 17–38 (p. 30). Cf. also M. de Certeau, 'La faiblesse de croire', at *FC* 307–14.

9 Cf. also 'L'épreuve du temps', *Christus*, 13 (1966), pp. 311–31, reprinted as 'Le mythe des origines' at *FC* 53–74.

10 L. Giard, 'Mystique et politique, ou l'institution comme objet second', in *Histoire, mystique et politique*, pp. 9–45 (p. 17).

11 *The Spiritual Canticle*, quoted and translated at *MF* 163/224 (the full text of the canticle can be found in *The Collected Works of St John of the Cross*, tr. K. Kavanaugh and O. Rodriguez (Washington, D.C.: ICS Publications, 1979), pp. 712–17).

12 Certeau gives the text of this preface at *MF* 179–80/246–7. This text and Certeau's notes are taken up in Jacques Prunair's subsequent edition of J.-J. Surin, *Triomphe de l'amour divin sur les puissances de l'enfer et Science expérimentale des choses de l'autre vie* (1653–1660; Grenoble: Jérôme Millon, 1990).

13 These passages appear in Latin in Surin's text (see *MF* 180/246), and represent modified quotations from the Vulgate Bible (see respectively the first letter of John, 1: 1–2, and John's gospel, 3: 11).

14 See Certeau's edition of Surin's *Correspondance*, pp. 241–414, and *PL* 287–306.

15 Cf. M. de Certeau, 'Introduction', in Surin, *Correspondance*, pp. 27–89 (p. 51).

16 On Surin's chronic compulsion to 'throw' himself (away), see M. de Certeau, 'Folie du nom et mystique du sujet: Surin', in J. Kristeva (ed.), *Folle vérité. Vérité et vraisemblance du texte psychotique* (Paris: Seuil, 1979), pp. 274–304.

17 Cited at *MF* 299/411. A comparable citation from Char appears on the covers of Michel Foucault's last two published historiographical works: 'The history of men is the long succession of the synonyms of the same word. To contradict it is a necessity'; see the French editions of vols 2 and 3 of *The History of Sexuality*, *L'Usage des plaisirs* and *Le souci de soi* (both Paris: Gallimard, 1984).

18 See the section 'Un non-lieu de la philosophie' in 'Historicités mystiques', *Recherches de Science Religieuse*, 73 (1985), pp. 325–54 (pp. 334–41).

19 Ibid., p. 330.

20 'Figures of the wildman', *MF* 203–93/275–405.

21 Surin comments repeatedly in his letters that 'I have nothing but a song', e.g. *Correspondance*, p. 1005.

22 Michel de Certeau and Mireille Cifali, 'Entretien, Mystique et

psychanalyse', *Le Bloc-Notes de la Psychanalyse*, 4 (1984), pp. 135–61 (p. 141).

23 The destabilizing implications of what may now appear as a debate about mere 'turns of phrase' are evident for example in Surin's obsessive references to his 'examiners' (*Guide spirituel*, pp. 248–60, etc.), or, as *mystics* was in Certeau's chronology about to break apart, in the texts arising from the 'quietist' controversy centred in France on Fénelon and Madame Guyon; for an introduction, see Louis Cognet, *Crépuscule des mystiques* (1958; Paris: Desclée de Brouwer, 1991).

24 For the textual history of Diego's introduction, see *MF* 331 n58/180 n59. Certeau uses Cyprien de la Nativité's 'revised and corrected' translation of the text as it was included in his French edition of the works of John of the Cross (Paris, 1642).

25 Translation by Cyprien de la Nativité quoted and corrected by Certeau, *MF* 133/184.

26 Quoted at *MF* 139/192.

27 See *MF* 293/405, and the 'Overture to a poetics of the body' which closes the volume, set in motion by Catherine Pozzi's poem 'Ave'.

28 On the function of the Dionysian corpus as a support or pretext for the emancipation of a mystic 'science' a thousand years later, see *MF* 101–4/138–43.

29 Quoted at *MF* 139/193.

30 For the problematic relation between the rhetorical effects of the 'secret' and the question of illusion or 'duplicity' see for example *MF* 97–9/132–5, and *PL* 307–26 (on the manipulative 'adaptability' and 'finesse' of Jeanne des Anges, the Prioress at Loudun who, as Surin put it, 'set up shop' as a mystic accredited by the stigmata of possession).

31 See 'Jean de la Croix et Jean-Joseph Surin', *AH* 41–70.

32 For the work of 'detachment' (*gelazenheit*, or *abgescheidenheit*) and 'silence' in Eckhart's sermons, see for example the *Sermons and Treatises*, vol. 1, tr. and ed. M. Walshe (Longmead: Element, 1987), pp. 1–13, 39–47, etc.

33 Surin, *Correspondance*, p. 749.

34 Cf. *MF* 175/240, and also Jacques Derrida, 'Nombre de oui', in Giard (ed.), *Michel de Certeau*, pp. 191–205. The quotation is taken from Galatians 2: 20. It is cited for example by Surin in *Correspondance*, p. 1111, or, more ambivalently, in a book which gives an account of the author's diabolic 'possession', in Surin, *Triomphe de l'amour . . . et Science expérimentale*, pp. 229, 288, 324.

35 Surin, *Correspondance*, p. 1256.

36 See e.g. ibid., pp. 599, 646–8, 804, 1158, 1507.

37 See for example the prologues to Teresa's *The Book of her Life* and *The Interior Castle*, and to John's *The Ascent of Mount Carmel*.

38 St Teresa of Avila, *The Interior Castle*, book I, ch. 1, quoted and translated

at *MF* 193/263; see also *The Collected Works of St Teresa of Avila*, vol. 2, tr. O. Rodriguez and K. Kavanaugh (Washington, D.C.: ICS Publications, 1980), p. 283.

39 Angelus Silesius, *The Cherubinic Wanderer* (1657), book II, verse 137, quoted and translated at *MF* 160/219–20.

40 Surin, *Correspondance*, pp. 139–43 (p. 142), letter of 8 May 1630; also cited in full at *MF* 207–10/281–5.

41 Ibid.

42 St Teresa, *The Interior Castle*, book I, ch. 1, quoted and translated at *MF* 194/264; see also *Collected Works*, vol. 2, p. 284.

43 Surin, *Triomphe de l'amour . . . et Science expérimentale*, p. 303.

44 See e.g. ibid., pp. 264–68.

45 Cf. e.g. E. Lévinas, *Totality and Infinity: An Essay on Exteriority* (1961; Dordrecht: Kluwer, 1991), pp. 85–9.

46 St Teresa, prologue to *The Interior Castle*, from *Collected Works*, vol. 2, p. 281.

47 J. Le Brun, 'Introduction', in Fénelon, *Oeuvres*, vol. 1 (Paris: Gallimard, 1983), p. ix.

48 Cf. Michel Foucault's essay 'What is an author?' (1969), included in *The Foucault Reader*, ed. P. Rabinow (Harmondsworth: Penguin, 1986), pp. 101–20, and the historical nuances of Roger Chartier, 'Figures of the author', in *The Order of Books: Readers, Authors and Libraries in Europe between the Fourteenth and Eighteenth Centuries*, tr. L. Cochrane (1992; Cambridge: Polity, 1994), pp. 25–59.

49 Daniel Defoe, *Robinson Crusoe* (1719; Harmondsworth: Penguin, 1985), pp. 162ff. See also *AH* 8–9, 177–180 and *PE* 152–6/223–8.

50 Quoted at *MF* 180/247.

51 Surin, *Guide spirituel*, p. 185.

52 One should note that Certeau had uncovered similar circulations in his earlier work on the geographical and spiritual travels of Pierre Favre through the labyrinth of sixteenth-century pretridentine Europe; see Certeau's introduction to Favre, *Mémorial*, esp. p. 56.

53 See *MF* ch. 7. This chapter reworks in part a much earlier article, 'L'illéttré éclairé dans l'histoire de la lettre de Surin sur le jeune homme du coche (1630)', *Revue d'Ascétique et de Mystique*, 44 (1968), pp. 369–412.

54 Cf. Chartier, *The Order of Books*, p. 23, where the expression is taken from Stanley Fish.

55 'Certainly, the question remains as to why it should be black or white, God or the Devil' (*WH* 249/254). In a note appended to his edition of Surin's *Guide spirituel*, Certeau recalls how Girolamo Frascatori argued in the sixteenth century that 'melancholy' facilitated the irruption of divine or diabolic possession – 'He shows that melancholy cannot explain divination or the foretelling of the future, but that it provides

a privileged site for the intervention of God, the angel or the demon' (p. 271 n3).

56 Certeau presents a short textual history of the writings and translations of John of the Cross at *MF* 129–32/179–83.

57 See the introduction to Surin's *Correspondance*, pp. 30–4; *AH* 41–50; *MF* 241–70/330–73.

58 Certeau and Cifali, 'Entretien, Mystique et psychanalyse', p. 159.

59 See *PE* v/11–12, and below, chapter 6.

60 See 'A preliminary: the *volo* (from Meister Eckhart to Madame Guyon)', *MF* 164–76/225–42.

61 For a highly prismatic and condensed treatment of this question, see Certeau's analysis of Freud's *Moses and Monotheism*, 'The fiction of history: the writing of *Moses and Monotheism*', at *WH* 308–54/312–58.

Chapter 5 Strategic Operations

1 The article originally appeared as 'La beauté du mort: le concept de "culture populaire"', in *Politique Aujourd'hui*, Dec. 1970, pp. 3–23. It can be found at *H* 119–36/*CP* 45–72.

2 Namely Robert Mandrou, *De la culture populaire aux XVIIe et XVIIIe siècles. La bibliothèque bleue de Troyes* (1964; Paris: Imago, 1985); Geneviève Bollème, *Les almanachs populaires aux XVIIe et XVIIIe siècles. Essai d'histoire sociale* (Paris: Mouton, 1969); Marc Soriano, *Les contes de Perrault. Culture savante et traditions populaires* (1968; Paris: Gallimard, 1977).

3 See C. Nisard, *Histoire des livres populaires ou de la littérature de colportage depuis l'origine de l'imprimerie jusqu'à l'établissement de la commission d'examen des livres de colportage* (Paris, 1854 and 1864). Mandrou cites this in his bibliography as remaining 'the essential book ... on the literature distributed by pedlars [*la littérature de colportage*]'; see Mandrou, *De la culture populaire*, p. 260.

4 Cf. e.g. Mandrou, *De la culture populaire*, p. 165, and Bollème, *Les almanachs populaires*, p. 43. Other factors also complicate the relation between the 'people' and this 'popular literature'. There is the question, for example, of who wrote such a literature, and indeed who for the most part read it (*H* 126/*CP* 56), as well as problems of internalized censorship and literary convention; see e.g. Roger Chartier, 'The Literature of Roguery in the *Bibliothèque bleue*', in *The Cultural Uses of Print in Early Modern France*, tr. L. Cochrane (Princeton: Princeton University Press, 1987), pp. 265–342.

5 Cf. e.g. Soriano, *Les contes de Perrault*, pp. xxiv–v, 130–1, 479–91, and Nisard, *Histoire des livres populaires*, p. iii.

6 There are other possible interpretations of such an 'aura': cf. e.g. Freud's analysis of 'naivety' in part 7 of *Jokes and their Relation to the Unconscious*, in Freud, *The Standard Edition of the Complete Psychological Works* (London: Hogarth Press and Institute of Psychoanalysis, 1953–74), vol. 8.

7 Brian Rigby goes so far as to detect a note of intellectual defeatism, or even masochism, in this article, although it also leads him to add 'somewhat ruefully... another dimension of self-consciousness and reflexivity' to his writing; B. Rigby, *Popular Culture in Modern France: A Study of Cultural Discourse* (London: Routledge, 1991), pp. 15–16.

8 Unless otherwise mentioned, the discussion which follows will be based on those parts of *UPdL* written by Certeau himself.

9 The text oɪ this report is included in the long appendix to *UPdL*, pp. 300–17.

10 Of course, Certeau and his co-authors are aware that such a centralizing thrust, in its various component parts, antedates the French Revolution as such; cf. e.g. Roger Chartier, *The Cultural Origins of the French Revolution*, tr. L. Cochrane (1990; Durham: Duke University Press, 1991), pp. 3–19.

11 For the text of Grégoire's questionnaire, see *UPdL* 12–14. A large number of the responses can be found in A. Gazier, *Lettres à Grégoire sur les patois de la France, 1790–1794. Documents inédits sur la langue, les moeurs et l'état des esprits dans les diverses régions de la France, au début de la Révolution*... (1880; Geneva: Slatkine, 1969). In addition, *UPdL* contains a number of replies which do not appear in Gazier's collection (pp. 173–249).

12 'Le rapport Grégoire', *UPdL* 307.

13 See Barrère's report, delivered to the National Convention on 8 Pluviôse, Year II (reproduced at *UPdL* 291–9).

14 A reply sent to Paris in the name of the 'Friends of the Constitution' of Auch informs Grégoire that '[our patois] is a brute form of the French language. Patois retains everything that the French language has eliminated from itself; it has none of the things through which French has enriched itself'; reproduced in Gazier, *Lettres à Grégoire*, p. 85. Cf. also Jacques Revel's comments at *UPdL* 145.

15 See Jacques Revel's comments at *UPdL* 136–8.

16 *UPdL* 188, in a reply to Grégoire from Pierre Bernadau (Guyenne).

17 See respectively *UPdL* 248, the reply from the 'Patriotic Society' of Saint-Calais, and *UPdL* 207, the reply from the Abbé Fonvielhe (Bergerac).

18 *Discipline and Punish: The Birth of the Prison*, tr. A. Sheridan (1975; Harmondsworth: Penguin, 1991), hereafter also cited as *DP*. I have occasionally modified the translation.

19 This formulation, taken from her introduction to the second French

edition of Certeau's *L'Invention du quotidien*, vol. 1: *Arts de faire* (p. xii),
is also intended by Giard to characterize Certeau's relation to the work
of Bourdieu (see the next section below). For Certeau's appreciation
and critique of *Discipline and Punish*, see 'Scattered technologies:
Foucault' (*PE* 45–9/75–81), and 'Micro-techniques and panoptic discourse: a quid pro quo' (*H* 185–92/*HP* 37–50).

20 See *DP* 257–92.

21 Admittedly, modes of 'resistance' are held out by Foucault in *Discipline
and Punish*, but always it seems as preludes to further tightenings of
the panoptic net: for example the ambivalence of criminal figures in
popular literature (pp. 67–8); industrial protests (pp. 272–5); a vaga-
bond being 'converted' into a delinquent (pp. 289–92), etc. Foucault also
adopted a dictum according to which there was 'no power without
resistance'. For further discussion of this, see H. L. Dreyfus and P.
Rabinow, *Michel Foucault: Beyond Structuralism and Hermeneutics*
(Brighton: Harvester Press, 1982), pp. 146–7, 206–7, and also the spe-
cially written afterword by Foucault, pp. 208–26. Finally, one should
note the new developments discernible in other parts of Foucault's late
writing, where he analyses what he calls 'techniques of the self' which
may presumably be set against the disciplinary techniques analysed in
DP; see vols 2 and 3 of *The History of Sexuality*, *The Use of Pleasure*
(1984; New York: Vintage, 1985) and *The Care of the Self* (1984; New
York: Pantheon, 1988), both tr. R. Hurley.

22 See ' "Docta ignorantia": Bourdieu', at *PE* 50–60/82–96. Certeau bases
his discussion largely on Bourdieu's *Esquisse d'une théorie de la pratique,
précédé de trois études d'ethnologie kabyle* (Geneva: Droz, 1972), hereafter
cited as *ETP*. Derek Robbins warns that the English version of *ETP* –
Outline of a Theory of Practice, tr. R. Nice (Cambridge: Cambridge
University Press, 1977) – was adapted by Bourdieu to such an extent
that it is best to treat it as a 'new text' rather than a translation; see D.
Robbins, *The Work of Pierre Bourdieu* (Milton Keynes: Open University
Press, 1991), p. 104. I therefore use here my own translations of the
ETP of 1972. Bourdieu has since written something like a further re-
vised and expanded version of *ETP*, available in translation as *The Logic
of Practice*, tr. R. Nice (1980; Cambridge: Polity, 1990), hereafter cited as
LP. For an account of the transition from *ETP* to *LP*, see Robbins, *The
Work of Pierre Bourdieu*, pp. 102–16, 132–50. The nature of this transi-
tion does not to my mind affect the substance of Certeau's critique.

23 See for example *ETP* 162–74, and the subsequent development of these
ideas at *LP* 30–41.

24 See in particular 'La maison ou le monde renversé' (*ETP* 45–59 and *LP*
271–83), Bourdieu's ethnological study of the spatial organization of
the Kabyle house. Significantly, this first appeared in *Échanges et
communications, mélanges offerts à Lévi-Strauss* . . . (Paris: Mouton, 1969).

For Bourdieu, this study pushed an objectifying 'structuralist' method towards a particular kind of limit (see *LP* 316 n1). It helped to lay the groundwork for his subsequent move beyond the 'reductions' of both structuralism and functionalism.

25 Bourdieu is careful to stress, both in *ETP* and in *LP*, that he is not seeking simply to 'rehabilitate' a practical disposition or logic, and that he does not want to sacrifice the gains made through practices of objectification by advocating a return to the putative immediacy of intuition. Certeau's theoretical standpoint is formally much the same in this respect, although his texts tend more than those of Bourdieu to be interrupted by significant moments of ambivalence or irony with regard to the benefits of 'proper' scientific procedure.

26 The English translation renders 'le démon de l'analogie' as 'irresistible analogy' (*LP* 200).

27 See e.g. *ETP* 73, 170–4, or *LP* 37–40, 107–10.

28 See 'La parenté comme représentation et comme volonté', at *ETP* 71–151, or 'The social uses of kinship', at *LP* 162–99.

29 P. Bourdieu, *Homo Academicus*, tr. Peter Collier (Cambridge: Polity, 1988), p. 279 n2. The term enters Bourdieu's writing via Aristotle, medieval scholasticism and Erwin Panofsky. For a more substantial definition of the 'habitus', see for example *ETP* 175, or *LP* 52–65.

30 See Certeau's comments, *PE* 60/95–6. Certeau's analysis also problematizes the relevance of the habitus, as a concept devised with reference to circumscribed, stable social groups, to the conditions of accelerated change and circulation characteristic of contemporary modernity (*PE* 55/89–90). The essential reference here would be Bourdieu's sociological classic *Distinction: A Social Critique of the Judgement of Taste*, tr. R. Nice (1979; London: Routledge, 1986), in which a panoply of interpretative devices (strategies of 'distinction' and of 'reconversion', a social dynamic of class 'grading, downgrading, regrading' etc.) introduce a greater degree of subtlety and flexibility into the notion of the habitus.

31 Cf. *MF* 187/255 and 280/387, and also *L'Invention du quotidien*, vol. 1, p. xxxiv (a preface not included in the English translation).

32 F. Choay, 'Tours et traverses du quotidien', in L. Giard (ed.), *Michel de Certeau*, (Paris: Éditions du Centre Pompidou, 1987), pp. 85–90 (p. 87).

Chapter 6 Turns and Diversions

1 R. Chartier, 'L'histoire ou le savoir de l'autre', in L. Giard (ed.), *Michel de Certeau* (Paris: Éditions du Centre Pompidou, 1987), pp. 155–67 (p. 155).

2 See e.g. Brian Rigby, *Popular Culture in Modern France: A Study of Cultural Discourse* (London: Routledge, 1991), pp. 1–38, 131–97.

3 Cf. M. de Certeau and J.-M. Domenach, *Le christianisme éclaté* (Paris: Seuil, 1974), developed from the transcripts of a radio debate transmitted on France-Culture in 1973.

4 Cf. Latin, *vertere*, to turn; Greek, *tropos*, a turn.

5 Cf. e.g. *PE* 26–8/47–9.

6 See e.g. Armand Mattelart, *Advertising International: The Privatisation of Public Space*, tr. M. Chanan (1989; London: Routledge, 1991).

7 M. Détienne and J.-P. Vernant, *Cunning Intelligence in Greek Culture and Society*, tr. J. Lloyd (1974; Hassocks: Harvester, 1978). On the 'occasion' (*kairos*), see pp. 15–16, 27, 203, etc.

8 The *Trésor de la langue française* defines the legal sense of 'insinuation' as the 'inscription d'un acte privé sur un registre public'.

9 For some useful suggestions about the relationship between reading and writing in scriptural economies, see Jean Hébrard and Anne-Marie Chartier, 'L'Invention du quotidien, une lecture, des usages', *Le Débat*, 49 (1988), pp. 97–108.

10 On the emergence of these theories in the field of literary studies, see e.g. Robert Holub, *Reception Theory: A Critical Introduction* (London: Methuen, 1984), or Terry Eagleton, *Literary Theory: An Introduction* (Oxford: Blackwell, 1983), pp. 54–90. On the development of audience research (including the appropriation of Certeau's work) in contemporary sociology and cultural studies, see David Morley, *Television, Audiences and Cultural Studies* (London: Routledge, 1992).

11 See e.g. R. Barthes, *The Pleasure of the Text*, tr. R. Howard (1973; London: Cape, 1976), and 'Sur la lecture', *Le Français Aujourd'hui*, 32 (Jan. 1976), pp. 11–18.

12 Barthes, 'Sur la lecture', p. 11.

13 M. Charles, *Rhétorique de la lecture* (Paris: Seuil, 1977), pp. 60–2.

14 R. Chartier and P. Bourdieu, 'La lecture: une pratique culturelle', in R. Chartier (ed.), *Pratiques de la lecture* (Marseilles: Rivages, 1985), pp. 218–39 (p. 230). See e.g. R. Chartier, *The Cultural Uses of Print in Early Modern France*, tr. L. Cochrane (Princeton: Princeton University Press, 1987), and *The Order of Books: Readers, Authors and Libraries in Europe between the Fourteenth and Eighteenth Centuries*, tr. L. Cochrane (1992; Cambridge: Polity, 1994), where he argues that Certeau provides 'an obligatory base and a disquieting challenge' for historians of reading (p. 1).

15 Chartier, *The Order of Books*, p. 23.

16 Cf. Chartier and Bourdieu, 'La lecture: une pratique culturelle', p. 237.

17 P. Ricoeur, 'The hermeneutical function of distanciation', in Ricoeur, *Hermeneutics and the Human Sciences*, tr. and ed. John B. Thompson (Cambridge: Cambridge University Press, 1981), pp. 131–44 (p. 139). See also the chapter on 'Appropriation', pp. 182–93.

18 Ibid., pp. 143–4.

19 I have derived the idea of a linguistic 'agonistics' or *agon* (the Greek word for a 'contest') from the work of Jean-François Lyotard; see *The Postmodern Condition: A Report on Knowledge*, tr. G. Bennington and B. Massumi (1979; Minneapolis: University of Minnesota, 1984), pp. 10, 16, etc. For the theory of hypertext, see notably Pierre Lévy, *Les technologies de l'intelligence. L'avenir de la pensée à l'ère informatique* (Paris: La Découverte, 1990), and 'Nous sommes le texte', *Esprit*, Feb. 1994, pp. 87–95.

20 On the function of the *lectio* in medieval intellectual life, see Jacques Le Goff, *Intellectuals in the Middle Ages*, tr. T. Fagan (1957; Oxford: Blackwell, 1993), pp. 89–90; on its function as a possible 'archaeology' of contemporary intellectual life, see Chartier and Bourdieu, 'La lecture: une pratique culturelle', pp. 228–9.

21 Certeau takes this expression from Guy Rosolato.

22 Cf. Richard Hoggart's proposition that 'people can remain little affected by the more advanced approaches of the advertisers; they take them in an oblique way'; in *The Uses of Literacy: Aspects of Working-Class Life with Special Reference to Publications and Entertainments* (1957; Harmondsworth: Penguin, 1990), p. 239.

23 See Jacques Revel, 'Michel de Certeau historien: l'institution et son contraire' in L. Giard, H. Martin and J. Revel, *Histoire, mystique et politique. Michel de Certeau* (Grenoble: Jérôme Millon, 1991), pp. 109–27 (p. 126).

24 Claude Lévi-Strauss, 'La science du concret', in *La pensée sauvage* (Paris: Plon, 1962), pp. 26, 27, 32; see also *The Savage Mind* (London: Weidenfeld and Nicolson, 1966), pp. 16, 17, 21. Lévi-Strauss uses 'bricolage' as an analogy or contemporary derivative of the 'prior science' which he sees at work in mythical thought.

25 Etymologically, 'metaphor' is a Greek term signifying a 'transport', or a 'carrying from one place to another'.

26 Cf. Catherine Pozzi's poem 'Ave', cited in full at *MF* 295/407.

27 'Du corps à l'écriture, un transit chrétien', *FC* 267–305 (p. 268). This piece was originally written for the publication of *Le christianisme éclaté* (1974), where it appeared in abridged form. One could usefully compare this definition with some of Jacques Derrida's work on 'writing' appearing around the same time – for example, 'Plato's pharmacy' (1968), in *Dissemination*, tr. B. Johnson (1972; London: Athlone, 1981), pp. 124, 143–4, etc.

28 S. Kinser, 'Everyday ordinary', *Diacritics*, 22/2 (1992), pp. 70–82 (p. 81).

29 Certeau is indebted in his analysis of a spatial rhetoric notably to J.-F. Augoyard's *Pas à pas. Essai sur le cheminement quotidien en milieu urbain* (Paris: Seuil, 1979).

30 *PE* 101–2/152–4; Augoyard, *Pas à pas*, pp. 60–9. The *Oxford English Dictionary* defines synecdoche as 'a figure of speech in which a more inclusive term is used for a less inclusive one or vice versa, as a whole

for a part or a part for a whole', and asyndeton as the 'omission of a conjunction'.

31 For interesting developments of Certeau's work on spatial 'itineraries' and 'stories', see David Harvey, *The Condition of Postmodernity: An Enquiry into the Origins of Cultural Change* (Oxford: Blackwell, 1989), and Marc Augé, *Non-Lieux. Introduction à une anthropologie de la surmodernité* (Paris: Seuil, 1992).

32 Cf. Françoise Choay, 'Tours et traverses du quotidien', in Giard (ed.), *Michel de Certeau*, pp. 85–90 (esp. pp. 89–90).

33 See M. de Certeau, L. Giard and P. Mayol, *L'Invention du quotidien*, vol. 2: *Habiter, cuisiner* (1980; Paris: Gallimard, 1994). Giard and Certeau also planned to write a third volume, entitled *Arts de dire* (see Giard's introduction to the French re-edition of *PE* (*L'Invention du quotidien*, vol. 1: *Arts de faire*, pp. xxi–xxii)). This was unfortunately never completed. They did, however, produce in 1983 a document for the Ministry of Culture entitled *L'ordinaire de la communication*, reprinted at *PP* 163–224.

34 For an account of 'miserabilist' and 'populist' approaches to the status of popular culture, see Rigby, *Popular Culture in Modern France*, pp. 64–66, 70, 96–130, etc., and Claude Grignon and Jean-Claude Passeron, *Le savant et le populaire. Misérabilisme et populisme en sociologie et en littérature* (Paris: Seuil, 1989).

35 Hoggart, *The Uses of Literacy*, p. 330.

36 This is not to say that the models refined by Certeau would be irrelevant in such cases. Cf. Alan Montefiore's discussion of Vaclav Havel's anecdote about a Czech greengrocer's disenchantment with the communist regime, see 'The political responsibility of intellectuals', in I. Maclean, A. Montefiore and P. Winch (eds), *The Political Responsibility of Intellectuals* (Cambridge: Cambridge University Press, 1990), pp. 201–28 (pp. 219–20).

37 Hoggart, *The Uses of Literacy*, p. 281.

38 Ibid., p. 282.

39 Cf. e.g. *CP* 17–32, *PE* 177–89/259–75.

40 Kinser, 'Everyday ordinary', pp. 76–7. For analogous forms of social dislocation and everyday distress in contemporary France, see the interviews, citations and analyses collected in P. Bourdieu (ed.), *La misère du monde* (Paris: Seuil, 1992).

41 See *PE* v/11–12.

42 Hoggart, *The Uses of Literacy*, p. 242.

43 On the 'ordinary' as operator of such a displacement, cf. *PE* 2–5/15–19. One should also compare the analyses elsewhere in Certeau's work which put into relief the quotidian pathological impulsions fermenting under the 'countenance of "normality"' (see e.g. *WH* 300–2/306–8; *PL* 7f., etc.). Luce Giard notes that Freud – 'the all too lucid author of a *Psychopathology of Everyday Life*' – is the writer most frequently cited in *PE*; in her introduction, *L'invention du quotidien*, vol. 1, p. xxvii.

44 Chartier and Bourdieu, 'La lecture: une pratique culturelle', p. 228.
45 See Revel: 'Michel de Certeau historien: l'institution et son contraire', p. 127.
46 There has not been space in this introductory book to focus on the extensive appropriation – both in francophone and anglophone countries – of that part of Certeau's oeuvre discussed in this chapter. This would require an investigation in its own right, both at the level of manifest textual citation – with its inevitable misprisions and 'alterations' – and at that of more subterranean 'circulations'. The following provide some points of departure. In French, see above all the references collected in Luce Giard's introductions to the re-editions of *L'Invention du quotidien*, vols 1 and 2 (respectively 1990 and 1994); also the articles grouped under the title 'La télématique, ou les nouvelles frontières du privé et du public', *Esprit*, Nov. 1992, pp. 97–139; and the discussions transcribed in *La culture des gens* (Aix-en-Provence: Association Espace des Deux Ormes, 1994), pp. 65–102, etc. In English, for the integration of Certeau's work into contemporary cultural studies, see e.g. Roger Silverstone, ' "Let us then return to the murmuring of everyday practices": a note on Michel de Certeau, television and everyday life', *Theory, Culture and Society*, 6/1 (1989), pp. 77–94; John Frow, 'Michel de Certeau and the practice of representation', *Cultural Studies*, 5/1 (1991), pp. 52–60; John Fiske, 'Cultural studies and the culture of everyday life', and Meaghan Morris, 'On the beach', both in L. Grossberg et al. (eds), *Cultural Studies*, (New York and London: Routledge, 1992), pp. 154–73, 450–78; Mark Poster, 'The question of agency: Michel de Certeau and the history of consumerism', *Diacritics*, 22/2 (1992), pp. 94–107.

Conclusion: Thought in Motion

1 One should note that Certeau's intellectual itinerary took him from the late 1950s on through a semantic space saturated with references to its own 'dilation'. See e.g. his editions of Favre's *Mémorial* (Paris: Desclée de Brouwer, 1960), pp. 133, 299 n3, 333 n3, 374, etc., and of Surin's *Correspondance* (Paris: Desclée de Brouwer, 1966), pp. 315, 505–6, 513, 1018, 1260, 1286, 1385–7, etc. For a mythical, fantasmatic expression of an 'absolute' dilation, see the prose poem 'Extase blanche' [White rapture], *Traverses*, 29 (1983), 16–18, republished at *FC* 315–18.
2 Cf. Surin, *Correspondance*, p. 49.
3 Cf. Marc Augé, *Le sens des autres. Actualité de l'anthropologie* (Paris: Fayard, 1994), pp. 9–11.

Select Bibliography

Readers in search of a comprehensive bibliography of Certeau's many published writings should consult Luce Giard's 'Bibliographie complète de Michel de Certeau', in L. Giard (ed.), *Le voyage mystique, Michel de Certeau* (see below), pp. 191–243 (also available in *Recherches de Science Religieuse*, 76/3 (1988), pp. 405–57). I recommend this bibliography highly as an instrument of research in its own right. Besides the books authored and edited by Certeau, I list below only those of his articles which have contributed significantly to this study, and which were not subsequently re-employed in one of his books. An asterisk after the details of a book indicates the existence of a forthcoming English translation.

BOOKS BY MICHEL DE CERTEAU

(Edited)   Bienheureux Pierre Favre, *Mémorial*, tr., ed. and introd. M. de Certeau (Paris: Desclée de Brouwer, 1960).

(Edited)   Jean-Joseph Surin, *Guide spirituel pour la perfection*, ed. and introd. M. de Certeau (Paris: Desclée de Brouwer, 1963).

(Edited)   Pierre Teilhard de Chardin, *Lettres à Léontine Zanta*, introd. R. Garric and H. de Lubac, ed. M. de Certeau (Paris: Desclée de Brouwer, 1965).

(Edited)   Jean-Joseph Surin, *Correspondance*, ed. and introd. M. de Certeau (Paris: Desclée de Brouwer, 1966).

La prise de parole et autres écrits politiques (1968; Paris: Seuil, 1994);* orig. title *La prise de parole. Pour une nouvelle culture.*

L'Étranger ou l'union dans la différence (1969; Paris: Desclée de Brouwer, 1991).

La possession de Loudun (1970; Paris: Gallimard/Julliard, 1990).*

L'Absent de l'histoire (n.p.: Mame, 1973).

La culture au pluriel (1974; Paris: Seuil, 1993).*

Le christianisme éclaté, with Jean-Marie Domenach (Paris: Seuil, 1974).

L'Écriture de l'histoire (1975; Paris: Gallimard, 1984); in English as *The Writing of History*, tr. and introd. Tom Conley (New York and Oxford: University of Columbia Press, 1988).

Une politique de la langue. La Révolution française et les patois: l'enquête de Grégoire, with Dominique Julia and Jacques Revel (Paris: Gallimard, 1975).

L'Invention du quotidien, vol. 1: *Arts de faire* (1980; Paris: Gallimard, 1990); in English as *The Practice of Everyday Life*, tr. Steven Rendall (Berkeley and London: University of California Press, 1984).

L'Invention du quotidien, vol. 2: *Habiter, cuisiner*, with Luce Giard and Pierre Mayol (1980; Paris: Gallimard, 1994); the 1980 edition contains only a brief preface by Certeau, whereas the re-edition also contains two chapters by him.

La fable mystique, vol. 1: *XVIe–XVIIe siècle* (1982; Paris: Gallimard, 1987); in English as *The Mystic Fable*, vol. 1: *The Sixteenth and Seventeenth Centuries*, tr. Michael B. Smith (Chicago and London: University of Chicago Press, 1992).

L'ordinaire de la communication, with Luce Giard and others (Paris: Dalloz, 1983); that part of the book written by Certeau and Giard can now be found in *La prise de parole et autres écrits politiques* (see above).

Heterologies: Discourse on the Other, tr. Brian Massumi, foreword by Wlad Godzich (Minneapolis: University of Minnesota Press; Manchester: Manchester University Press, 1986)

Histoire et psychanalyse entre science et fiction, ed. L. Giard (Paris: Gallimard, 1987).

La faiblesse de croire, ed. L. Giard (Paris: Seuil, 1987).

SELECTED ARTICLES BY CERTEAU

'Mystique', in the *Encyclopedia Universalis* (1971), reprinted in the 1990 edition (translation by M. Brammer in *Diacritics*, 22/2 (1992), pp. 11–25).

'Une épistémologie de transition: Paul Veyne', *Annales ESC*, 27 (1972), pp. 1317–27.

'Qu'est-ce qu'un séminaire?', *Esprit*, Nov.–Dec. 1978, pp. 176–81.

'Folie du nom et mystique du sujet: Surin', in J. Kristeva (ed.), *Folle vérité. Vérité et vraisemblance du texte psychotique* (Paris: Seuil, 1979), pp. 274–304.

'Croire: une pratique de la différence', in *Documents de travail et prépublications*, Centro Internazionale di Semioticạ e Linguistica, University of Urbino, no. 106 (1981), serie A, pp. 1–19.

'La lecture absolue', in L. Dällenbach and J. Ricardou (eds), *Problèmes actuels de la lecture* (Paris: Éditions Clancier-Guenaud, 1982), pp. 65–79.

With M. Cifali, 'Entretien, Mystique et psychanalyse', *Le Bloc-Notes de la Psychanalyse*, 4 (1984), pp. 135–61.

'Marguerite Duras: on dit', in D. Bajomée and R. Heyndels (eds), *Écrire dit-elle. Imaginaires de Marguerite Duras* (Brussels: University of Brussels, 1985), pp. 257–65.

'Le dire en éclats', preface to John of the Cross, *Les dits de lumière et d'amour*, tr. B. Sesé (1985; Paris: José Corti, 1990).

'Historicités mystiques', *Recherches de Science Religieuse*, 73 (1985), pp. 325–54.

'Notes de voyage. Mexico (1980)', in L. Giard (ed.), *Michel de Certeau* (Paris: Centre Georges Pompidou, 1987), pp. 101–21.

ARTICLES AND COLLECTIONS OF ARTICLES ON CERTEAU

Bogue, R., '*The Practice of Everyday Life*. By Michel de Certeau. Trans. by Steven F. Rendall', *Comparative Literature*, 38/4 (1986), pp. 367–70.

Champion, F., 'La "fable mystique" et la modernité', *Archives de Sciences Sociales des Religions*, 58/2 (1984), pp. 195–203.

Diacritics, 22/2 (1992), special issue on Michel de Certeau, ed. T. Conley and R. Terdiman (articles by Marsanne Brammer, Roger Chartier, Tom Conley, François Hartog, Samuel Kinser, Richard Terdiman, Steven Ungar, Mark Poster).

Frow, J., 'Michel de Certeau and the practice of representation', *Cultural Studies*, 5/1 (1991), pp. 52–60.

Geffré, C., *Michel de Certeau ou la différence chrétienne* (Paris: Cerf, 1991) (articles by Dominique Bertrand, Christian Duquoc, Claude Geffré, Pierre Gibert, Joseph Moingt, Louis Panier, Joël Roman).

Giard, L., 'Epilogue: Michel de Certeau's heterology and the New World', *Representations*, 33 (1991), pp. 212–21.

Giard, L., (ed.), *Michel de Certeau* (Paris: Centre Georges Pompidou, coll. 'Cahiers pour un temps', 1987) (articles by Alain Arnaud, Marc Augé, Christine Buci-Glucksmann, Roger Chartier, Françoise Choay, Jacques Derrida, Luce Giard, François Hartog, Danièle Hervieu-Léger, Edmond Jabès, Charles Malamoud, Louis Marin, Luis Mizon, Paul Rabinow, Jean Louis Schefer, Monique Schneider, Richard Terdiman, Pierre Vidal-Naquet).

Giard, L., (ed.), *Le voyage mystique. Michel de Certeau*, (Paris: RSR/Cerf, 1988) (articles by Stanislas Breton, Luce Giard, Marc Guillaume, Dominique Julia, Claude Langlois, Jacques Le Brun, Joseph Moingt, Guy Petitdemange, Claude Rabant).

Giard, L., H. Martin and J. Revel, *Histoire, mystique et politique. Michel de Certeau* (Grenoble: Jérôme Millon, 1991).

Le Débat, 49 (1988), special section entitled 'Michel de Certeau, historien' (articles by Philippe Boutry, Anne-Marie Chartier and Jean Hébrard, Jacques Le Brun, Michelle Perrot).

Le Roy Ladurie, E., 'Le diable archiviste', in *Le territoire de l'historien* (Paris: Gallimard, 1973), pp. 404–7.

Libération, 11–12 Jan. 1986, pp. 22–3 (obituaries by Roger Chartier, Louis Marin, Julia Kristeva, Jean Louis Schefer, Georges Vigarello).

Lion, A., 'Le discours blessé. Sur le langage mystique selon Michel de Certeau', *Revue des Sciences Philosophiques et Théologiques*, 71 (1987), pp. 405–20.

Littoral, 9 (1983), section on *The Mystic Fable* entitled 'La mystique: fable ou discours' (articles by Alain de Libéra and Frédéric Nef, Guy Le Gaufey (which are followed by a short critical response from Certeau), Philippe Julien).

Maclean, I. W. F., 'The heterologies of Michel de Certeau', *Paragraph*, 9 (1987), pp. 83–7.

Petitdemange, G., 'L'Invention du commencement. *La fable mystique*, de Michel de Certeau. Première lecture', *Recherches de Science Religieuse*, 71 (1983), pp. 497–520.

Schirato, T., 'My space or yours?: De Certeau, Frow and the meanings of popular culture', *Cultural Studies*, 7/2 (1993), pp. 282–91.

Silverstone, R., ' "Let us then return to the murmuring of everyday practices": a note on Michel de Certeau, television and everyday life', *Theory, Culture and Society*, 6/1 (1989), pp. 77–94.

Vidal, D., 'Figures de la mystique: le dit de Michel de Certeau', *Archives de Sciences Sociales des Religions*, 58/2 (1984), pp. 187–94.

Index

Numbers in **bold** type indicate pages where particular terms are explained or redefined